all we're meant to be

Word Books, Publisher
Waco, Texas

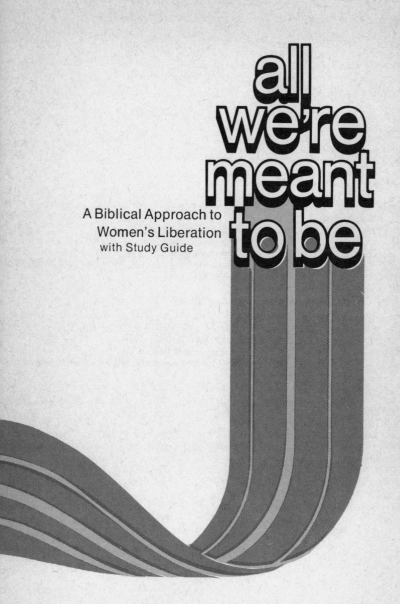

all we're meant to be

A Biblical Approach to
Women's Liberation
with Study Guide

to be

Letha Scanzoni • Nancy Hardesty

ALL WE'RE MEANT TO BE

First Printing—August 1974
Second Printing—April 1975
First Paperback Printing—September 1975
Second Paperback Printing—June 1976
Third Paperback Printing—October 1976
Fourth Paperback Printing—June 1977
Fifth Paperback Printing—May 1978

Printed in the United States of America
ISBN 0-87680-897-6
Library of Congress catalog card number: 74-78041

Unless otherwise noted, all Scripture quotations are from the Revised Standard Version of the Bible, copyrighted 1946 (renewed 1973), 1956 and © 1971 by the Division of Christian Education of the National Council of the Churches of Christ in the U.S.A., and are used by permission.

Quotations from *The New English Bible* (NEB), © The Delegates of The Oxford University Press and The Syndics of the Cambridge University Press, 1961, 1970, are used by permission.

Quotations from *The Jerusalem Bible* (JB), copyright © 1966 by Darton, Longman & Todd, Ltd. and Doubleday and Company, Inc., are used by permission of the publisher.

Quotations marked KJV are from the King James or Authorized Version of the Bible.

Quotations from Today's English Version of the New Testament (TEV), copyright © American Bible Society 1966, are used by permission.

Contents

Preface

SEVERAL YEARS AGO, after observing reactions of fellow Christians to some of my views on woman's role in the home, church, and society, it occurred to me that all too little creative Christian thought had been given the subject. The phrase "women's liberation" was not yet in use, but stirrings indicating a new surge of feminism were apparent. Betty Friedan's *The Feminine Mystique* was on the bestseller list, and articles on "trapped housewives" were beginning to appear in the popular press. Yet, for the most part, it seemed that Christians were sitting on the sidelines saying nothing about the "woman question"—except once in awhile to voice dismay at the way things were going and to warn of dire consequences for society if women were to forget that their place is in the home.

The idea of writing a book on the subject began to grow in my mind, and I wrote a few articles on woman's role in Christian perspective for *Eternity* magazine. Reader reaction varied, but I was especially encouraged by the interest shown by an assistant editor, Nancy Hardesty. We corresponded only briefly and infrequently; but from the clippings she sometimes sent for my files, I perceived that we had similar viewpoints. The thought of inviting her to join me as coauthor of a book about women flashed through my mind. But I dismissed it, thinking she was too busy with her editorial responsibilities even to consider it. I laid the project aside to accept other writing assignments.

In 1969, a visit from an unmarried missionary friend rekindled my interest in the projected book. She freely confided her heartaches, struggles, and questionings and urged me to write on the woman issue and especially to include some help for single women. Again I thought of Nancy. She had once recommended a book dealing with this topic, and I knew she must have thought a great deal about singleness on the personal level.

However, I debated about writing her. For one thing, I hesitated to invite someone I didn't even know to join me in such a major project. Also there was the matter of timing. In spite of my writing

activities, something of the "restless housewife problem" was
creeping up in my own life. I felt this might be the time to return
to school to complete my interrupted college education and wondered about the wisdom of getting involved in writing another book.
On the other hand, perhaps the book would be just the outlet
I needed.

I asked the small group of Christian friends who met weekly
in our home for prayer and sharing to pray with me for God's
guidance. I then planned to write to Nancy Hardesty and ask if
she would like to join me in writing such a book. At the same
time, I would investigate the possibilities of applying college cred-
its from years before to a degree in religion at Indiana University.
Whichever of the two paths opened up I would accept as God's leading. I never expected *both* to be his answer—but that is what
happened.

God's timing was perfect. Unknown to me, Nancy had just moved
to the Chicago area, only a five-hour drive from my home, making
it possible for us to meet soon after I wrote her and to have
many delightful visits together since. I expected to find in her a
writing partner, and I did. But more than that, I found a friend.
And sister. During my year of completing my university studies,
she stood by me with constant encouragement and faithful prayers.
She also tried to help me work through the many practical problems of combining family responsibilities with the time and energy
demands of a writing career, just as I've tried to help her work
through the challenges of living as a single woman in a couple-
oriented society. Both of us have come to understand the "woman
issue" in a broader and deeper sense than ever before, in relation
to both married and unmarried women, because we have learned
to understand, love, and appreciate each other.

Special thanks are due to my husband John who encouraged us
all the way. We are grateful for his willingness to serve as a
sounding board for our ideas and for the many research suggestions
he gave us. (It helps to be married to a sociology professor who
is also doing research and writing in the area of women's roles!)
And we want to thank him for those times when, during Nancy's
visits, he somehow managed to put up with *two* "liberated women,"
whose long talkathons sometimes lasted until two or three in the
morning and whose engrossment in putting together the book sometimes seemed to take precedence over putting together his dinner!
But he bore up well, as did sons Steve and Dave. Our thanks to
all three.

—LETHA SCANZONI

THE YEAR 1969 marked a turning point in my life. Bitter about the way my life was going and homesick for the Midwest, I agreed to take a teaching position at Trinity College in Deerfield, Ill. This involved two things I had vowed never to do: teach, and work for another Christian organization.

During my first frustrating month I received a letter from a woman I had never met and knew only by name from her writing, Letha Scanzoni. She asked if I were interested in joining her as coauthor of a book on women. She warned me that the project was a lonely and controversial one, but suggested that we seemed to have the same views and so might stimulate each other's thinking. In my reply I warned her that I was no longer a professional writer but an "old maid schoolteacher" and had no answers to the problems of singleness. But I accepted the offer to share the search for some answers to the whole "woman question."

As Robert Frost says in his poem "The Road Not Taken," "that has made all the difference." In the past few years I have been traveling an entirely different road, one which God set me on despite my own logical calculations to the contrary. I have found that I enjoy teaching immensely—enough to motivate me to go back to graduate school for the necessary Ph.D. My writing career has blossomed in several directions. And my relationship with Letha, nurtured by sometimes almost daily letters and frequent visits, has radically changed many areas of my life.

We have written a book together. It could have been merely an intellectual and business collaboration. Instead it has been a union of two souls. I came to her a bitter, lonely, insecure, frustrated, and troubled person. And I found in Letha someone who was interested not only in my intellectual ideas, but also in the wounds of my heart. I found acceptance, empathy, and love. It revolutionized my life. She has shown me God's love until I can now truly believe that he loves me. She has understood and supported me until now I can accept myself and step out onto new pathways. She has probed and challenged my thinking as I have probed and challenged hers. Together we have struggled with all aspects of what it means to be a woman, married or single, in today's society.

You have in your hands our answers. We hope that our thoughts will stretch your mind, inspire your spirit, and deepen the love in your heart for all of your sisters.

—NANCY HARDESTY

Introduction

JESUS CHRIST spoke a great deal about liberation. He saw the world in terms of slavery to sin, suffering, selfishness, and the fear of death. And he exposed the futility of man's own efforts to extricate himself from such bondage, pointing out that man-made traditions have a way of "making void the law of God" and tightening the bonds rather than bringing freedom to do God's will. But "if the Son makes you free, you will be free indeed," Jesus said (John 8:36). He described his mission in Isaiah's words: "He has sent me to proclaim release to the captives and recovering of sight to the blind, to set at liberty those who are oppressed" (Luke 4:18).

Women were certainly a class of oppressed people at the time that Jesus walked upon the earth. Both pagan culture and Jewish custom insisted that women be kept in their place—and that place was clearly spelled out. Opportunities for self-fulfillment, personal development, and for achievement and leadership in public life or organized religion were greatly restricted. Women were expected to stay behind the scenes, keep the home fires burning, bear and rear children, and remain apart from the busy, important world of men.

Yet, Jesus' attitude toward women gave promise of liberation from the chains of custom. Women who followed him, served him, spoke with him, and listened to his teaching could not help but contrast his treatment of them with the way other religious leaders regarded them. Could it be that his message of God's love and redemption contained the seeds from which could sprout possibilities for human dignity and authentic personhood for all people—regardless of class or race or *sex?* Could it be that here was woman's liberator? We believe the answer is yes!

In speaking of liberation for the Christian woman, we are not thinking of an organization or movement, but rather a *state of mind* in which a woman comes to view herself as Jesus Christ sees her—as a person created in God's image whom he wants to make free to be whole, to grow, to learn, to utilize fully the talents and gifts God has given her as a unique individual. It is a

realization that men and women alike may be freed from sex role
stereotypes and traditions which hinder development into the true
humanness that God intended when he created male and female
in his own image to delight in fellowship with him and with one
another.

The first two chapters of Genesis show us that God didn't plan
for man and woman to be in conflict or competition. Rather they
are to be partners—both in family life (the two are to "become one
flesh," and "be fruitful and multiply") and in carrying out God's
will on earth ("subdue it; and have dominion"). The redeeming
power of Christ makes it possible to go back to the ideals of Para-
dise, for he came to make the crooked straight. That straightening
includes not only our relationship with God but also our twisted,
out-of-joint relationships with other people, including male-female
relationships.

The liberated Christian woman learns to appreciate her worth as
a person created by and for God, possessing unique gifts bestowed
upon her for use in honoring him and benefiting mankind. She is
not content to settle without thought into the constricting pattern
society expects of its members who happen to have been born
female. Instead, she is free to know herself, be herself, and develop herself in her own special way, creatively using to the full
her intellect and talents. It is in the hope of waking more Christian women to the possibility of such a life that this book has been
written.

1. Religion and the Male/Female Polarity

> Men have broad and large chests, and small narrow hips, and more understanding than women, who have but small and narrow chests, and broad hips, to the end they should remain at home, sit still, keep house, and bear and bring up children.
> —MARTIN LUTHER, *Table-Talk*, DCCXXV, 1569

> Man for the field, and woman for the hearth;
> Man for the sword, and for the needle she;
> Man with the head, and woman with the heart;
> Man to command, and woman to obey;
> All else confusion.
> —ALFRED LORD TENNYSON, *The Princess*, Part V

"WHEN GOD CREATED MAN, he made him in the likeness of God. Male and female he created them, and he blessed them and named them Man when they were created" (Gen. 5:1–2). Thus, at the very beginning, we see the basic division of the human race, the division into two parts—two sexes. (The English word *sex* itself conveys the thought of separateness. It is derived from the Latin *secare,* which means to cut or divide.)

But what does this quality of "otherness" or separateness mean? What *is* maleness and femaleness in relation to humanness? These are the questions being asked today. And in this reexamination of the roles and relationships of men and women, an agonizing reappraisal of religion's part in female subordination is occurring. Current books and articles calling for woman's liberation are sprinkled liberally with quotations and illustrations of misogyny from the Judeo-Christian tradition, as well as from among the teachings and practices of other religions, such as Islam and Hinduism.

Psychoanalyst Karen Horney has discussed the attitudes of men toward women in various cultures and in different periods of history, and has described the role of religion and philosophy in the conflict between the sexes.[1] She points out that the very fact of *differences* between the sexes inevitably results in *comparison.* That is, one of the sexes comes to be thought of as superior to the other. An ideology is then set up to justify roles assigned to each sex on the basis of such comparison. Furthermore, if this ideology is claimed to be divinely ordained and carries the label of "God's

13

will," its potency is great indeed. Discrimination becomes not only
condoned or excused, but it is actually encouraged—on the basis
of principle!

In recognizing the differentiation between the sexes, religious
systems the world over have found a variety of ways to deal with
it. The noted historian of religions, Mircea Eliade, has written of
archaic man's fascination with polarities—both cosmic polarities
(heaven/earth, right/left, day/night, life/death) and the polarities
of human existence (male/female, we/they, etc.).[2] He points out
that where dichotomies exist, there is "opposition, clash, and
combat," which raises the question of how this conflict may be
mediated or resolved.

An examination of myths, customs, and rites of a variety of
cultures indicates four major ways in which the religions of man
have attempted to deal with the male/female polarity. First, there
is the approach which strongly emphasizes the distinctiveness of the
sexes, setting male and female in opposition to one another. Antithesis is stressed through patterned exclusiveness or segregation.
The world of men and the world of women are separate ones.
In choosing a title for this approach to the polarity problem,
debarment seems fitting.

Complementarity is a second approach. Here the sexes are viewed
as different but complementary. Each sex is considered equal in
worth but has its own sphere to fill. An overlapping of the spheres
is precluded or at least discouraged; rather, they are considered
counterparts, rounding out, reinforcing, and supplementing one
another. As an example, we might think of the Yin-Yang philosophy
of ancient China in which opposition is looked upon as counter-
balance. Yin is the term applied to the female principle of the
universe which is regarded as passive and negative, whereas Yang
is the "active, positive, or male principle."[3] The two principles
maintain an equilibrium—alternating, rotating, and balancing one
another in perfect complementarity for the smooth running of the
universe.

Synthesis, a third method of dealing with the male/female polarity enigma, refers to integration. The two antithetical elements
are united. There is a blending or merging of male and female to
form a new entity. Eliade speaks of various cultures in which
ritual enactments periodically take place to call attention to the
new third form that emerges when male and female elements
unite.[4]

Lastly, there is *transcendency,* which overlooks or denies any
sexual distinctiveness insofar as the realm of the sacred is concerned. The rupture and separateness that result from stressing

sexual differentiation are transcended. Such a view suggests the existence of an altogether new dimension where the polarity is somehow dissolved or rendered meaningless. Eliade sees such an approach, for example, in certain ideas of the Absolute in eastern religions where "the *summum bonum* is situated beyond polarities." [5] The Absolute may be thought of in terms of the ultimate liberation *(moksha* or *mukti)* of Hinduism or the "awakening" and deliverance implied in the Buddhist nirvana. The important point is that there is some notion of a realm or state of being in which the male-female dichotomy no longer matters.

Many people are confused and puzzled about Judeo-Christian teachings and customs with regard to women. We believe such confusion has occurred because *all four* of the above streams of thought are found in the Bible. At one time, one may surface; at another time, it may be a different one. And occasionally, two or three seem to bubble up at the same time—either to go at cross currents or to blend together.

For example, we sometimes see the *debarment* approach. Women were set apart during menstruation and after childbirth. Men and women were segregated in the synagogue and temple. In certain places and times, women were debarred from teaching in religious services and were told to keep silent in church. On the other hand, *complementarity* is often stressed—particularly in New Testament passages that give instructions on husband and wife roles and duties, or in Paul's comment about the interdependence of the sexes in 1 Corinthians 11:11–12.

The most obvious example of *synthesis* or a union of the sexes is marriage. There is a fusion into a new entity: man and woman are united so that a new family unit comes into being. "The two shall become one. So they are no longer two but one" (Matt. 19: 5–6). The fourth approach, *transcendency,* is perhaps most clearly summed up in Galatians 3:28: "There is neither Jew nor Greek, there is neither slave nor free, there is neither male nor female; for you are all one in Christ Jesus."

Christianity has the potential of offering transcendency as the solution to the problem of suspiciousness and separation between the sexes—a transcendency made possible because men and women stand on equal footing as fellow members of the kingdom of God. Galatians 3:28, in our opinion, holds the key to bringing harmony and removing the dissonant clash that is bound to exist as long as one sex is looked upon as superior and the other as being inferior and the source of evil.

Only as *all* human beings—male and female—are regarded as being equally in a condition of need before God and equally recipients of his love and grace can the message of Christ be considered good news for women. All mankind, not just the distaff side, is in a state of estrangement from God; and the word of reconciliation in Christ is offered to all. The description of Jesus as "the Lamb of God, who takes away the sin of the world" (John 1:29) certainly implies that women are included in that world. To suggest that the curse upon man is lifted through the redemption offered in Christ, but that the curse upon woman somehow remains (with the result that all women must forever be penalized because of Eve's transgression) seems to be a false and inconsistent theological assumption.

Yet a tension exists within the Christian tradition because, while transcendency seems to be presented as the ideal of the kingdom, there are at the same time certain biblical passages that may be interpreted as perpetuating what one writer calls "the myth of feminine evil," [6] and other passages that seem to suggest a hierarchical view of the sexes, with male above female. This tension has caused and continues to cause great confusion in attempts to understand the teachings of Scripture in relation to woman's role in the home, in public life, and in organized religion.

For this reason, it is imperative that we next turn our attention to an exploration of what the Bible has to say about women. *Does the Bible put women down?* What causes some voices to shout that Christianity has kept women in an inferior and degraded position, while other voices counter by claiming that Christianity has exalted womankind to a position never known before? The following chapters endeavor to provide some answers to these and other related questions.

2. Understanding the Bible

> The Word has to be free to remake and reform the Church over and over again. The moment the Church loses interest in working the mines of the Word because it thinks it has seen all there is to see, that moment the Church also loses its power and its credibility in the world. When the Church thinks it knows all there is to know, the opportunity for surprising discovery is closed. The Church then becomes old, without perspective, and without light and labor and fruitfulness.
>
> —G. C. BERKOUWER[1]

TO STUDY THE BIBLE'S teaching on women, or any other subject, one must first be aware of the subject of *hermeneutics*—the principles for interpreting Scripture. Except for some of the Wisdom literature (such as Proverbs), most of the Bible is not written in pithy aphorisms but in logically developed paragraphs, sections, books.

Thus, in studying Scripture, we must continually ask: What is the author really saying? What is the context? Under what circumstances was this written? What do we know from history, archaeology, or other disciplines that might shed light on the culture of the people to whom this particular portion was addressed or from which it sprang? How can this knowledge help us better understand the meaning of this passage? What is its application for today and for my life?

Any thoughtful Christian recognizes that such questions are not attempts to destroy the Bible but are rather efforts to comprehend what it has to say to us. This is nothing new. The Old Testament describes the efforts of Ezra and his assistants. They "helped the people to understand the law. . . . And they read from the book, from the law of God, clearly; and they gave the sense, so that the people understood the reading" (Neh. 8:7–8). Scripture had to be interpreted for full comprehension and application.

Such efforts are common in approaching the Bible. We view certain passages as allegorical or figurative and others as literal. We understand certain instructions to be addressed to a particular person or group (e.g., 2 Tim. 4:21; 1 Tim. 5:23). To interpret other instructions, we must know the customs of the times in which they were given. The teachings on meats offered to idols (1 Cor. 8 and

17

10), for example, require some understanding of the situation in Corinth when Paul was writing. From this understanding we go on to find principles of Christian liberty that can be applied in today's world.

Most Christians do not feel that they are breaking a divine command by not following the "letter of the law" in regard to some matter seen to be culturally conditioned. Men wear longer hair styles in spite of 1 Corinthians 11:14. Few Christian women feel they are sinning if they wear jewelry, attractive clothing, robes, or braided hair—even though 1 Timothy 2:9 and 1 Peter 3:3 are on the pages of Scripture. Churches do not require men to lift their hands while praying (1 Tim. 2:8). Modern translations have not hesitated to change the "holy kiss" of 1 Corinthians 16:20 into a handshake. This is interpretation and application.

Christians who claim to follow "exactly what the Bible says" are nevertheless *interpreting* its meaning. Otherwise, there would be complete uniformity. Matters of church polity would be settled once for all; there would be no episcopal, presbyterian, and congregational forms of government each claiming the Bible's support for its position. Questions about prophecy would be resolved in total agreement. Opinions about the Lord's Supper and baptismal practices would show no variance throughout Christendom. Questions about dress, customs, and proper conduct for Christians would have one final answer. Yet we know that these are all areas of disagreement among Christians—Christians who take the Bible seriously, yet who interpret its meaning differently on various issues.

This brings us to the matter of *theology*—the stepping-stone that lies between revelation and application. The theologian tries to understand the whole of Scripture in order to make generalizations about the nature and destiny of human beings and the will of God for human life. Based on the Bible, theology is also open to other ways of understanding God's world. If all truth is God's truth, then insights from philosophy, the physical sciences, and the behavioral sciences may help us understand the biblical message.

The biblical theologian does not build on isolated proof texts but first seeks the *locus classicus,* the major biblical statement, on a given matter. (The doctrine of creation and fall, for example, is to be found most clearly spelled out in Gen. 1–3 and Rom. 5:12–21, not in 1 Cor. 11:2–16 or 1 Tim. 2:13–14.) Passages which deal with an issue systematically are used to help understand incidental references elsewhere. Passages which are theological and doctrinal in content are used to interpret those where the writer is dealing with practical local cultural problems. (Except for Gal. 3:28, all of the references to women in the New Testament are contained in passages dealing with practical concerns about personal relationships or behavior in worship services.)

Some Christians, of course, feel they don't need a theological interpretation—that there is no need for a bridge between God's revelation in the Bible and its meaning for today. They claim to apply the Bible in a literalistic manner, asserting that the Bible *is* God's will rather than the means by which God's will may be ascertained. "The Bible means exactly what it says," they assert. However, they often betray inconsistencies when it comes to literalistic applications of such commands as "if any one would sue you and take your coat, let him have your cloak as well" (Matt. 5:40), "if your eye causes you to sin, pluck it out" (Mark 9:47).

By theology, then, we mean an attempt to go behind the letter to the spirit of biblical teachings. Jesus interpreted theologically the commandment about not committing adultery. He went beyond the letter of the law to disclose its *spirit*—a spirit that can be violated in thought and attitude completely apart from a sexual act (Matt. 5:27–28). Similarly, his theological interpretation of "Thou shalt not kill" included violating our brother through hatred, insult, contempt, and neglect as well as actual murder. Never was Jesus satisfied merely to repeat traditional interpretations of Scripture; he constantly sought to uncover fresh meanings and new insights that escaped others. He revealed the heart of God's message to his hearers. (See Luke 24:27, which contains the Greek word from which "hermeneutics" is derived.)

Dr. G. C. Berkouwer has written that this attitude toward the Scriptures has characterized people of God through the ages. The fear and hesitancy that some Christians display at present in view of the search for new insights from the Bible is unnecessary. Berkouwer points out that "if the men of the sixteenth century had been content to go along with tradition, we would never have known the blessing of the Reformation." But matters were not easy for the Reformers because Rome accused them of acting "as ingrates in the face of the Holy Spirit's guidance of the Church." [2] This did not stop the Reformers, however, because they knew that it is possible for traditions to place "a veil of misunderstanding" over crucial portions of God's Word to us.

The matter of hermeneutics is central in discussing the question of woman's role and status. For too long, proof texts from the Bible have been hurled at women to "keep them in their place." Now the church is beginning to take a new look at scriptural teachings on human personhood and human relationships with regard to both sexes.

Specifically, with respect to the church's attitude toward woman's status, seminary professor Julius Bodensieck has suggested some guidelines. Interpretations of Scripture relative to women must not conflict with either the unequivocal, universal, and identical sinfulness of both sexes, or the grace bestowed on both sexes through Jesus Christ. Likewise, any interpretation that does not stress equal responsibility of both sexes in the kingdom of God must be rejected. An interpretation that "absolutizes a given historical social order" is unacceptable, as is one that is based on only isolated texts. And, Bodensieck concludes, we should reject any interpretation that does not apply just as well to women in a modern society; in totalitarian, welfare, and democratic states; inside and outside marriage; in the home and in the working world.[3]

In other words, any teaching in regard to women must square with the basic theological thrust of the Bible. It must not contradict the truth of the gospel. And it must apply to all women, yesterday, today, and tomorrow, whatever the social situation.

Since we believe the Bible to be God's Word, we also feel it reveals the divine nature. Throughout Scripture God is spoken of as the Father, the Son, "he." Is God then masculine? Some people are convinced that he is. C. S. Lewis once declared, "God Himself has taught us how to speak of Him. To say that it does not matter is to say either that all the masculine imagery is not inspired, is merely human in origin, or else that, though inspired, it is quite arbitrary and unessential. And this is surely intolerable." [4]

To speak of God otherwise is considered nearly blasphemy. Many were shocked to hear singer Helen Reddy accept her Grammy Award with "I'd like to thank God because She made everything possible." Any pastor who began by praying, "Our Mother, who art in heaven . . ." would probably be defrocked forthwith. Yet the Bible is not afraid to use that image of God. In Isaiah 42:14 God says, "I will cry out like a woman in travail, I will gasp and pant." Isaiah 46:3 continues the image: "Hearken to me, O house of Jacob, all the remnant of the house of Israel, who have been borne by me from your birth, carried from the womb." Again in Isaiah 49:15, God asks Israel, " 'Can a woman forget her sucking child, that she should have no compassion on the son of her womb?' Even these may forget, yet I will not forget you." The same image is used in Isaiah 66:13 where God promises, "As one whom his mother comforts, so I will comfort you." (All of which might lead one to ask if "Second Isaiah" was really Isaiah's wife, the prophetess.) The Psalmist also sees God as a mother when he says, "I have calmed and quieted my soul, like a child quieted at its mother's breast" (Ps. 131:2).

Christ used a maternal image when, overlooking the city of

Jerusalem, he cried, "How often would I have gathered your children together as a hen gathers her brood under her wings, and you would not!" (Matt. 23:37). We often think of God as the father welcoming home the prodigal son or the shepherd seeking his lost sheep, but how often do we think of God as the woman who swept out her entire house in search of one precious coin (Luke 15: 8–10)?

In essence, however, God is neither masculine or feminine. As Jesus told the Samaritan woman at the well, "God is spirit, and those who worship him must worship in spirit and truth" (John 4:24). Israel was careful to distinguish its God from the divine couples of the fertility cults. While the Israelites spoke of him in masculine imagery somewhat, growing no doubt out of their patriarchal culture, they emphasized that their God was not an anthropomorphic, terrestrial being, not a progenitor, but the Creator, the high and lofty One, God of the universe. He could not be located in just one place nor described by one name. Thus he is revealed by analogies: ruler, judge, general, shepherd, friend, lion, lamb, bread, vine, fire. The Old Testament speaks of Wisdom ("She is more precious than jewels. . . . Long life is in her right hand; in her left hand are riches and honor. Her ways are ways of pleasantness, and all her paths are peace" says Prov. 3:15–17). In the New Testament Wisdom (feminine) becomes Word (cf. Proverbs 8 and John 1:1–18).

The adjectives we use of God are not intended to indicate sexuality but generic personhood. God is a person, a union of three persons. In all languages persons can only be referred to by masculine or feminine pronouns. Usually in referring to members of a group or a person whose sex is unknown, we use the masculine. It is generic, whereas the feminine is used in reference only to individuals known to be female. God is neither and both. He contains all personhood; we are all made in his image, male and female. In thinking of God we should use neither "he" nor "she" but "Thou" in whose presence we stand at all times.

Our thinking about God is important because it colors our self-image and our interactions with others. Our children get the message early, as this epistle from *Children's Letters to God* indicates: "Dear God, Are boys better than girls? I know you are one but try to be fair." [5] Women have just as much right as men to think of themselves in God's image and of God as similar to them. Men have no more right than women to think of themselves as God's image bearers, God's representatives.

The God revealed in Scripture is not only the Holy One of Israel; he is also Jesus of Nazareth and the Spirit poured out at

Pentecost. The nature of this triune God is not explained by the New Testament, and thus our doctrine of the Trinity has been hammered out subsequently by the church. Artistically we sometimes symbolize the Trinity by a triangle inside a circle. The circle represents God's unity and eternality while the points of the triangle suggest his three distinct persons. In relation to the world it is as though the circle has revolved, revealing one point at a time pointing downward. Yet in essence the Trinity is characterized by mutuality and reciprocity in love.

The nature of the Trinity is relevant to our study of the Christian woman because of 1 Corinthians 11:3: "the head of every man is Christ, the head of a woman is her husband, and the head of Christ is God." Many have interpreted this to portray a "chain of command" in which authority passes downward from God to Christ to the Holy Spirit to the man to the woman and thence to the child, the slave, and the dog. Clearly, however, Paul did not intend that image, or he would have begun logically with either God at the top or woman at the bottom. Instead he begins with a middle member, and speaks in a more circular manner. As Chrysostom argued fifteen hundred years ago, the emphasis is on unity, not hierarchy.[6] As Christ is one with God in substance, so the husband is one flesh with his wife. Every Christian is united with Christ. The purpose of head-coverings (the point made in 1 Cor. 11:2–16) is to display the marital union and thus glorify the triune God in whose image male and female are created.

Is Christ subordinate to the Father? "The Father is greater than I," he says in John 14:28. "My Father . . . is greater than all," he declares in John 10:29, but the very next verse says, "I and the Father are one." And what are we to make of John 14:9: "He who has seen me has seen the Father"? Christ as God and man both rules and submits. He voluntarily, out of love, set aside the privileges of the Godhead to assume the work of redemption as a man, but he has now ascended into heaven to resume all his divine attributes. He is no longer subordinate to the Father as he was on earth, but coequal, as the creed says, "very God of very God" (see Heb. 1:3; 1 Cor. 15:27–28).

All of us as Christians are called to forsake the ways of the world which include domination and lording it over others (Mark 10:42). We are to "be subject to one another out of reverence for Christ" (Eph. 5:21), and "in humility count others better than" ourselves (Phil. 2:3), for "God opposes the proud, but gives grace to the humble" (1 Pet. 5:5). In Christ there is no chain of command but a community founded and formed by self-giving love.

3. It All Started with Eve

> We are borne ruinous
> For that first marriage was our funerall:
> One woman at one blow, then kill'd us all.
> —JOHN DONNE, "First Anniversary"

> Then God said, "Let us make man in our image, after our likeness; and let them have dominion over the fish of the sea, and over the birds of the air, and over the cattle, and over all the earth, and over every creeping thing that creeps upon the earth." So God created man in his own image, in the image of God he created him; male and female he created them. And God blessed them, and God said to them, "Be fruitful and multiply, and fill the earth and subdue it; and have dominion over the fish of the sea and over the birds of the air and over every living thing that moves upon the earth."
> —Genesis 1:26–28

THIS IS HOW we as human beings began and where we must begin if we are to understand ourselves. In the beginning we are told that, male and female, we are created by God, created in his image, created to be fruitful and to subdue the earth.

What does it mean to say that male and female are created in the image and likeness of God? Those who stress the differences between the sexes sometimes talk as if God's attributes of justice and love, righteousness and mercy, wisdom and goodness were divided between the sexes. Thus each person contains only half of God's image, which can only be completely realized within a married couple.

Some theologians have stressed the intellectual nature of the image. We are rational creatures capable of comprehending God and thinking his thoughts after him. Thus our bodies are not part of the image and indeed are irrelevant to it, they contend. The purpose of sexual differentiation is simply procreation.

We believe that the image of God is not only rationality but "relationality." All persons, male and female, are created by God with rational self-awareness and also with the capacity for self-transcendence. The fellowship of husband and wife, of parents and child, and even the fellowship within the church reflect the dynamic mutuality and reciprocity of the Trinity, which agreed, "Let us make man in our image." God wanted a person who could not only understand and communicate with him but also respond to him in love. And so he made human beings who could also so relate to each other.

After the Fall the fact of mankind in God's image is reaffirmed (Gen. 5:1). Although the Fall marred the image, cracked our mirror, the New Testament promises Christians that we "have put on the new nature, which is being renewed in knowledge after the image of its creator" (Col. 3:10). Although our human nature has been corrupted, we can "be renewed in the spirit of [our] minds, and put on the new nature, created after the likeness of God in true righteousness and holiness" (Eph. 4:23–24).

What part does sexual differentiation play in this image? Obviously it does not reflect any sexual differentiation in the Godhead. Yet it is important because God created it and pronounced it good. Those who see sexuality as evil and part of our fallen nature are more Platonic and gnostic than Judeo-Christian. Sexuality is necessary in order that we might fulfill God's first command to propagate the race. Yet God could have devised some other method, perhaps on the parthenogenetic model of some lower animals. Instead he chose to make men and women dependent on each other to carry out this task and thus to have two people responsible for each child. The necessity for fellowship is "built in" to human nature.

While marriage is a unique and ultimate expression of such communion, it is not the only way in which human beings reflect the relational dimension of God's image. God's statement that "it is not good that the man should be alone" has implications beyond the marital union. It shows us that no human being is self-sufficient but all experience humanness only in relation to others and to God. We need each other—old people, young people, men, women, children—both within and across sex lines. Jesus desired that his followers experience the oneness and glory that he shared within the Trinity (John 17:22–23). Such interdependence and unity is surely a manifestation of his image.

Sexual differentiation does not dictate social roles. Genesis 1: 26–28 does not say, as a leading evangelist would have it, that "the biological assignment was basic and simple: Eve was to be the child-bearer, and Adam was to be the breadwinner. . . . Wife, mother, homemaker—this the appointed destiny of real womanhood." [1] Scripture speaks of no "separate spheres" or "different functions." Both sexes were created with the biological and psychological capability for parenthood and both were also given what theologians call the "cultural mandate." Agriculture, animal hus-

bandry, education, industry, government, commerce, the arts—
every human being is equally responsible under God for all aspects of life on this earth.

"And God saw everything that he had made, and behold it was
very good. . . . God finished his work which he had done, and he
rested . . ." (Gen. 1:31; 2:2).

MAN AND THEN WOMAN

Genesis 2 seems to begin the story all over again. Rather than
an ordered progression from the creation of earth, light, waters,
vegetation, sun and moon, birds, fish, and animals to mankind, it
tells the story from another angle, focusing the spotlight on man,
created before animals and before woman. Many have found reconciliation of the two accounts impossible. On the surface they are
contradictory. So the temptation has been to build one's theology
on one and ignore the other. Paul, for example, seldom refers to
the first story at all. According to biblical scholarship, the second
chapter is older, imbedded in Jewish folklore from more primitive
times.[2] Genesis 1 is a more recent account and may be seen as
an editorial attempt to counter some of the more anti-feminine
and anthropomorphic interpretations which chapter 2 had occasioned. Read as a unit, however, the first three chapters of Genesis
seem to answer different questions that people have always pondered: How did the world begin? What is the relationship of the
sexes in marriage? How did the world get in such a mess?

Genesis 2 tells us that God created man from the dust of the
ground and breathed into him the breath of life (2:7). Giving
Adam a perfect garden in which to live and talking with him face
to face, God still felt that "it is not good that man should be
alone" (2:18). The animals were created and brought to Adam. He
rationally understood the essence of each and so named them, but
among them he could not find one with whom he could relate.
God did not suddenly realize at this point that he had erred, that
his creation was not so perfect after all. Nor did he look at man
and conclude, "That human is a rather scruffy model. Maybe we
could improve with another try."

Rather, within God's gracious plan, after showing man that it
was not good to be alone, that the animals could not meet his
needs, "God caused a deep sleep to fall upon the man, and while he
slept took one of his ribs and . . . made [it] into a woman"
(2:21–22). Those who see in Genesis 2 an old man fashioning a
clay doll beside a river bed or a white-gowned plastic surgeon
building a human body around one rib miss the point of the narra-

tive. Details of the actual creation of both male and female are
shrouded in mystery. We do know, however, that in each case
creation was a direct act of God. God did not simply saw an original androgynous being in half, as Plato and Jewish speculation
suggest.[3] God's use of Adam's rib has provoked preachers to note
that woman was "taken from his side to be his equal," "taken
from under his heart" to be his beloved, etc. Perhaps more instruc-
tive is linguistic evidence that "rib" is related to "life." [4] For
both Adam and Eve shared the same life; they were not two species
but "one flesh." Woman is not simply an object within the created
world, as sinful men have been prone to view her, but a complete
human person, synonymous with man's very self.

God created Eve to be "an help meet for him" (2:18, 20, KJV).
From this King James rendering stem many of the warped ideas
that surround the woman's role. Subsequent translations have
corrupted the phrase into "helpmate" which has engendered visions
of an assistant, if not a servant. The key Hebrew words here are
ezer, "help," and *neged,* "meet."

Neged is a preposition meaning "before," "in the presence of,"
"in the sight of." Psalm 16:8 says, "I keep the Lord always *before*
me." The familiar Psalm 23:5 promises, "Thou preparest a table
before me *in the presence of* my enemies." "Suitable," "correspond-
ing to" or "adequate" to meet all man's needs for physical, intellectual, and social communion might be better translations for
the old English "meet."

Ezer, used as a noun meaning "help" or "helper," appears twenty-
one times in the Old Testament. Sixteen of these occasions refer
to a *super*ordinate helper, not a *sub*ordinate. "From whence does
my *help* come? My *help* comes from the Lord," says Psalm 121:
1–2. Psalm 146:3, 5 tells us, "Put not your trust in princes, in
a son of man, in whom there is no *help.* . . . Happy is he whose
help is the God of Jacob." At no time is *ezer* used to indicate a
subordinate helper unless the references in Genesis 2 are taken to
be exceptions to the general rule.[5]

Then exactly what does "an help meet for him" mean? Bible
scholars offer such phrases as "a mirror of himself, in which he
recognizes himself," one who will "assist him in the work given
him to do, carrying it on in the same spirit," "a vis-à-vis which
has the character of a Thou." [6] Woman was created in every way
the equal of man, one to whom he could relate at every level of
his being.

Adam's response upon awakening assures us that he realized
woman's complementary nature at once. He saw her not as different
but as one like himself. Hebrew scholars tell us that the grammar

at this point is chaotic—Adam's response was much like ours when we are surprised and delighted. The repetition of the word "this" indicates that he was at a loss for words to describe his joy and could only point:

> *This* at last is bone from my bones,
> and flesh from my flesh!
> *This* is to be called woman,
> for *this* was taken from man' (Gen. 2:23, JB, italics ours).[7]

The biblical writer immediately underscores the point of the story with the editorial comment, "Therefore a man leaves his father and his mother and cleaves to his wife, and they become one flesh" (2:24). Interestingly it is the *man,* not the woman, who leaves and cleaves, suggesting a matriarchal family model, rather than the patriarchal one which prevailed in the Old Testament. The term "leave" means "to abandon" or "to forsake" and is generally used of forsaking strange gods. "To cleave" means to establish a deep personal attachment. The word is used of Ruth and Naomi (Ruth 1:14), of the people and King David (2 Sam. 20:2), and eight times of Israel and Jehovah.[8] The verse establishes a strong basis for marriage as an egalitarian partnership, though Israel did not practice it.

Jesus harmonizes Genesis 1 and 2 by joining 1:27 and 2:24: "Have you not read that he who made them from the beginning made them male and female, and said, 'For this reason a man shall leave his father and mother and be joined to his wife, and the two shall become one flesh'?" (Matt. 19:4–5). He used the reference to assert the fact that marriage and consequently divorce are not a masculine institution and prerogative, but an indissoluble union of male and female. He makes no comment about sexual or marital roles.

Yet Christian theologians have taught with Augustine that God created us male and female in "a kind of friendly and genuine union of the one ruling and the other obeying."[9] Usually termed "the order of creation," this assertion is sometimes said to be based on the order in which human beings were created (males first, females second) or more broadly on a general belief in the subordination of women to men due to woman's weaker nature (sometimes more bluntly referred to as her "inferiority").

IS ONE BETTER?

Is the *order* of creation of cosmic significance? 1 Timothy 2:13 prohibits women from teaching because "Adam was formed first,

then Eve." As we have seen, Genesis 1 and 2 vary in the matter
of order. In Genesis 1 male and female are said to be created
simultaneously by God as the culmination of his work. If beings
created first are to have precedence, then the animals are clearly
our betters. In Genesis 2 Adam is created prior to the animals
but the culmination of God's creative activity is clearly Eve. And
how order of creation relates to abilities in teaching is not explained.

Paul approaches the issue from a different angle in 1 Corinthians
11:8–9 where he argues that "man was not made from woman,
but woman from man. Neither was man created for woman, but
woman for man." The second creation narrative does say that
woman was made from and for man, but the theological leap from
this to woman's subordination is a traditional rabbinic (and one
might add "Christian") understanding that is not supported by the
text.[10] After all man was made from dust but this does not make
him subordinate to the earth.

Paul himself seems to realize immediately that this argument
has inevitably led to a subordination of women which is incompatible with the gospel he expounded in Galatians 3:28 and elsewhere. So lest readers be misled, he declares: "Nevertheless, in the
Lord woman is not independent of man nor man of woman; for as
woman was made from man, so man is now born of woman. And
all things are from God" (1 Cor. 11:11–12). As Jewett comments: "Here we have what may be the first expression of an
uneasy conscience on the part of a Christian theologian who argues
for the subordination of the female to the male." [11] Unfortunately
few theologians since have had such tender consciences!

This passage (1 Cor. 11) raises at least two other questions
relating to our understanding of Genesis and the "order of creation."
Verse 7 contains the curious statement that "a man ought not to
cover his head, since he is the image and glory of God; but woman
is the glory of man." Some have tried to avoid apparent problems
by suggesting that "image" here refers to the "order established
for marriage" rather than the *imago Dei,* but the verse itself
stands in seeming contradiction to Genesis 1:27, which says both
male and female were created in the image of God. Is Paul here
saying that women do not bear the image of God? No, he does
not say that and probably does not have the Genesis 1 account
in mind at all.

Rather than concentrating on "image," Paul is concerned with
"glory," *doxa.* To be "the glory of" someone is to manifest, reveal,
or represent that person (see Ezek. 1:26–28; Exod. 33:18; Isa.
40:5; John 1:14–18). Paul argues that mankind reflects the God-

head as Christ, the Second Adam, reflected God in the flesh. Woman reflects humanity or perhaps more precisely in this passage the wife represents her husband. Paul is not here making a major theological point but simply using what seems to us a rather curious rabbinic interpretation to underscore his instruction that in order to glorify God alone in worship men should have uncovered heads while women should veil their heads (to obscure the "glory of man").[12]

As Helmut Thielicke points out,[13] this passage sounds almost like the Gnostic doctrine of emanation by which man, being created first, was a higher emanation and contained a more clear and direct representation of God; while woman, created later, was a dimmer, more indirect reflection. Similar thinking has portrayed woman as earthy, sensual, less spiritually capable, more concerned with inferior, corporeal, temporal things.[14] It has led even in our own times to such comments as the following:

[Paul says that] God's purpose was to express Himself fully and crown all His works by bringing into being a creature made in His image, able to subdue, and rule, and develop all that is in the world. This creature was man, a masculine, resolved capable creature. And just as it appeals to our sense of fitness that when God became incarnate He should appear as a man, and not as woman, so does it appeal to our sense of fitness that it is man, and not woman, who should be thought of as created to be God's representative on earth. . . . By nature woman is endowed with a symbol of modesty and retirement. The veil, which signifies her devotement to home duties, is merely the artificial continuation of her natural gift of hair. . . . And nature, speaking through this visible sign of woman's hair, tells her that her place is in private, not in public, in the home, not in the city or the camp, in the attitude of free and loving subordination, not in the seat of authority and rule. In other respects also the physical constitution of woman points to a similar conclusion. Her shorter stature and slighter frame, her higher pitch of voice, her more graceful form and movement, indicate that she is intended for the gentler ministries of home life rather than for the rough work of the world. And similar indications are found in her mental peculiarities. . . .[15]

No one has ever asked women if this appealed to their sense of fitness!

Man is made in God's image, so the argument goes, and the facet of that image which he represents is God's authority, dominion, supremacy.[16] God rules the whole created universe but he has delegated some of his authority to man. While Genesis 1:28 clearly states that such authority has been given to both men and women, theologians have insisted that it has been delegated to males only. They have done so largely based on an understanding of the

Greek word "head," *kephalē*. Some scholars use the phrase *"kephalē*-structure" as a synonym for "order of creation." [17]

HEAD

The word *kephalē* is used in several different ways in the New Testament. "The hairs of your head are all numbered" (Matt. 10: 30) and "they struck his head with a reed" (Mark 15:19) illustrate its most common, literal use. Five times it is used of Christ as "the head of the corner" (e.g., Matt. 21:42). Christ is spoken of as head of the body in Ephesians 1:22, 4:15; 5:23 and Colossians 1:18; 2:19. Men (husbands) are mentioned in parallel with Christ only in 1 Corinthians 11:3 and Ephesians 5:23. Colossians 2:10 speaks of Christ as head but in a different respect which we will examine shortly. 1 Corinthians 12:12–27 speaks of the church as the body of Christ, but does not speak of Christ as its head, and members of the church appear to be included in the head or at least such parts as ears and eyes. Incidentally, "head" in Scripture has nothing to do with either thinking or making intellectual decisions, functions which we associate with the brain. Rather the heart was thought to be the source of such activity.[18]

What do these figurative references to "head" (found primarily in 1 Cor., Eph. and Col.) add up to? Do they reveal a *"kephalē*-structure," an "order of creation," which determines that males are to lead and rule while females are to submit and follow? This has been the traditional interpretation. But nowhere does the New Testament say positively that the "head" rules. Colossians 2:9–10 states of Christ, "in him the whole fulness of deity dwells bodily, and you [all Christians] have come to fulness of life in him, who is the head of all rule and authority." "Head" here obviously means "source." And we have been made one with that source, not subject to it. A similar thought is found in Ephesians 1:22 where God is said to have raised Christ above every rule and authority, submitting all things under his feet and making him head over his body the church. Again, what is in subjection is not the "body" but the world which is "under his feet" (a reminder of Gen. 3: 15?).

The concepts of headship and submission in regard to husbands and wives come together only in Ephesians 5:23–24. The general principle (5:21) is that all Christians should submit to each other (not all women to all men). Then Christian wives are asked to submit to their husbands as the church submits to Christ. Husbands in turn are not told to emulate Christ in his rulership of the universe (certainly a prerogative of Christ alone as God) but rather to follow his example of self-giving oneness with his body, the church. As we will see in our chapter on the marriage partnership, Paul was beginning with his readers' traditional understanding of patriarchal marriage and attempting to point them to a new understanding in Christ.

"Head," as used metaphorically in the New Testament, points overwhelmingly, *not* to a corporate organizational chart, but to a dynamic, organic, living unity—a "one flesh" relationship, if you will. As Christians we have all been baptized into one body, all made to drink of one spirit. Christ is the head "from whom the whole body, nourished and knit together through its joints and ligaments, grows with a growth that is from God" (Col. 2:19; cf. Eph. 4:16). The goal of this growth process is that every one of us might be conformed to his image, might grow "to the measure of the stature of the fulness of Christ" (Eph. 4:13).

The "head" of this living, growing organism is not its ruler but the source of its life. *Kephalē* is used almost synonymously with *archē,* "beginning," somewhat similar to our use of the "headwaters of a river" or "fountainhead." Colossians 1:15–18 sums it up perfectly (and notice the similarities to Paul's thinking in 1 Cor. 11): "He is the image of the invisible God, the first-born of all creation; for in him all things were created . . . all things were created through him and for him. He is before all things, and in him all things hold together. He is the head of the body, the church; he is the beginning [*archē*], the first-born from the dead, that in every thing he might be preeminent." The same image is clear in Ephesians 5:23: "Christ is the head of the church, his body, and is himself its Savior," its lifegiver. "Christ loved the church and gave himself up for her, that he might sanctify her. . . . For no man ever hates his own flesh, but nourishes and cherishes it, as Christ does the church, because we are members of his body" (Eph. 5: 25–30).

Christ is our "head" in the sense that he is the "first fruits" of the dead (1 Cor. 15:20). Adam was the first to die. But "priority of time neither necessarily nor irreversibly leads to priority in rank." [19] As Paul indicates in 1 Corinthians 11:11–12, while man may have come first in the original creation, men and women now live in mutuality and reciprocity with each other and with God. His point is precisely that of Genesis 2: men and women are not separate species with differing functions, capabilities, and value. Both are created by God from one substance to be "one flesh." Just as the Godhead is not a hierarchy or a pantheon of gods, but a loving union of three equal persons, so God has created us male and female in his image.

THE FALL

That image, however, was defaced by the Fall; that unity with God and with each other was broken. The biblical story begins with the observation, "Now the serpent was more subtle than any other wild creature that the Lord God had made" (Gen. 3:1). Although diverse explanations are offered of who or what appeared to Eve, the words it spoke were those of Satan himself.

And he addressed the woman. Luther speaks for a majority of commentators when he explains that "the subtlety of Satan showed itself also when he attacked human nature where it was weakest, namely, in Eve, and not in Adam. I believe that had Satan first tempted the man, Adam would have gained the victory." [20] Others agree that Eve was singled out for temptation because she was not too smart (after all, who goes around talking to snakes?). Woman's nature has thus been seen as naturally defective and gullible, making her less fit for any intellectual pursuit, particularly theological activity. This explanation, however, seems to cast a slur on God's wisdom in saying that woman's creation was in his image and "very good."

Another equally valid interpretation is that both Adam and Eve were there (v. 6), but Eve alone leaped to God's defense when Satan sought to discredit him. Genesis 3:2 could be translated, "The woman interrupted the serpent." [21] The serpent asked if God had been so niggardly as to forbid eating from any tree. Contrary to those who say Eve did not take God's prohibition seriously because she may have only received it secondhand from Adam, Eve not only sets the serpent straight—saying they could certainly eat of all the trees except one—but she adds to God's instructions: " 'You shall not eat of the fruit of the tree . . . neither shall you touch it' " (3:3). Actually God had only forbidden eating, but perhaps Eve realized that looking and touching would lead to the temptation to eat.

Then the devil shifted ground; he contradicted what God had said would happen if they ate and instead suggested that the results would be beneficial. By denying the threat outright, he made it sound as though God was just withholding something good for his own enjoyment. To this attack Eve did not know how to respond. After all, she was in dialogue with "the most subtle of all," Satan himself!

So she ate. "And gave also unto her husband with her; and he did eat. And the eyes of them both were opened, and they knew that they were naked" (Gen. 3:6–7, KJV). Had Adam been listening to the conversation? Did he watch her reach out to pluck the fruit without trying to dissuade her? Did he search her eyes for signs of change before accepting the fruit from her hand? Scripture offers us no further insights into details of or motives for the action. It merely records that both man and woman disobeyed God's command.

What was the original sin? From the biblical account the answer to this question may seem simple and self-evident, but theologians offer many curious speculations. A very old tradition says the sin was sexual intercourse (though how Eve would receive so much individual blame for an act that takes two is puzzling). This interpretation was offered by some early church fathers who, influenced by gnosticism, felt that sexuality was the major source of sin in the world anyway. But even Augustine reportedly said of this theory: "Illud est ridiculum!" The Hebrew people themselves held no gnostic ideas concerning marriage—rather they honored and glorified marital union as Genesis 2 illustrates.

Several theories lay the blame on Eve's tendency toward liberation.[22] Early feminist Judith Murray put the case positively. She said Eve's downfall resulted from a noble motive—to adorn her mind, to quench her thirst for intellectual knowledge.[23] A contemporary writer puts it more negatively: "she unlawfully assumed the religious responsibility for the first community. . . . By the 'theological' conversation with the serpent Eve assumed a function which God had not given her." Adam was supposedly responsible for all "theological negotiations."[24] Thus by taking the lead, Eve "emasculates the man. She doesn't consult her husband. Although she was supposed to be a helper fit for him, she snatches away the meaning of his masculinity."[25] Medieval schoolmen argued that while Adam sinned only against himself and God, Eve's crime was worse because she sinned not only against herself and God but also against her husband. And after her own sin, they argue—contrary to any shred of biblical evidence—that she lured, seduced, enticed her husband to sin.

Adam does, however, come in for condemnation by some theologians. He was ungentlemanly in letting her talk with a dangerous snake and eat a fruit already advertised as deadly. Out of "fond affection" and "the drawings of kindred"[26] he forsook his God and cleaved to his wife. Thus some say his sin was actually greater. Some medieval scholars (some still alive today), believers in Aristotelian biology, say that Adam's sin was worse because since he is the active principle in procreation, children would not have inherited the disease if only their mother had sinned.

None of these explanations square with the biblical teaching on original sin. All of them imply various sinful motives and sometimes actions prior to the act of eating. We know nothing, however, of the minds and hearts of Adam and Eve, except that God says they were created in his image and pronounced "very good." He says their sin was disobedience to his command not to eat the fruit of a certain tree. They ate and *then* sin took hold. As one scholar puts it, "Adam, then, must have fallen exactly as Eve had, with as little excuse, with as great a guilt." [27] Dietrich Bonhoeffer declares, "Eve only falls totally when Adam falls, for the two are one. In their guilt too they are two and yet one. They fall together as one and each carries all the guilt alone. Male and female he created them—and man fell away from him—male and female." [28] Whenever the New Testament speaks of the Fall, it uses Adam in the generic sense and *anthropos,* "mankind," rather than *anēr,* "man," in such verses as "sin came into the world through one man and death through sin, and so death spread to all men" (Rom. 5:12, cf. 5:14–19; 1 Cor. 15:22, 45–49).

The immediate result of sin was a shattering of that perfect communion the two human beings had known in the garden with God and with each other. They realized their nakedness, became self-conscious, and hid. E. J. Young puts it poignantly, "Sin is secretive and breaks a pure and open fellowship . . . for sin is essentially divisive. . . . Sin renders men lonely." [29]

Immediately Adam tried to pass the buck, to blame the woman God gave him. Following her "leader," Eve blamed the serpent. God accepted neither evasion. The consequences fell on all—and equally. Estrangement is the result of the Fall—alienation from God, from others, and from nature. All participants suffer a loss of freedom, a limitation of their potential.

But first God promises redemption, release, restoration. The broken communion, the severed cord of intimacy, would some day be healed by woman's seed (Gen. 3:15). She who was first to sin would be the first to know the Messiah.

In the meantime, mankind would suffer for their disobedience. God speaks not in wrath but in gentle reproof. He speaks of what *will* be, not what *should* be; his words are *descriptive,* not *prescriptive.* He does not institute or condone role stereotypes for the sexes, but his words point to the sinful ways in which men and women would be limited by cultural constructions.

Genesis 3:16 outlines three ways in which woman would suffer from the Fall. First, her labor in childbearing would be multiplied.[30] Luther called this a "gracious and joyous punishment" because even in childbearing woman was sustained by the hope that her child might be the Messiah. Other theologians have seemingly gotten almost sadistic pleasure from this verse, commenting that

"Eve . . . had disobeyed God and sought for enjoyment contrary to God's law. She therefore will be punished in her sexual life, for not only will her pregnancy be unpleasant, but her entire life." [31] Some have used such thinking (as they have used Jesus' comment, "The poor you will have with you always") as an excuse for oppression of women in the name of God's will.

"Your desire shall be for your husband" (3:16) has also tempted scholars to speculation: "This yearning is morbid. . . . It may be normal. It often is not but takes a perverted form. . . . It is a just penalty. She who sought to strive apart from man and to act independently of him in the temptation finds a continual attraction to him to be her unavoidable lot." [32] Another describes this desire as "practically bordering on disease." [33] One whose God seems a bit sadistic suggests that desire was added to insure the first penalty of multiplied sorrow in childbearing.[34]

Actually there is nothing morbid or pathogenic about woman's desire—it is the same as man's for restoration of the communion with his mate and with his God. Just as our communion with God is restored in Christ Jesus, so the marriage relationship in Christ can become a true "one-flesh" relationship. The Song of Solomon, which gives us an ideal picture of marriage, says, "My beloved is mine and I am his. . . . I am my beloved's and his desire is for me" (2:16; 7:10).

Perhaps the most famous of God's pronouncements to women is the last one in 3:16: "he shall rule over you." A better translation is the Jerusalem Bible's "he will lord it over you." Contrary to *Fascinating Womanhood,* which declares this to be "the first commandment which God gave unto the woman," [35] even those who believe woman is subordinate in the order of creation realize that this verse represents a sinful perversion:

> God is not here issuing a special commandment, "Be thou ruled by him!" or, "Thou shalt not rule!" But here in Genesis 3:16 we have a statement, a prediction, a prophecy, of how man, degenerated by sin, would take advantage of his headship as a husband to dominate, lord it over, his wife. Nowhere in the Bible is Genesis 3:16 quoted or referred to as establishing a general subordination of woman to man.[36]

Man's rule over woman "is not an imperative order of creation but rather the element of disorder that disturbs the original peace of creation." [37] Even Luther, despite all that he says elsewhere, concedes in his commentary on this verse, "Had Eve not sinned she would have raised children without any pain or sorrow. Nor would she have been subject to her husband." [38] He says this places a very heavy burden on men because it is easier to rule animals than human beings! But Adam tries. Whereas in Genesis 2:23 Eve was called "Woman," in 3:20 she is reduced to "mother of all living." Her function and sphere has been cut in half.

The consequences of sin fell not just on the serpent or on woman but also on all of mankind and indeed all creation. We all toil for our food, we earn our bread by the sweat of our brows, and we return to the dust at death.

THE FALL THROUGHOUT THE BIBLE

Despite the importance attributed Genesis 3 by Christians, the Old Testament writers seem to have paid little attention to it—so much so that it is uncertain as to whether they referred to it at all. Possible exceptions are Job 31:33 ("If I covered my transgressions as Adam. . ." KJV), in which modern versions of the Bible favor the translation "man" instead of the proper name, and Hosea 6:7 ("But at Adam they transgressed the covenant"), which some scholars believe is a reference to the place Admah, rather than to the man, Adam. The only clear reference is in the apocryphal book Ecclesiasticus 25:24 (NEB): "Woman is the origin of sin, and it is through her that we all die" (cf. Rom. 5:12).

For the Hebrew people, as we have said, the first three chapters of Genesis answer particular questions concerning the creation of the world, the institution of marriage, the source of sin. Though the Hebrews obviously accepted these explanations as given, they did not use them to explain or excuse their own problems. When calamity befell the nation, the prophets did not stand up and say, "Our father Adam sinned and thus we are being punished," but "All *we* like sheep have gone astray!"

Other than four references to the "one-flesh" relationship, the New Testament only refers to Genesis 1–3 in five passages. Only two of these deal specifically with women, and they are an effort to settle very practical, cultural issues concerning behavior in church meetings. Eve is named or referred to twice in the New Testament: "I am afraid that as the serpent deceived Eve by his cunning, your thoughts will be led astray from a sincere and pure devotion to Christ" (2 Cor. 11:3); "Adam was not deceived, but the woman was deceived and became a transgressor" (1 Tim. 2:14).

These verses are surely not saying that Adam did not sin, since this would certainly contradict Genesis and the great theological teaching of Romans 5. Nor are they arguing for Eve's greater guilt or weaker mind because she was deceived. As Ambrose pointed out long ago, "In the Fall of our first parents, there is more excuse for the woman. For the man allowed himself to be tempted by his sister, his equal. Whereas Eve was tempted by an angel—a fallen angel, it is true, but nevertheless a creature superior to a human." [39] Nor would it seem logical that Eve who was deceived should be less apt as a teacher than Adam who apparently sinned with eyes wide open.

No, both 2 Corinthians 11:3 and 1 Timothy 2:14 are more concerned with deception and false teaching than with women. All Christians must beware lest false teachers deceive them as the serpent did Eve. Apparently some women in Timothy's church in Ephesus had been so misled (2 Tim. 3:6–7) and so they were barred from teaching.

Interestingly, nowhere does Jesus refer to the Fall. He does not suggest that the woman is weak and easily deceived. He does not forbid her to study theology or teach his word. He does not blame her for the first sin or remind her that men will rule over her because of it. Rather he treats all daughters of Eve as persons created and re-creatable in his image and likeness.

4. Women in the Bible World

> Look at the index of any cultural history: ancient Greece, medieval Europe, Renaissance Italy, postwar America. There, after pages of the familiar headings under which we classify the phenomena of human experience—art and architecture, games and pastimes, medicine, politics, trade, war, etc. —the reader will almost always come upon the entry "Women," in nearly every case followed by some such phrase as "position of." What won't be found is the entry, "Men, position of," for the very good reason that the history of men has been synonymous in the minds of nearly all historians with the history of civilization itself.
>
> —RICHARD GILMAN[1]

TO UNDERSTAND the social position of women during Bible times, we must keep two things in mind. First, the Bible was written over a long period of time and spans thousands of years of history. In any society, time brings various changes. Second, the "Bible world" did not exist in a vacuum as some strange storybook land somehow located outside time and space. The life described in both Old and New Testaments took place surrounded by, and often influenced by, other cultures that were also working out social customs. The question, "What was life like for women during Bible times?" can only be answered by seeing woman's position in historical, cross-cultural perspective.

Woman's status in a given society greatly depends upon her power and position within the economic-opportunity structure of that society. As Simone de Beauvoir points out, where a woman is permitted to own nothing she cannot experience the dignity of being a person; she herself is part of a man's property.[2] In a patriarchal society with a patrimonial system of inheritance (as in ancient Israel), woman's position is one of subordination (though not necessarily degradation). In societies where economic opportunities for women are greater, women hold a higher position. For example, there are African tribes in which, though the land is owned by the men, the women have ownership of the crops and control all food supplies—which obviously places tremendous power in their hands.[3]

In addition to the degree of property rights and privileges held by women in ancient cultures, another significant factor affected their position—the matter of a particular society's attitudes toward fertility cult practices and reverence for female deities. Societies which felt deep awe toward woman's maternal powers and associated her with the soil and fecundity of crops revered woman as the giver of life. Societies convinced of a "female principle" in the universe and devoted to female divinities were likely to value earthly women as well.

If these two factors (economic/legal privileges and fertility goddess religions) affected woman's social status in ancient cultures, what about Israel? Israel's patriarchal family form limited woman's social-economic-legal privileges greatly; but in other respects, the Israelites gave significant honor and legal protection to women. Also, the official stand of Israel was one of opposition to fertility cults and female deities. Would this result in a higher or lower status for Israelite women when compared to surrounding cultures? The answer requires some understanding of these other societies.

OLD TESTAMENT PERIOD

Woman's Social Position among Israel's Neighbors

Sumerian Culture

Saggs speaks of an initial high status for women in Sumerian culture which gradually deteriorated, and he shows a direct relationship between the society's religion and the position of women. In the early days of the city-state, women served as priestesses and temple prostitutes. Their service was valued as highly as that of the men and was rewarded with allotments from the temple. But over time this changed, and the change was related to the disappearance of goddesses in Sumerian religion.

The early myths had given the goddesses an important role in the divine decision-making assembly. In fact, the Sumerians originally believed the underworld was ruled by a goddess alone, and one myth tells how she came to take a consort.[4] Evidently, marriage ended even the "liberation" of a goddess, and the male gods gradually took over the running of things. Woman's lowered position in society reflected the situation in the world of the divinities.

Assyria

One indication of a high regard for women in early Assyrian civilization is an amazing legend about a queen named Semiramis, whose marvelous exploits and accomplishments captivated the minds of the Mesopotamian world of long ago. Abandoned by her mother (a goddess who had been involved in an amorous affair with a young mortal), the infant was found and reared by a shepherd. As a young woman, Semiramis posed as a soldier and became a war hero, whereupon she became the wife of the founder of Nineveh. Upon his death, she reigned over a vast territory that she extended in every direction, conquering kings, building great cities, and accomplishing fantastic engineering feats.

While it is generally conceded that Semiramis was mythical, Pollard makes the point that such a legend could have developed only in an atmosphere where female intellectual and leadership talents were recognized and appreciated.[5] As expressed in words attributed to Semiramis herself: "Nature gave me the body of a woman, but my deeds have equalled those of the most valiant men."

In later periods, although Assyrian girls as well as boys were taught to read and write, the amount of social freedom for women depended on their rank in society. Bare feet and bare heads characterized lower class women as they went to the marketplace or visited the homes of friends. Higher status women were expected to remain secluded in their homes.

The queens and women of the kings' harems were shut up as virtual prisoners in surroundings of great opulence. Occasionally the king visited his women or invited them to dine with him, but most of the time the women were idle and sought to alleviate boredom through embroidery, music and dance, conversation, and attention to dress. The average Assyrian housewife, on the other hand, filled her days with household chores. Many tasks (kneading bread, hanging the wash, and so on) were done upon the flat rooftops, making it easy for neighbor women to chat across the terraces as they worked.

Veils became important during certain periods of Assyrian history. Laws of the late second millennium B.C. required the veiling of married women and concubines. Harlots were commanded by law to keep their heads uncovered; if they dared to put on veils, they were beaten fifty stripes and pitch was poured on their heads.[6] (An awareness of the significance of veils for women in different cultures is helpful in understanding otherwise baffling Bible passages, such as 1 Corinthians 11. Even in modern times, there remain places where veiling customs have caused problems for women desiring equality. When Princess Llalla Aiche in the late 1960s publicly removed her veil to call attention to the demands of many Moroccan women for higher rights, conservatives were shocked and whispered that the princess must surely be a prostitute! To lower one's veil in public seemed extremely risqué.[7])

All in all, we may conclude that Assyrian women had many rights during Old Testament times, but they were somewhat more restricted than another of Israel's neighbors—Babylon.

Babylon

Babylonian culture provided a fairly high status for its women.[8] Women could own property, attend to their own business, appear in public, plead in courts of justice, even hold office. Marriage regulations, property rights for widows (including the privilege of conducting business in their own names), and other provisions of the Code of Hammurabi indicate a genuine concern for female citizens' rights. Women could be judges, elders, and secretaries. They were recognized as witnesses to documents. The Code of Hammurabi speaks of businesswomen who ran wineshops. Women were by no means mere chattels in Babylonian society.

One praiseworthy provision of the law had to do with a married woman's property rights. Her dowry (often including land or other valuable property) remained in the wife's possession and passed from her to her children. Marriage in Hammurabi's Code was more than a sale of a woman by her father to her husband (though legally there were some elements of this practice). It was also viewed as a contract between a husband and wife.

Divorce privileges, however, favored men more than women. A woman could obtain a judicial separation only by proving her husband had been cruel to her, and such proof often demanded that she undergo a strange trial by ordeal which was to serve as a sort of lie detector test. In contrast, a man could apparently divorce his wife for any cause, provided that he would return her dowry, let her keep custody of the children, and agree to pay for their upbringing. Thus, even though the husband had greater privileges in *initiating* a divorce, there was ample provision for the wife's rights and protection.

Persia

In Persia, despite the fact that fathers chose husbands for their daughters, that wives were required to be absolutely obedient to husbands (see Est. 1:10–21), and that polygamy was common, women were (according to de Beauvoir) "held in honor more than among most Oriental peoples." [9]

Marriage was the main purpose of a Persian woman's life, and posterity for the husband was considered the main purpose of marriage. Persian mothers were responsible for educating sons up to the age of seven, and daughters until marriage. If a son somehow had shown he was unworthy to receive his share of his father's estate, his mother received it. If a husband died leaving no adult son, the wife became the guardian of minor children and manager of her husband's business affairs.

Egypt

Women were highly esteemed in ancient Egypt. Even the Pharaoh recognized his queen as his equal or even superior, for as Seltman points out, "to her belonged the land of Egypt itself, and the king was the man who married the daughter of his predecessor." [10] Simone de Beauvoir also calls attention to woman's high social status in the land of the Nile, including equality with men in court and the right to own property. [11]

As late as the period of the Ptolemies, marriage contracts were not unusual in which the whole of a man's property was assigned to his wife. *Either* wife or husband might own their house and fields, and husbands and wives were expected to show loving respect toward one another regardless of who was considered the owner. Ancient Egyptian writings give advice to husbands living in homes owned by their wives, warning the husbands not to be rude or demanding but to appreciate their wives and find joy in them. On the other hand, if the husband owned the home, he must likewise make his wife happy, provide well for her, and show love. [12]

However, despite the many positive aspects, woman's situation was not utopian. For all her praise of woman's lot in the Egyptian world of long ago, de Beauvoir is enough of a realist to make the following observation:

> But even at the time when they had a privileged status, unique in the ancient world, women were not socially the equals of men. Sharing in religion and in government, they could act as regent, but the pharaoh was male; the priests and soldiers were men; women took only a secondary part in public life; and in private life there was demanded of them a fidelity without reciprocity. [13]

Women's Social Position in Ancient Israelite Society

Before looking at four aspects of woman's social position in Hebrew culture (legal rights, education, occupations outside the home, and political participation), there are some general observations worth noting.

First, a woman in Israel found her identity not as a separate individual but as a member of a family. She was a daughter, then a wife, and then a mother. Second, there is no denying the patriarchal nature of Israel's culture. Old Testament scholar Roland de Vaux says that the proper word to describe the Israelite family is *bêth 'ab,* the "house of one's father." Genealogies recorded the father's line, and "the father had absolute authority over his children, even over his married sons if they lived with him, and over their wives" in addition to authority over his own wife.[14] De Vaux concludes that "the social and legal position of an Israelite wife was . . . inferior to the position a wife occupied in the great countries round about." [15]

We are reminded of Krister Stendahl's comment about the strongly masculine structure of Jewish society and religion:

> All the way from circumcision to burial rites it is only the male who is an Israelite in the true sense of the word. . . . The feminine ideal is in line with tradition's picture of Rabbi Akiba's wife, the student's and scholar's wife who sacrifices everything for her husband's studies, the mother who manages her own affairs subject to her husband.[16]

Legal Rights

In his book, *Hebrew Law in Biblical Times,* Ze'ev Falk warns against defining Hebrew society in terms of its laws alone. He reminds us that "the law, for instance, treated woman harshly, whereas custom operated in her favor," and also that the legal position of a married woman must be distinguished from that of a *femme sole.*[17] In discussing many aspects of the position of woman in a given society, what may be under consideration is the position of a *wife* rather than woman as woman.

However, despite Falk's plea for caution, marital status seemed to make little difference in rights for the Israelite woman. Whether single or married, she was under the jurisdiction of some male; she was never her own person. Betrothal terms were the same as those of purchase. The word *ba'al,* which referred to a husband, meant owner or master; and a man's wife was included in lists of his possessions (e.g., Exod. 20:17). A childless widow was required to submit to the right of levirate and marry her husband's brother in order to produce offspring who would bear the name and inherit the property of her deceased husband (see Deut. 25:5 ff.; Gen. 38:8). Falk concludes that although women were considered capable of committing most offenses and incurring penalties just as in the case of men (cf. Num. 5:6 ff.), the women of Israel clearly "did not enjoy equality of rights."

Yet we must not overlook the fact that legal protection was offered to persons regardless of sex. There was no sexual differentiation in the commandment that children should honor their parents (father *and mother* [Exod. 20:12; Lev. 19:3]), and a death penalty was prescribed for anyone who struck or cursed either his father or his mother (Exod. 21:15, 17). Likewise, Exodus 21 lists penalties for slave owners who hurt or killed slaves of either sex, and penalties for farmers whose oxen gored anyone, male or female.

However, from the vantage point of our own day and our own values, it is easy to see glaring inequities in the treatment of the sexes under Israelite law—particularly in regard to inheritance laws, laws about adultery and fornication, and laws about vows.

INHERITANCE LAWS

In ancient Israel, only sons had a right to inheritance, with a double portion going to the firstborn (cf. Deut. 21:16–17). If sons survived the father, neither the widow nor daughters had any share in the inheritance. However, if there were no sons, the estate went to the daughters, and in their default passed to the deceased man's relatives.[18]

The origin of the custom granting inheritance privileges to daughters in the absence of sons is an interesting anecdote in the history of feminism, for it was a bona fide case of agitation for women's rights! The daughters of Zelophehad had come to Moses to protest the unfairness of their father's name dying out simply because he left no sons. The five sisters asked to be given a possession among their father's brethren. "Moses brought their case before the Lord. And the Lord said to Moses, 'The daughters of Zelophehad are right. . . . "If a man dies, and has no son, then you shall cause his inheritance to pass to his daughter." ' " (Num. 27:5–8).

However, custom decreed that a woman left her old family upon marriage. Having passed into a new family, she was to assist in continuing the name of her husband's family. Thus, a proviso was added to the ruling made for Zelophehad's daughters (Num. 36: 1–9). Girls must marry within their father's tribe to avoid transference of the family property to another tribe. This addition to the law again insured masculine dominance and offset whatever gains were made for women in Numbers 27.

If a man died without children, none of his inheritance went to his widow. Rather, it passed to his male kinsmen on his father's side or to his brothers. Childless Israelite widows either returned to their own fathers or remained a part of their husbands' families through the practice of levirate marriage. In cases where a widow had adult children, she depended on them for support. If a husband died while his children were small, the widow became the trustee of the money left to them and was responsible for its management. Later Jewish law recognized greater inheritance rights for widows.[19]

LAWS REGARDING FORNICATION AND ADULTERY

In Israel, a woman was expected to be chaste before marriage and faithful afterwards. This was undoubtedly related to every Israelite man's desire for sons—sons that he could be sure were his own. But judging from at least some of the legislation, this emphasis seems to have given rise to a kind of double standard.

For example, a man could accuse his bride of not being a virgin (Deut. 22:13–21). If the woman could not *prove* she was virginal at the time the marriage was consummated, the law required her to be stoned to death at the door of her father's house. However, if the bridegroom's charge could be proven untrue (because the girl's parents produced "tokens of virginity" to show to the town elders), the young man would be whipped, fined, and forced to keep the woman as his wife for life, with no divorce privileges permitted. (One wonders if the wife wasn't being unjustly punished by being required to stay married to such a man!)

The law may have seemed unfair to women on two other counts. First, it demanded virginity of the woman and provided a "test" to assure the husband that he was the first one to have sexual intercourse with her. But there was no similar provision to guarantee women that their husbands had come to the marriage bed "pure."

Second, attempts to prove virginity are unreliable. The "tokens of virginity" are usually thought to be blood-stained bedsheets or cloths smeared from the breaking of the bride's hymen during the first experience of coitus. Various cultures have had such tests over the ages, with some even requiring that items stained with hymenal blood be displayed to wedding guests.

However, the hymens of many women have been ruptured during childhood through means totally unrelated to sex relations; and there are other women whose hymens stretch rather than tear when the penis enters the vagina. The absence of bleeding during the first intercourse does not prove a woman is not virginal. Such a test could easily yield false results, and an innocent woman could be condemned to death because her parents had no "tokens of virginity" to show on her behalf.

Possibly the "tokens of virginity" were something other than this—perhaps special garments that served as "chastity belts" for unmarried girls. According to this theory, girls under their parents' supervision would have to wear such garments and submit to frequent inspection for signs of disarray.[20]

If a married woman were suspected of adultery, she might be forced to undergo a "trial by ordeal." Behind any such trial is the idea that God (or "the gods") must decide guilt or innocence and

deliver the final verdict. Although such procedures were not unusual among ancient peoples, Israel rarely had anything resembling them (with the exception of casting lots to discern God's will).
Thus, the "bitter water ordeal" (Num. 5:11–31) seems strange.

A man who suspected his wife of adultery but could find no
witnesses to prove it could bring her to the priest for a special
"experiment." After taking an oath spelling out the details of what
might happen to her, the wife was forced to drink a bitter liquid
concocted by the priest. (It was a mixture of holy water and dust
from the tabernacle into which had been dipped the "writing
pad" that contained the list of the curses.) If guilty of adultery,
the wife's body was expected to swell and her "thigh fall away."
If innocent, she would escape the signs of the curse and be able
to bear children.

A woman could be compelled to undergo this shameful and
frightening experience for no other reason than her husband's
jealousy or suspicions. Yet, the law provided no means for her
to check up on him if she felt he had been unfaithful to her.

Israel's requirement of a trial by ordeal for suspected adultery is
by no means unique. Anthropologist Mary Douglas tells of groups
having deep anxieties about "adultery pollution." A wife's unfaithfulness is thought to defile her, and this defilement would endanger
her husband upon contact with her. In some cases, it is feared the
couple's children (living or yet unborn) will be contaminated in
some way. In one present-day tribe, if a man suffers from diarrhea
after a meal, he automatically assumes that one of his wives has
committed adultery. In the past, this tribe sought to determine
guilt through the poison ordeal. If the woman vomited instead of
suffering from the poison's deadly effects, she was considered innocent. But if she died, it supposedly proved she had committed
adultery.[21]

Among Israel's neighbors, the Assyro-Babylonian river ordeal
existed for the same purpose. A woman accused of adultery, who
had not been caught in the act, was required to jump into the
holy river. The belief was that a guilty woman would drown; an
innocent one would float.

Actually, Israel's trial by ordeal was less severe than those of
other cultures where women were expected to *die* if guilty (and
the designated tests made death almost certain). Perhaps Israel
wanted a "detection system" such as other societies had; yet the
Israelite legal penalty for adultery (death) could only be applied
if the woman were caught in the actual act. Therefore, a more
merciful way was provided for cases where suspicious husbands
accused their wives of unfaithfulness but had no real proof. The

"bitter waters" ordeal had less severe consequences than other methods of dealing with adultery. At worst, a woman might have a miscarriage (the usual interpretation of Num. 5:27), preserving her own life at the same time it removed her husband's worst fear—that she would bear a child that was not his own.

We must keep in mind that overall there was equality of treatment in Israel's adultery laws. Not only women, but their lovers as well, were stoned to death if caught in an adulterous act (Deut. 22:22 ff.). If a double standard does appear in some form, we must remember what adultery meant in ancient Israel. Since a wife was considered one of her husband's possessions, an act of adultery on her part meant disloyalty to her owner. But if a man committed adultery, his crime wasn't unfaithfulness to his own wife so much as it was an injury inflicted on the other woman's husband or betrothed (by stealing that man's exclusive sexual rights to that woman).

On the other hand, as de Vaux points out, Leviticus 18:20 ranks adultery among "sins against marriage." "Adultery was a sin against one's neighbor, but the text of Lev. 18:20 adds a religious consideration, and the stories of Gen. 20:1–13; 26:7–11 represent adultery as a sin against God." [22]

As time went on, attitudes toward adultery reflected much more consideration for the wife's rights to her husband as well as vice versa. Proverbs 5:15–19 and Malachi 2:15 exhort husbands to be faithful to their wives for this is the will of God. Hosea 4:13–14 makes clear that no double standard was in effect at this stage of Israel's history; both men and women were alike condemned for their adultery (here connected with idolatry). The Apocrypha speaks of a wife's adultery as first of all *sin against God,* next against her husband, and third against herself and any illegitimate children she might bear (Ecclus. 23:22 ff.).

WOMEN AND VOWS

A third category of laws that seem discriminatory with regard to women concerned vows. Numbers 30 shows that a woman was considered a minor all her life. Either her father or her husband was responsible for her actions. Thus, if she made a voluntary religious promise, her father's consent or her husband's consent (depending on her marital status) was necessary in order for her vow to be valid.

If father or husband withheld consent, a woman's pledge became null and void. A widow or divorcee, however, was held responsible for her own vows, just as was a man; but all other women were under a kind of perpetual tutelage. In a patriarchal society, where a woman was under some man's authority and without independent status or means of support, the law about vows and pledges was probably given for the men's protection. Otherwise, they might be required to pay for obligations incurred by the women under them.

Another passage on vows, Leviticus 27, evidently refers to pledges for the service of the Lord. If a person pledged himself or someone under his charge for such service, he did not necessarily have to serve in the sanctuary. In lieu of such service, he could offer money to God, according to a specified rate scale. The amounts varied according to age and sex, with the highest valuation being placed on males from twenty to fifty years of age. Females in that age category were assigned a valuation of half as much. Although the percentage differed according to age level, girls and women were consistently rated at a lower monetary value than boys and men.

Apparently, value was based upon assumed physical strength; and in a society that measured strength in traditional masculine terms (muscle power, ability to perform heavy manual labor, military might), women, old people, and small children would be considered of less worth in work potential.

To use this passage as a proof text giving biblical justification for unfair pay scales based on sex is ridiculous. Occupational value today depends upon mental ability, skill, training, and talents. Christians who try to universalize this passage as God's will for all time, insisting that it "proves" women deserve lower wages than men, put themselves in an absurd position. To be consistent, they would also have to conclude from this passage that a sixty-year-old neurosurgeon should be paid less than one-third as much as a twenty-year-old grade school drop-out who washes dishes at a grill!

Education

During earliest childhood, Israelite boys and girls alike learned from their mother—especially moral teachings. Parents were responsible before God for the religious training of both sons and daughters (Deut. 6:4 ff.), and the various festivals and holy days were designed to incite children's questions and educate them in the meaning of Israel's religion (cf. Deut. 6:20; Exod. 12:25–27).

However, as children grew, boys and girls were separated in their training. Girls remained under their mothers' control, learning to perform household tasks in preparation for marriage and housewifery. Boys were turned over to their fathers for education in crafts and trades, for instruction in their national heritage, and for specialized religious training. Prophets, priests, and elders also played a part in educating boys, because a knowledge of the Torah was considered vital in the life of every Israelite male. Boys were educated for manhood, girls for wifehood and motherhood.

Occupations Outside the Home

Since caring for husband, children, and home was considered the main purpose of a woman's life, it is not surprising that Israelite women were little concerned with outside careers. The heavy tasks of working in the fields, looking after flocks, cooking, spinning, sewing and caring for many offspring made Israel's women "working mothers" in a very real sense, even though they didn't have outside paying jobs.

However, the Israelites did not so rigidly believe that "woman's place is in the home" that all outside occupational activity was forbidden. At least by the time of the Wisdom Literature, some women did have additional careers, and they were able to combine such occupations with marriage quite successfully—as the idealization of the "virtuous woman" in Proverbs 31 shows. Apparently, it was not unusual in the later period of Israel's history for women to have income from spinning, sewing, weaving, needlecraft, and so on. The Apocrypha tells of Anna who earned money by "women's work" (weaving) and was not only paid wages by her employer but was also sometimes given a bonus, such as a goat. (See Tobit 2:11–12.)

Political Participation

In a patriarchal society where men were considered the authorities, women had little opportunity to participate in political affairs. Deborah's position of power during the times of the Judges was the exception rather than the rule (Judg. 4:4 ff.). But she and Jael (the other wartime heroine in the battle with Sisera) were highly honored by Israel, and there seems to have been no disparagement of their sex. The book of Esther and the apocryphal book of Judith both extol women for saving the nation. Likewise, Huldah, a prophetess during the times of the kings, played an important role in public affairs (2 Kings 22:14–20). In 1 Chronicles 7:24, the listing of sons in the genealogies is broken to mention a daughter named Sheerah who built and fortified three cities.

During the monarchy, women were excluded from the throne. (Athaliah's rule was illegal—2 Kings 11:1–16.) The line of succession went from father to son. If there were no male heirs, the rulership passed to the deceased king's brother. Clearly, the affairs of Israel as a nation were in charge of the men. Women supported, encouraged, influenced, and generally served behind the scenes if at all.

NEW TESTAMENT PERIOD

In the New Testament, we see a convergence of many cultural influences—Greek, Roman, Oriental, Jewish, and more. Each of these contain inconsistencies, fluctuations over time, and much that is ambiguous. Therefore, to understand the position of women in Christianity, we must give attention to the Jewish milieu and the Greco-Roman world at the time Christianity began and then spread.

In comparing Greek and Roman culture as regards women, we see strange paradoxes. For example, Rome's upper-class women had more prominence in public life than did the women of Athens. Yet, opportunities for education were seldom extended to Roman girls (except for study in the home and sometimes at the primary school level, i.e., through about age eleven). For Greek girls, on the other hand, education even up through the secondary level was quite common. The Athenian Academy even had women professors.[23] Simone de Beauvoir makes the point that Greek women were, legally speaking, less enslaved than Roman women; but paradoxically, Roman women were "much more deeply integrated in society."[24]

Greek Culture

In the world of the Greeks, Macedonia stands out like the ancient Greek state of Sparta as being exemplary in granting high status and freedom of opportunity to the female sex. Classics professor E. M. Blaiklock points out that "Macedonian inscriptions bear witness to the respected and responsible position of women in the northern Greek communities," and suggests that the exaltation of womanhood in the Gospel of Luke and the book of Acts fits well with the tradition that Luke was a Macedonian.[25]

Throughout the history of Greece, attitudes toward women varied—as is reflected, for example, in the great Greek plays. The philosophers disagreed about women. Plato suggested that girls be given a liberal education and that women be granted a share in the government of the republic. He wrote: "There is no occupation concerned with the management of social affairs which belongs either to woman or to man, as such. Natural gifts are to be found here and there in both creatures alike."[26] Aristotle, however, disagreed. He viewed woman's nature as being inherently defective and inferior.

Some of the Greek ambivalence no doubt stemmed from the

categories into which women were placed. Demosthenes summed up the three major classes in his famous remark: "We have hetairai for the pleasures of the spirit, concubines for sensual pleasure, and wives to give us sons." [27]

Wives were secluded and closely guarded to insure that all off-spring were those of the husband. Regarded as permanent minors, a woman's person and property were controlled by a guardian—father, husband, husband's heir, or even the state. However, ancient monuments show that many men of Athens deeply respected and loved their wives, honoring them as mothers of their children and managers of their homes.

Yet, since it was considered improper to take one's wife out in public, men often found intellectual female companionship from among the *hetairai* (the word means "companion," "girl friend," or "mistress"). Artistic, cultured, often well educated and intellectual, the hetairai were free to do as they pleased and were treated essentially as equals by men. Many of the great Greek scholars had mistresses from among these women; and it was common custom for a married man to invite a hetaira to attend a social gathering with him. Men admired the talents and highly cultivated minds of these women, whom Seltman describes as generally having been "foreigners from other Greek states and cities, earning a living sometimes in commerce, business girls, bachelor girls, models." [28] Because they were considered courtesans, however, they were not free to marry Greek citizens. They lived on the fringes of society, free from family obligations (and the seclusion this meant for Greek women).

Demosthenes' third category, concubines, were women husbands took as temporary replacements for their wives while the wives were ill, pregnant, or recovering from childbirth. Often a man took a concubine from among his household servants.

There were other categories of Greek women who served as prostitutes. Some were slaves and others were streetwalkers who lived a miserable existence. In a somewhat higher position on the prostitute stratification scale were the musically talented dancing flute girls. Lastly, there was the specialized category of prostitute-priestesses, such as the temple girls who served in the Temple of Aphrodite at Corinth.

Roman Culture

In Rome, the condition of women was somewhat better than in Greece—not so much legally, but in practice. During the days of the Republic, women had been quite restricted and were under the authority of father or husband with little rights of their own.

But with the establishment of the Empire, things began looking up for women. Marriage laws were changed, giving greater rights to the wife. Women were highly esteemed as wives and mothers, shared responsibilities with their husbands with regard to children and property, were not confined to their homes, ate with their husbands and dined with invited guests also, went to the public baths, and accompanied their husbands to the theater, races, and other public entertainments.

The growing emancipation of women disturbed many people, who feared a deterioration of morals and a breakdown of family life would be inevitable by-products of such female freedom. Basing their conclusions on antifeminist writings (such as the *Epigrams* of Martial and the *Satires* of Juvenal), as well as records of notorious scandals among upper-class society where wealth and leisure were often misused, some scholars paint a picture of gloom and degeneration, and pin much of the blame for Rome's troubles on women's liberation.[29]

In view of this, some Bible scholars have sought to justify early restrictions on Christian women, concluding that Paul and others were reacting to the damage caused by Rome's granting "too much freedom" to women. Such reasoning is wrong on at least two counts.

First, *men* dissolved family ties just as much, if not more so, than women. The famous Cicero, after thirty years of marriage, cast off his wife in order to marry a rich young woman. The self-righteous moralist Cato also divorced his wife, but he took her back years later after learning that her second husband had died leaving her a large estate.

It was also not unusual for men to dissolve marriages if the wife bore no children (infertility was always assumed to be the woman's fault). And the changing of mates for political advantage was very common—one sad example being the Emperor Augustus's demand that his stepson Tiberius divorce his beloved wife in order to marry Augustus's daughter Julia. The marriage was painful and disgusting to Tiberius because of Julia's flagrant unfaithfulness. If one turns to the rumors of adultery, homosexual practices, and various scandals recorded by Suetonius showing unsavory sides of Roman life, it is not difficult to conclude that the male sex played an even greater role than the female sex in the loosening of moral standards.[30]

The second point to be made is that wifely virtues were still praised in the days of the Empire. Morals and family stability did *not* disappear. Tombstones indicate great devotion between husbands and wives. And although divorce was not unusual, the high rates of remarriage were largely due to the death of a spouse.

Other Influences

With trade, immigration, and the movement of the Roman army, ideas from the east had spread throughout the Roman Empire. Of particular importance were the mystery cults, which stressed secret revelations for the initiate and had a triple appeal—to the *intellect* (by emphasizing knowledge), to the *senses* (by stressing terror, love, hope, ecstasy, emotional frenzy, music, dance, drama, and sometimes sexual debauchery) and to the *conscience* (through ascetic practices in efforts to gain eternal rewards).

Women played a prominent role in many of these religions, especially in the cult of the wine god Dionysus or that of Cybele, the great mother-goddess of Asia. There were temples to the goddesses Artemis (Diana) in Ephesus and Aphrodite (Venus) in Corinth. Worship of the Egyptian goddess Isis had a powerful appeal to the female sex. Called "the Glory of Women," Isis promised her women followers equality with men.[31]

Christianity spread in areas affected not only by Greco-Roman culture, but also influenced by these various religions and their excesses. At the same time, there was its heritage from Judaism—both the strict masculine structure of the Palestinian form and the Judaism of the dispersion which Stendahl feels was different enough to seem quite attractive to women of the Hellenistic world.[32]

Thus, at first glance, there sometimes seems to be tension and inconsistency with regard to "woman's place" as seen in the New Testament writings—a subject to be explored in the following chapters.

5. Woman's Best Friend: Jesus

> Jesus was a feminist to a degree far beyond that of His fellows and followers. . . . No other Western prophet, seer, or would-be redeemer of humanity was so devoted to the feminine half of mankind.
>
> —CHARLES SELTMAN[1]

"BUT WHEN THE TIME had fully come, God sent forth his Son, born of a woman, born under the law, to redeem those who were under the law . . ." (Gal. 4:4–5). At last the seed of the woman was come to strike the serpent dead and break the power of his law. No one was more bound by that law than women.

And from the moment the preparations for his coming were set in motion, the Messiah's special mission to women was evident. In the light of his culture, Jesus' behavior in regard to women is so extraordinary that one theologian cites it as evidence for the New Testament's supernatural authenticity: "the Gospel portrait of Jesus would seem to have fairly forced its way through an atmosphere still . . . alien to it and still scarcely comprehending." [2]

As Dorothy Sayers has said so eloquently, many women then and now find Jesus a compelling figure because he never made jokes about them, treated them as either "The women, God help us!" or "The ladies, God bless them!" He always took women seriously and never "urged them to be feminine or jeered at them for being female." He did not have a patriarchal ax to grind or a "male ego" to defend. He simply treated women as human beings.[3]

Women responded gratefully and wholeheartedly from the very beginning. Men were somewhat more dubious. When Elizabeth learned that she would bear the forerunner of the Messiah, she acknowledged immediately, "Thus the Lord has done to me" (Luke 1:25). When the angel Gabriel told her husband Zechariah that his aged wife would conceive, he realized at once the scientific improbability and questioned the angel's veracity—which left him speechless.

When the angel told Mary she would bear the Messiah, she responded, "I am the handmaid of the Lord; let it be to me according to your word" (Luke 1:38). Joseph, on the other hand, found Mary's story of a "virgin birth" a bit difficult to believe and so sought "to divorce her quietly" until an angel told him not to (Matt.

1:18–25). Some radical feminists have charged that Mary was
a pawn in this affair, that she was "used" by God. Yet in an
extremely patriarchal society, a God who has been accused of
patriarchal tendencies himself did not send his angel to ask permission of Mary's father or of Joseph. He came instead directly to a
young woman and presented her with his plan. She, with admirable
courage, accepted.

Scholars have presented Mary as having a "retiring nature, unobtrusive, reticent, perhaps even shrinking from observation so that
the impress of her personality was confined to the sweet sanctities
of the home circle." [4] While we would not cast aspersions on Mary's
behavior, an unwed pregnant girl who sets off on a journey to
visit relatives does not seem like a reticent homebody! The joyous poetry of the Magnificat does not sound like the response of
one retiring and shy.

She bore her baby among strangers. She, not Joseph, called her
young son to account for staying in Jerusalem. She initiated
Christ's miracle working. She once came to fetch him home. She
went to Calvary to witness his death. And she was in the Upper
Room at Pentecost. All of which does not exactly add up to the
image of one who shrank from the public eye. Luke 2:19 summarizes
her response to the events of her life: "Mary kept all these things,
pondering them in her heart." A proper, quiet, "feminine" attitude? The verse is modeled on similar responses by Jacob and
Daniel (Gen. 37:11; Dan. 7:28). Mary reacted, not as a woman,
but as a person to the mystery of God's Incarnation.

Part of that mystery is that Mary brought forth a *son*. Why
did God choose to become flesh in male form? Philippians 2:7–8
says that Christ "emptied himself, taking the form of a servant,
being born in the likeness of men. And being found in human
form he humbled himself and became obedient unto death. . . ."
Men usually do not think of themselves as the "form of a servant."
Feminists have noted that if God really did want to condescend
to those of lowest estate, he should have become a woman!

God had only two choices. A hermaphrodite or a divine couple,
while popular in some forms of religion, would have been inconsistent with the particularistic God of Israel. Given the setting of
patriarchal Judaism, Jesus had to be male. He came as the Messiah,
the heir to David's throne, our great high priest, and a lamb
without spot or blemish to be an offering for our sin.[5] In addition
to these symbolic reasons, Christ was male for practical reasons.
Jewish women were kept in subjection and sometimes even seclusion. A female Messiah would have had little scriptural knowledge (according to the Talmud, the Torah should rather be burned

than transmitted to a woman), and would not have been allowed to teach publicly in the synagogue, or have been believed if she had. And with her monthly "uncleanness" making her ritually impure for a fourth of the time, a female Messiah would have taken at least an extra year to complete God's mission!

Jesus was a man, but he was also Man. English obscures the distinction, but New Testament writers are careful to distinguish between *anēr* (male) and *anthropos* (human). When speaking of the Incarnation, they invariably choose *anthropos* (e.g., Phil. 2:7; Rom. 5:12, 15; etc.).

Jesus came to earth not primarily as a male but as a person. He treated women not primarily as females but as human beings. Without sentimentality, condescension, or undemanding indulgence, he accepted them as persons in a way that moved them to repentance and love. The "Bleeding Pharisees" were so named because they closed their eyes at the approach of any woman—and so proceeded to bump into all kinds of things! Yet Christ associated with all sorts of women. He drew those wealthy and politically prominent as well as those poor and morally disreputable. Some, like the Samaritan and the Syro-Phoenician women, were even outsiders altogether.

Despite a leading evangelist's assertion that "with all the new freedom that Christ brought women, He did not free them from the home," [6] Jesus seems to have encouraged women just as much as men to become his followers. He commended Mary for listening to his teachings and reprimanded Martha for being overly concerned with household chores (Luke 10:38–42). As Dorothy Sayers comments of that story: "God, of course, may have His own opinion, but the Church is reluctant to endorse it. . . . Mary's, of course, was the better part—the Lord said so, and we must not precisely contradict Him. But we will be careful not to despise Martha. No doubt, He approved of her too. We could not get on without her, and indeed (having paid lip-service to God's opinion) we must admit that we greatly prefer her. For Martha was doing a really feminine job, whereas Mary was just behaving like any other disciple, male or female; and that is a hard pill to swallow." [7] "If you love me, you will keep my commandments" (John 14:15) was Jesus' instructions to all his disciples.

Women responded by following him, traveling in the band of disciples, and supporting him financially (Matt. 27:55; Luke 8:2–3). Interestingly the Bible mentions no other monetary contributions to his ministry.

In a day when most rabbis refused to teach women because their minds were supposedly incapable of grasping God's truth,

Jesus taught women openly, even in the temple Court of the Women (Luke 21:1–4). He did not confine himself to "feminine" subjects either. Some of his greatest truths were revealed to women. To the Samaritan at the well in John 4 he first declared that he was the Messiah. He also reminded her that God is a spirit, that true faith can be found and practiced without regard to national and religious boundaries. Christ's assertion "I am the resurrection and the life" brought comfort to Martha, grieving over her dead brother Lazarus, and provoked from her an affirmation identical to Peter's: "Yes, Lord; I believe that you are the Christ, the Son of God" (John 11:25, 27).

Jesus also incorporated in his teaching objects and incidents with which women were familiar: wedding feasts, lost coins, grinding corn, putting yeast in bread. Never is a woman or something "feminine" ridiculed or rebuked. C. I. Scofield (whose reference Bible is widely used in conservative circles) had no basis for the footnote: "A woman, in the bad ethical sense, is always a symbol of that which, religiously, is out of its place. The 'woman' in Matt. 13:33 is dealing with doctrine, a sphere forbidden to her (1 Tim. 2:12)." Rather Jesus was simply teaching his disciples that the kingdom of heaven will spread throughout the earth if they will be like yeast, or salt, or a lamp set on a stand.[8]

Jesus did not only talk with women, but he went so far as to touch them publicly—something unheard of in Jewish society where a man would not allow a woman to count change into his hand for fear of contact. Luke 13:10 ff. records how Jesus' healing touch brought relief to a woman crippled for eighteen years. He even calls her a "daughter of Abraham," a distinction rarely used though men are often called "sons of Abraham." But rather than rejoice in her wholeness, the men standing nearby condemned Christ's "working" on the Sabbath.

In return women felt free to touch Jesus. A most poignant illustration is the healing of the woman with a hemorrhage. For twelve years she had spent all her money on doctors who could not relieve her constant menstrual flow (Mark 5:25 ff.). Thus she was ritually unclean and beyond all human contact (see Lev. 15:19–30). Realizing this, she dared not address the Master, but with courageous faith reached out to secretly touch the hem of his robe. Christ, on his way to heal the only daughter of a temple official, obviously an important mission, immediately stopped and demanded, "Who touched me?" The poor woman must have been frozen with terror: she had been discovered. Surely the rabbi would rebuke her sternly for imparting her uncleanness to him. Trembling she came forward and, falling at his feet, confessed. Instead of a

tirade or instructions for cleansing rituals, she heard those beautiful words: "Daughter, your faith has made you well; go in peace"
(Mark 5:34).

Though Jesus knew who had touched him and why, several
explanations could be given for his actions. Perhaps he wanted to
insure that her relationship with him would be based not merely
on "magic" but a personal encounter. In addition to physical healing, his public recognition brought social and psychological wholeness to this outcast. Others have cited this as an instance of Jesus'
encouraging women to public ministry. Undoubtedly this woman
would have praised God for her cure among family and friends,
but Jesus gave her opportunity for a wider ministry that continues
today.

Christ publicly accepted more intimate gestures of love on several
occasions from women who washed, dried, and anointed his feet.
For a single young man to allow a woman to kiss and fondle his
feet was most unusual. For a woman, particularly a chaste single
woman like Mary of Bethany (John 12:1–8), to take down her hair
was considered most immodest. Yet in his presence Mary felt free
and pure. In accepting the affection of the "sinner" (Luke 7:36–
50), Jesus did not acquiesce to her former moral standards. He
rebuked neither of the women but only his fellow diners who saw
the women as either sex objects of unsavory reputation or as irresponsible spendthrifts. The women he commended for their
devotion.

While one of his disciples betrayed him, one denied him, and all
forsook him, the women followed Jesus to the end and beyond.
Risking life and virtue, they dared to stand among the Roman
soldiers at the foot of his cross and to come at dawn to his guarded
tomb, full of faith that the sealed stone would somehow move. Their
perseverance was rewarded by the sight of the radiantly empty
tomb and angels who announced, "He has risen, he is not here;
. . . go, tell his disciples" (Mark 16:6–7).

And so they bore first witness to the fact that he, their beloved,
was alive.[9] But to the disciples "these words seemed . . . an idle
tale, and they did not believe them" (Luke 24:11). Though Christ
had repeatedly foretold his death and resurrection, the disciples
"did not believe them" (Mark 16:13). Only Peter and John were
moved to go and see for themselves. After a rational, analytic
appraisal of an empty hole in the ground, the men went away
scientifically satisfied.

But John tells us that Mary Magdalene lingered, lovingly, want-
ing to remain at least close to where Jesus last lay. And when
she saw one whom she took to be the gardener, she emphatically,

passionately, assertively demanded: "Tell me where you have laid him, and I will take him away!" He did not ridicule her strength to accomplish such a task, or rebuke her for such audacity. He rewarded her with a revelation of himself, and a loving affirmation of her self, "Mary!"[10]

One could argue that the women's being first at the empty tomb was only an accident of history. But the appearances of angels and of Christ himself were deliberate acts of God. Jesus appeared first not to Peter, the "vicar" of his church, nor even to John, the "beloved." Women were the first to receive the central fact of the gospel and the first to be instructed to tell it abroad.[11]

Thus Jesus' life on earth from beginning to end outlines a paradigm for women's place. His actions upset and appalled his contemporaries, dumbfounded his critics, and flabbergasted his disciples.[12] Since that day the church has struggled, if sometimes unenthusiastically and unsuccessfully, to cut through the barbed wire of cultural custom and taboo in order to emulate the one who promised both men and women, "If the Son makes you free, you will be free indeed"!

6. Your Daughters Shall Prophesy

> St. Bernard, who had a great devotion to the
> Virgin Mary, was allegedly kneeling one day be-
> fore a statue of her when the stone lips parted
> as if to speak. "Silence!" he cried. "It is not per-
> mitted for a woman to speak in church!"

WHEN ASKED what Scripture has to say about women's role in the
church, many people would agree with Bernard's summary. The
New Testament's direct advice to women seems encapsulated
in 1 Corinthians 14:34 and 1 Timothy 2:11–12. Yet such proof texts
focus on only one small corner of a very large picture.

Given the social role of women in the first-century world, Christian women were extraordinarily active. We have seen how Jesus
throughout his ministry accepted women fully. They learned from
him and ministered to him on a par with men. Although the apostles
had great difficulty understanding, let alone imitating, Christ's
attitude, women continued to play a wide role in the early church.

Originally Christianity was simply a Jewish sect. Judaism was,
and still is, a "man's religion not only in substance and in practice,
but also in its symbolic theology." [1] The law commanded Israelites
to "set apart to the Lord all that first opens the womb" (Exod.
13:12), but the context makes it clear God only wanted sons. Only
men were required to attend the great festivals (Deut. 16:16); a
woman could and did go along but her first duty was to serve her
husband and free him to worship God. In the Hellenistic period,
Jewish women were not only barred from all religious leadership
but even from worshiping alongside men. In the Jerusalem temple
and local synagogues they were walled off into a separate area. Ten
men were required before a service could begin; women did not
count. Women were not taught the oral law and even today a woman
with the stature of Golda Meir is not permitted to touch the Torah.

FULL PARTICIPANTS

In the Christian church, women's place was quite different. From
the beginning women participated fully and equally with men. At
Pentecost three thousand souls accepted the Christian message—not
so many men *plus* women and children as Jews would have

60

reckoned (Acts 2:41; cf. 5:14; 8:12 with Matt. 15:38). Paul's first convert in Europe was Lydia (Acts 16:14–15) and other prominent women were among his followers in other cities (Acts 17:4, 12; 17:34; 18:2). In Romans 16 among the twenty-nine people greeted by Paul ten are women.[2] Baptism, the sign of the new covenant as circumcision had been of the old, was given to both men and women believers. Both sexes worshiped together in one room, though probably divided by an aisle. Women were present in the Upper Room (Acts 1:14) and received the filling of the Holy Spirit (2:3) which signaled the founding of the church.

From the moment of the resurrection, women were active witnesses to the Living Christ, as indeed they had been before. Paul came to rely on several women as fellow workers in spreading the gospel (Phil. 4:2–3; Rom. 16:3, 6, 12). As the prophet Joel had predicted (2:28–32), Peter discovered that both men and women received the gift of prophecy, the call of God to proclaim his word to others (Acts 2:17–18). Perhaps this was spoken of in Psalm 68:11 which reads: "The Lord gave the command, and many women carried the news" (TEV).

Many Jewish women had been prophets—Miriam (Exod. 15:20), Deborah (Judg. 4:4), Huldah (whom Josiah consulted on the authenticity of a book found in the Temple and whose advice he enacted into important reforms, 2 Kings 22:14 ff.; 2 Chron. 34:22 ff.), Noadiah (Neh. 6:14), Isaiah's wife (Isa. 8:3), and Anna (Luke 2:36–38). Christian women continued in that tradition (1 Cor. 11:5)—particularly Philip's four daughters (Acts 21:9). Prophecy was a highly valued gift in the early church, earnestly to be sought (1 Cor. 14:1) and prophets were listed right after apostles in lists of gifts (1 Cor. 12:28–29; Eph. 4:11). The purpose of prophecy was primarily to convict and call sinners to account (1 Cor. 14:24–25) and for the "edification, and exhortation, and comfort" of the church (14:3–4, KJV).

Women were also teachers, and teaching is listed third after the ministries of apostle and prophet. In Acts 18:24 ff. Priscilla (along with Aquila her husband) took the learned Apollos of Alexandria aside and "expounded to him the way of God more accurately." Older women in the church were expected to "teach what is good" (Titus 2:3), as Timothy's mother and grandmother evidently did (2 Tim. 1:5). In fact all mature Christians (Heb. 5:12) should be able to "teach and admonish one another in all wisdom" (Col. 3:16). Teaching in the New Testament was not connected with any specific office but was the explication of Scripture by anyone with sufficient knowledge and piety (Rom. 15:14). Since education of women was very limited, few may have had opportunity to develop this gift. Yet some like Priscilla, who may well have been a wealthy Roman with access to private tutors, did exhibit such gifts to the extent that many have suggested her name as the author of Hebrews.[3]

Jewish women were permitted no voice in the local synagogue or the Sanhedrin, which governed national affairs. Yet in the church, women were active in official capacities from the beginning. Women were among those who chose a successor to Judas (Acts 1:13–26). Many influential women opened their homes as meeting places for the first assemblies—John Mark's mother (Acts 12:12); Nympha (Col. 4:15); Priscilla (Rom. 16:5).

ADMINISTRATORS

Phoebe, of suburban Corinth and seemingly the courier for the book of Romans, is given two titles (Rom. 16:1–2): *diakonos* and *prostatis*. The latter word (translated "helper" in RSV) usually means "one who presides," the "chief of a party," a president, ruler, patron, superintendent. The noun form is used only in this passage, but the verb form appears many times. Usually translated "rule" or "manage," it refers to bishops, deacons, and elders (see 1 Tim. 3:4–5; 5:17; Rom. 12:8). A better translation would be "she was designated as a ruler over many by me" (Rom. 16:2).[4]

Phoebe's first title, *diakonos* (deacon), is a word which has the same endings for both masculine and feminine forms. Paul uses the word twenty-two times, eighteen of which the King James Version translates as "minister" and three as "deacon." Phoebe, however, is called "servant"! While 1 Timothy 3:11 is sometimes translated to refer to deacons' wives, it more logically refers to women deacons. Although those named in Acts 6 (to "serve tables"!) were all men (and not specifically called "deacons"), both men and women were ordained to this office in some areas throughout the church's first millennium.[5] The duties of both sexes included the practical work of the community: serving the communal meal, taking Communion to those unable to attend services, instructing converts, assisting in baptisms, distributing food and funds to the needy, visiting the sick and imprisoned, consoling the bereaved, arranging funerals, caring for orphans. Obviously it was a very important post in the church. Women were necessary because they could visit, instruct, and physically baptize other women, whereas society would nòt have permitted a man such contact. Women deacons became obsolete with the adoption of infant baptism.

Another official group within the church was the widows. 1 Timothy 5:3–16 speaks of them as a definite order into which mature

women of good reputation were enrolled. Early church fathers Igna-
tius and Polycarp as well as early church documents indicate such a
group also. The widows' primary ministry seems to have been
intercessory prayer, although they also went from house to house
collecting gifts, helping others, and caring for orphans.[6]

Dorcas, mentioned in Acts 9:36–42, may well have been a widow,
since others mourned her death. She may also have been part of a
group of consecrated virgins who are spoken of in 1 Corinthians 7
and who emerge in the second-century Western church as a large
and respected group. A third-century Syrian document speaks of
two groups of virgins, divided at age fifty. They made clothes for
the needy, fasted and prayed for those in distress, visited and even
laid hands on the sick.[7] It is from this group that nuns evolved.

As the church developed a more structured ministry, the "elders"
or "presbyters" took precedence over the deacons. Though it is often
said that there is no evidence for women holding this office (which
is often compared to today's "preachers" in nonhierarchical
churches), 1 Timothy 5:1–2 refers to both *presbuterō,* "an elder,"
and *presbuteras,* "female elders." These references are usually
camouflaged by translating them "an older man" and "older
women." However, the chapter is clearly talking about established
orders of ministry, because it goes on to speak of the enrolling of
widows (v. 9) and of *presbuteroi,* the plural form of "elders," who
rule well and labor in preaching and teaching (v. 17). Nothing in
verses 17–22 indicates that only men are being referred to. Titus 2:3
refers to *presbutidas,* which can more justifiably be translated
"older women," but here they are called "reverent" (*hieroprepeis,*
a word that comes the closest of any in the New Testament to
describing a priestly, sacred or liturgical function but is not applied
to male presbyters or deacons), and they are specifically told to
teach and not necessarily just other women.

Sunergos is another word used to describe what may be another
ministerial office. It is usually translated "fellow laborer," or "coworkers" in the plural, and is applied to Timothy (Rom. 16:21),
Apollos and Paul (1 Cor. 3:9), Titus (2 Cor. 8:23), Clement
(Phil. 4:3), Demas and Luke (Philem. 24), and others. It is also
used of several women: Priscilla (Rom. 16:3), Euodia and Syntyche
(Phil. 4:2–3). There is evidence that the word may have been inter-
changeable with *diakonos.*[8]

One woman "apostle" is even mentioned in the Bible! Junia,
saluted by Paul in Romans 16:7 (KJV), is a common Roman name
for a woman, but since she is identified as an "apostle," many
translators have assumed the name to be a contraction for a much
less common male one. Chrysostom, fourth-century bishop of

Constantinople, however, had no difficulty identifying her: "Oh, how great is the devotion of this woman that she should be counted worthy of the appellation of apostle!" [9] Actually if the qualification for becoming an apostle, as Acts 1:22 suggests, is having witnessed the resurrection, several women were highly qualified.

Into a very structured and restrictive society, the gospel of Jesus Christ came as a very liberating, mighty rushing wind, overturning racial, social, and sexual differences. In Christ all are a "chosen race, a royal priesthood, a holy nation, God's own people" (1 Pet. 2:9). As Tertullian commented of men and women: "Together they pray, together they prostrate themselves, together they perform their fasts, mutually teaching, mutually exhorting, mutually sustaining. Equally are they both found in the church of God." [10]

But such freedom was not fully understood by those outside the church and even by some within. From outsiders the church was beset by several accusations including allegations that Christians did away with marriage and the family (did they really hold *all* things in common?) and that they were disloyal to Rome (they did call Jesus rather than the emperor "Lord"). Inside the church some also made liberty into license—Christians considered leaving their non-Christian spouses, slaves ran away from their masters, some flaunted the fact that they ate meat offered to idols, others courted martyrdom by openly thumbing their noses at statues of Caesar. And so early church leaders offered some strong suggestions.

Rule one was, don't rock the boat quite so hard! Christians were repeatedly admonished to respect and obey the government. Christian spouses were absolved of their marital commitments only if the unbeliever left them. Women in particular were warned to do nothing which would discredit the word of God (Titus 2:5) or "give the enemy . . . occasion to revile us" (1 Tim. 5:14). Within the church "all things should be done decently and in order" because "God is not a God of confusion but of peace" (1 Cor. 14:40, 33).

HEAD-COVERINGS

Thus the longest passage in the New Testament devoted solely to the issue of women in the church concerns the wearing of certain head-coverings or the arrangement of the hair during worship services (1 Cor. 11:2–16).[11] The exact composition and cultural background of Corinthian church members is uncertain, but Corinth was a wide-open industrial and commercial center, dominated by a famous temple of Aphrodite, whose priestesses accounted for much of the city's proverbial immorality. On the other hand, according to Acts 18:7-8, the local church met next door to the Jewish synagogue and may have had many Jews as members. Thus it is difficult to know in what context Paul is speaking.

In Jewish circles there was great aversion toward women praying with heads uncovered. (Jewish men did not begin to wear the yarmulke until the fourth century, though Old Testament priests wore elaborate headgear.) A Jewish woman seen in public without her veil was considered to be flouting her marriage vows, and the Talmud commanded her husband to divorce her. Veiling was important because Jewish teachings considered both a woman's hair and her voice sexual enticements.[12]

Greek custom is a bit more complicated. Highborn wives generally wore veils in public. Concubines and second-rank wives could wear them but not in the presence of the first wife. Single women generally did not wear veils. Prostitutes and slaves were forbidden by law to veil themselves. In cultic worship both men and women were bare-headed; temple priestesses never wore head-coverings. In their homes no one wore veils. Thus some Corinthian Christians may have argued that within the "household of faith," particularly if it met in a private home as many churches did, they could dispense with the veil. Perhaps eventually a compromise was worked out, because early Christian art shows a woman speaking to a mixed assembly with a head-covering pulled back and fastened with a fashionable ornament.[13]

Both Jews and Greeks considered the veil and certain hair styles symbolic of marriage. Paul did not want Christian women to act in such a manner that people would confuse them with either the pagan orgiastic cults where women loosed their hair in ecstatic frenzy, or the gnostics who degraded the body and marriage. He would not have understood modern Christians who almost unanimously disregard this injunction as cultural while clinging to silence for women, because as a Jew he considered unveiling a far more serious offense to public decency than speaking.

The exact purpose of the veil and thus the clear meaning of this passage has been debated by theologians for centuries. Those who interpret "head" as authority and rule see the repeated puns on the word in regard to the wife as meaning that her veil symbolizes her acceptance of her husband's authority. The key word is *exousia* (1 Cor. 11:10, translated "veils," RSV), meaning "power." The question is whose? The traditional answer, "her husband's," is philologically questionable and raises two questions: If the veil is

a symbol of one under authority, why does the husband not wear
one to indicate that he is under God's authority. And is not the
worshiping woman responsible to God alone?

Even more creative are suggestions that the word is simply a play
on an Aramaic word for veil that is related to a Hebrew word
for "rule"—a nifty word game surely, but it undoubtedly would
have totally bypassed Paul's Greek readers. Another interesting
theory is that the veil represented magical power which would
ward off evil spirits. A bit more understandable is an interpretation based on verse 7. It suggests that the goal of worship is to
glorify God. Since the man, according to verse 7 (though not
Gen. 1:26–27), is made in the image and glory *(doxa)* of God, his
uncovered head glorifies God. Since the woman reflects the glory
of the man she must be veiled before she can glorify God alone.[14]

The most textually plausible suggestion is "her own power." An
insignia of respect, the marriage head-covering or hair style would
offer protection for a woman's dignity. To arrange one's head is
to exercise control; to expose one's head is to court shame. Some
argue that this passage is directed primarily at women exercising
the gift of prophecy and that Ezekiel 13:17–23 indicates that
women prophets may have worn specific veils or headbands indicating prophetic office. 1 Kings 20:41 indicates that male prophets
also wore some insignia on their head to identify themselves. Within
this context, the "angels" were considered the intermediaries who
gave the prophets their message from God.[15]

On the other hand, Joseph Yoder argues that the first ten verses
of 1 Corinthians 11 are simply a restatement of traditional Jewish teachings, but that a great change begins with the words,
"Nevertheless, in the Lord. . . ." From here on, says Yoder, Paul
is moving away from Jewish arguments for subordination and
enunciating a doctrine of liberty for the Christian woman. She
needs no veil "for her hair is given to her for a covering" (11:15).
Obviously some people might be upset by such radical teaching, but
to "any one . . . disposed to be contentious," Paul, according to
Yoder, simply says, "we recognize no other practice, nor do the
churches of God" (11:16).[16] That is, women need no covering other
than their hair. Thus this passage would be similar to those putting
down Judaizers who insisted that Gentiles be circumcised.

Though it is hardly a major issue, the "angels" referred to in
11:10 have intrigued and befuddled scholars. One pastor finally
conceded that it was probably a phrase Paul tossed in for effect,
much like we use "for heaven's sake!" But he does seem to offer
it as a justification, in addition to the "headship" argument and

his rabbinic exegesis of Genesis which we have discussed earlier. Some say the angels are good ones who oversee the created order, guard individuals, and evidence God's presence in public worship. On the other hand, they might be bad angels, perhaps those who got confused at creation and worshiped man rather than God. Tertullian was the first to suggest that they might be evil and attracted by a woman's seductiveness unveiled. The angels may also be learning from the church and for them women should set an example of Christian modesty. Or maybe women should learn from the example of the angels in Isaiah 6:2 who modestly covered themselves in God's presence. A more down-to-earth suggestion is simply that "angels" was a euphemism for ministers who, standing before a congregation, might be distracted by the beauty of unveiled women.[17]

The essential justification for the wearing of veils was simply social custom: "Give no offense to Jews or to Greeks or to the church" (1 Cor. 10:32); "maintain the traditions . . . as I have delivered them to you" (11:2); and "we have no such custom" (11:16, KJV). In between, Paul appeals to "nature," saying it obviously teaches that for a man to wear long hair is degrading. But this is certainly an appeal to social custom since nature unprevented would veil a man's face and head in hair much more than a woman's. Actually this is a strange comment since Jewish men often let their hair grow as part of religious vows (something Paul and his friends had evidently done in Acts 21:24), and Greeks honored the ancient long-haired Spartans as well as their contemporaries whose long hair was a sign either of asceticism or of devotion to philosophy.[18]

SILENCE IN SERVICES

Basically the church was concerned with what was "fitting" in its social context (1 Cor. 11:13; Eph. 5:3; 1 Tim. 2:10; Titus 2:1). A broader view of 1 Corinthians illumines the issues. *The New English Bible* titles the section beginning in chapter 7 "The Christian in a pagan society." Chapter 11 in *The Jerusalem Bible* is labeled "Decorum in Public Worship" with subtitles "Women's behaviour at services," "The Lord's Supper," and "Spiritual gifts." A cursory glance at the book reveals the multitude of serious problems facing this large, active congregation. The church was obviously endowed by the Spirit with an abundance of gifts (1:7), but even these required discipline if the entire group was to be edified. Women in the group were given two instructions: "any woman who prays or prophesies with her head unveiled dishonors her head" (11:5) and "women should keep silence in the churches" (14:34). On the face of it, these two commands are contradictory, but the context offers an explanation.

Immediately following the instructions concerning veils Paul discusses the Lord's Supper. Indications throughout the New Testament as well as other early church writings show that meetings were divided into two parts. The first half was open to anyone who wanted to come and hear the gospel. This is sometimes called the "mass of the catechumens" because, just as in liturgical churches today, it was devoted to the reading of Scripture and discussing it, praying, and perhaps singing. Catechumens were those interested in becoming Christians but who had not finished instruction or been baptized. Thus they were barred from the second half of the service, the "mass of the faithful" who were permitted to take Communion.

Chapter 11 falls within the latter context where only bona fide Christians were present. Women could prophesy and pray, but they should not offend other Christians or give rise to rumors of looseness by their behavior. In 1 Corinthians 14 the discussion has turned to the first half of the service where "uninitiated," "unlearned," "unbelievers" (vv. 16, 23, 24) are present. Here Paul lays down another rule because, as he says in 14:23, "If, therefore, the whole church assembles and all speak in tongues, and outsiders or unbelievers enter, will they not say that you are mad?" His intent is clearly to preserve order and decorum.

Exactly what is Paul prohibiting women to do in 1 Corinthians 14:34–35? Says one author, it is "a command not to take charge of the public worship service. . . . This prohibition of women into the pastoral office is a universal prohibition." [19]

But is Paul prohibiting women from speaking altogether? Could he really silence women in the home church of Priscilla, Chloe, and possibly Phoebe? No. Although there are textual questions about the authenticity of these verses,[20] they do fit perfectly with the linguistic and thought pattern of the chapter. The word for "speak" here is used twenty-four times in the chapter. Everybody in Corinth seemingly wanted to speak during their services. The word does *not* mean a formal lecture, exhortation, or teaching, but simply *talking,* idle talk or chatter. It is used of the women in 1 Timothy 5:13 who are also described as "idlers . . . gossips and busybodies."

Contemporary orthodox synagogues still have the same problem. Women are usually confined to a screened-off balcony or side room where they can barely hear. And since they are still not allowed to learn as much of the liturgy, the Torah, and the oral laws of Judaism as men do, they simply do not understand what is going on. So they chatter and gossip to the point where it becomes quite noisy.[21]

Paul goes on to say that "if there is anything they desire to know, let them ask their husbands at home." Obviously these women were interrupting the meetings with questions. Inquirers, converts from paganism, uneducated women—they probably had many questions more appropriate for a catechetical situation. This certainly could not be a definitive pronouncement—of whom would single women, widows, or those with pagan husbands or fathers ask questions? But one can imagine how disturbing it could be for spouses separated by an aisle to call questions back and forth!

And so Paul forbids women so to speak; he tells them to keep silence. Again the word for silence is one that has already appeared in verses 28 and 30. If these orders of silence had been applied as rigorously as the one concerning women, our services would be silent indeed! Paul is not simply telling women to be totally silent but rather he is asking all Christians to defer to each other in order that the services might be orderly and edifying. Utterances inspired by the Spirit were permitted; other talking should cease.

In support of this injunction he uses simply a reference to "the law." In some translations the word is capitalized as if to refer to the Law of Moses in some way, but nothing in the Old Testament prohibits women's speaking in worship contexts, nor is there any verse that specifically says she should be in subjection. Bibles with cross-references usually cite 1 Timothy 2:11–12 and Genesis 3:16. Since Timothy was undoubtedly written later, Paul could not have been referring to that. Genesis 3:16 says that as a result of the Fall men will dominate women. Surely Paul would not have the church perpetuate a sinful condition.

The word "law" used here rather means "what is proper, what is assigned to someone," [22] thus their role. Again he appeals to social custom. If the Corinthian church were meeting in a Jewish synagogue or home, the orthodox would feel it a desecration to allow women to speak. The Talmud says a woman is subject to divorce for "conversing with all sorts of men." Another suggestion is that Chloe, mentioned in 1:11, was a highborn Greek woman who was offended by the forward outspokenness of converted lower class women and hetairai. Whatever the reason, the verses do not prohibit a ministry for women in the church but simply assert that Christian meetings should be orderly.

TEACHING

1 Timothy 2:8–15, though usually considered synonymous with 1 Corinthians 14:34–35, presents many different questions, some of which we have dealt with elsewhere. Some modern biblical scholars regard the book as non-Pauline, written at a much later period when the church was more structured and institutionalized.[23] Timothy's church was in Ephesus, home of the great temple of Diana, and some of the women there seem very unstable. Although some were deacons and official widows, the younger women were "burdened with sins and swayed by various impulses, who will listen to anybody and can never arrive at a knowledge of the truth" (2 Tim. 3:6–7) and "idlers, gadding about from house to house" (1 Tim. 5:13). Such young widows were advised to remarry, contrary to Paul's advice to Corinthian widows in 1 Corinthians 7:40.

The immediate context in 1 Timothy 2 is behavior in public worship, presumably the first part of the service with unbelievers present, since Communion is not mentioned. First, men are instructed to pray without anger or quarreling—which makes one wonder what was going on, though perhaps the reference is to Matthew 5:23–24. Then women are told to adorn themselves modestly, though they must not have been wearing veils or no one would have noticed their hair. Both 1 Timothy 2:9 and 1 Peter 3:3 inveigh against "gold-braided hair," not simply braids but an especially elaborate style including false hair and jewelry interwoven—a favorite style of courtesans. Judging by the space devoted to the subject, New Testament writers seem most concerned about how women wore their hair and jewelry! These instructions are almost totally dismissed by today's church as cultural and irrelevant, yet the verses following are proclaimed as eternal principles.

"Let a woman learn in silence with all submissiveness. . . . she is to keep silent" (1 Tim. 2:11–12b). Though this sounds identical to 1 Corinthians 14:34–35, the word for "silence" is different. It means to "desist from bustle" or to "refrain from the use of language." It suggests decorum. The adjectival form of the word was used in 1 Timothy 2:2 to describe the type of life all Christians should lead.

"I permit no woman to teach" (1 Tim. 2:12). In Greek the word for "teach" comes first in the sentence and is the word for formal instruction, though as we have seen, in the early church many members, including women, had this gift and exercised it. The primary concern here is not so much the role of women as the possibility of false teaching. Timothy's parishioners had already shown themselves to be confused in doctrinal matters (2 Tim. 3:6–7) and "some have already strayed after Satan" (1 Tim. 5:15). The prohibition is buttressed by a reference to Eve's being deceived, an occurrence cited elsewhere only in 2 Corinthians 11:3 where, as we have seen, Paul warns all Christians to beware lest the serpent deceive them too. Insubordinate men who were "empty talkers and deceivers" were likewise silenced in Titus 1:10–11.

The fascinating element in this instruction to Timothy comes in verse 12: "or to have authority over men." The men referred to are probably husbands. The verb is *authentein,* used just this once in the New Testament. Possible translations are "interrupt" (Dibelius), "dictate to" (Moffatt) or "domineer over" (NEB). In noun form, as used by the great Greek dramatists, it meant a "suicide" or a "family murderer." Later the noun came to mean "lord" or "autocrat." In the first century it was rather a slang word, and one can sense the writer's relish at throwing in such a juicy word. Because suicide involves deciding for oneself, taking one's life into one's own hands, to do so for others meant to become a "dictator." Thus the word came to mean "self-willed" or "arbitrary," interfering in what was not properly one's own domain, trespassing the socially proper limits.

Thus we see again a concern for maintaining the cultural status quo, for not transgressing the marital social roles. The passage seems directed at a particular situation rather than at stating a general principle. Of all the passages concerning women in the New Testament, only Galatians 3:28 is in a doctrinal setting; the remainder are all concerned with practical matters. In 1 Timothy the problem seems to be women who usurped authority from others, teaching when they had neither gift nor training. Perhaps one of the wealthier women thought her social position guaranteed her a leadership post. Or perhaps the church was even meeting in the home of a woman who was bossy and domineering. Maybe some women were putting their husbands down publicly. Whatever the local situation, we must be careful not to consider this passage the only and final word to women.

Although the New Testament does not repudiate the social order, neither does it make the maintenance of the order the goal of the Christian church. With "one Lord, one faith, one baptism, one God and Father of us all, who is above all and through all and in all" (Eph. 4:5–6), the church's goal is to be one building (Eph. 2:19–22) and one body (1 Cor. 12:12–26). "There is neither Jew nor Greek, there is neither slave nor free, there is neither male nor female; for you are all one in Christ Jesus" (Gal. 3:28). This verse

directly contradicts the prayer of every orthodox Jew: "Blessed
are you, Lord our God . . . who has not created me a heathen . . .
a slave . . . a woman." Christ prayed "that they may all be one"
(John 17:21), and the church's goal has always been unity. But
somehow the church has continually come unglued: Judaizers and
Gentiles, East and West, clergy and laity, catholics and anabaptists,
Catholics and Protestants, masters and slaves, evangelicals and
liberals, men and women. Rather than being healed, the divisions
have festered.

Yet Paul in Galatians was serious; he did not get carried away
with rhetoric; his words are intentional. The last phrase, *arsen kai
thēlu,* uses the technical terms which parallel Genesis 1:27 as
quoted by Jesus in Matthew 19:4. Although the three pairs given
by Paul are usually translated with identical syntax, the first two
are "neither . . . nor" constructions but the last is literally "there
is not male and female." [24]

Paul here is not denying certain distinctions between groups. A
person could not change what he was born—Jew, Greek, slave,
free, male, female. Paul was not following certain gnostics who
tried to deny man's biological nature. None of the apostles ad-
vocated the immediate overthrow of cultural custom—Christianity
was controversial enough without that! Yet they did not shy away
from the radical cutting edge of the gospel which would gradually
undermine society's oppressive policies and restore God's intended
harmony. Both Greeks and Jews were accepted by Christianity on
an equal footing. Slaves and free men became brothers. Men and
women worked side by side in spreading the gospel. There were no
second-class citizens in Christ's church.

Social distinctions are meant to be transcended—not perpetuated
—within the body of Christ. Paul was certainly not talking to the
Galatians in purely "spiritual" terms as some have contended
"in Christ" means. He did not advise the conflicting groups to
sing one chorus of "We are one in the Spirit, we are one in the
Lord" and then each go off to separate meals. In fact, that is precisely what he reprimanded Peter for doing (Gal. 2:11–21). In asking Philemon to receive back his slave, he pointedly tells him to
treat Onesimus "no longer as a slave but more than a slave,
as a beloved brother . . . both in the flesh and in the Lord"
(Philem. 16).

All social distinctions between men and women should have been
erased in the church. Yet, they have been perpetuated with a vengeance. Just how sincere has been our prayer, "Thy will be done on
earth, as it is in heaven"?

7. He, She, or We?

Throughout history people have knocked their heads against the riddle of the nature of femininity. . . . Nor will you have escaped worrying over this problem—those of you who are men; to those of you who are women this will not apply— you are yourselves the problem.

SIGMUND FREUD[1]

"VIVE LA DIFFERENCE!" someone is sure to shout whenever the discussion turns to the natures of men and women. Most people assume that innate differences exist between the sexes, that they are "sexually differentiated in their entire humanness," and that this antithesis is "a part of nature," "a God-given principle, his creation order." [2]

Strength, action, sound reason, decisiveness, aggressiveness, ambition, energy, drive, courage, inventiveness are thought to characterize "masculine nature." The male biological symbol is that used in astronomy for Mars, god of war, and represents his shield and spear: ♂. The mirror of Venus, ♀, goddess of love and beauty, is the female symbol because "feminine nature" is thought to be narcissistic, subjective, dependent, passive, intuitive, tender, fragile, irrational, frivolous.

Not only do the sexes inhabit differently shaped bodies, but we have been taught that God created us with "masculine" or "feminine" minds and souls as well. Thus men are innately the spokesmen, the leaders, the builders of society, while women's greatest joy and fulfillment are found in marriage, motherhood, and housewifery.

Masculinity in our society, *machismo,* is characterized by power. The male is expected to prove his manhood through achievements in athletics, education, occupation, and even in bed. Sex becomes conquest; the object is to "score." Violence too is part of the real he-man image.

"The feminine mystique" on the other hand lies in woman's supposed innate passivity. A man chooses her as his wife and "gets her pregnant." Without her help the baby grows mysteriously inside her. All her maternal and nurturing "instincts" are devoted to her child. She finds total fulfillment in mothering her children and responding to the wishes of her husband. Her goal in life is to

73

please other people, to sacrifice herself for them. She lives through their achievements.[3]

Are men and women as radically dissimilar as our society constantly tells and shows us that they are? Are we *innately* so different?

BIOLOGY

"Male and female he created them"—that is all the Bible tells us about sexual differences. The biological givens are assumed; they are never defined further or explored. Instead Scripture continually reaffirms the unity of the human race, not our distinctives but our similarities.

What are the biological givens? Are not men and women radically different in their chromosomal, hormonal, and structural makeups? The answer to that question is yes and no, and the question which must follow it is: Do biological differences lead inevitably to behavioral differences?

Let's begin at the beginning. Of the forty-six chromosomes in every fertilized egg, forty-four have nothing to do with sexuality but simply constitute a human being, plus either XY chromosomes designating a male or XX denoting a female. Some males have an extra chromosome in an XXY or XYY pattern and some females have X or XXX patterns. The female genetic pattern appears to be the stronger. Though many more males are conceived than females, yet 12 percent more male fetuses die *in utero*. Though 105 boys are born for every 100 girls, boys have a 32 percent higher mortality rate during the first week of life. The male Y chromosome has been called a fragment of an X and a blank. Attributed to it have been such sex-linked abnormalities as hemophilia, color blindness, bark-like skin, dense hairy growths on the ears, hard lesions on the feet, and webbed toes, among other things.[4] But there is no evidence that genetic differences account for "masculine" or "feminine" behavior or temperament.

In fact "genetic sex alone does not exercise a direct and peremptory power over psychosexual differentiation." Whatever the genetic pattern of the fetus, "nature's first choice or primal impulse is to differentiate a female."[5] Something must be added to obtain a male: the male hormone androgen. Everyone contains a certain amount of all three sex hormones: androgen, estrogen, and progestin. In biochemical structure the sex hormones are cousins and the body can convert one into the other. Hormonally the sexes are not antithetical in their makeup. Rather the spectrum is more like a continuum with most people having a preponderance of either androgen (male) or estrogen (female).

Other than their role in the prenatal differentiation of our external genital structure,[6] most of the hormones' work is done later in life, confirming with appropriate secondary sex characteristics in puberty the sex role which we were assigned and learned from birth. Yet individual characteristics vary widely depending on bodily build and hormonal balance. Some women have facial and chest hair while some men have very little. Some women's breasts develop hardly at all while some men have pronounced breasts. But such differences and/or similarities do not determine how a person will feel and function.[7] A woman with small breasts, for example, can feel just as feminine and function just as well in her capacity as wife and mother as a woman with larger breasts.

On the adult level, female hormones supposedly make women unfit for political and intellectual leadership. Their bodies are allegedly swept periodically by raging hormonal imbalances which wreak havoc with any decision-making powers they might have. Both men and women, however, are subject to biologically determined ups and downs in physical, emotional, and intellectual functioning in roughly monthly cycles. Both men and women eventually go through a "change of life" when their hormonal balances change, sometimes causing distressing symptoms. Most women learn to recognize and adjust to their own menstrual cycle with little difficulty. Hormone therapy is now available for those with extreme problems, as it is for both menopausal men and women.[8]

Other physical differences between men and women do exist, of course. Men have a higher ratio of muscle to fat tissue than women. Women have a lower center of gravity so that they can float in water and a pelvic structure specialized for childbirth. Men have an elbow structure specialized for throwing baseballs overhand. In all societies men have taller and larger skeletons. Yet the differences between the sexes vary. Among American Indian tribes two to six inches is the average variation in mean height between men and women. Among a certain African tribe the mean difference is eight inches. But what are these compared to the fact that the average Tutsi man is six feet one inch while the average Mbuti pygmy man is four feet six inches and the woman four feet five inches? Obviously such differences must have something to do with racial stock, diet, life-style, etc.

Doesn't the Bible say that women are the "weaker sex"?[9] Before the advent of birth control when most women spent most of their adult lives pregnant, they certainly did appear weaker. And because we have stressed and encouraged muscular development in men, they do generally exhibit greater bodily strength. If, however, this is still a measure of superiority, then civilization has advanced no further than our cave-dwelling, club-wielding ancestors. In our society, at least, women appear to have greater stamina and endurance under stress—witness men's earlier death due to heart attacks, their high rates of ulcers and suicide. There is also evidence that testosterone, one of the androgens which regulate male sexuality, induces a slightly higher metabolic rate which seems to cause men to "burn out" faster. It also does not retard the aging of blood vessels and the build-up of cholesterol as the female's estrogen does.

But what difference do all these differences make? Why should individuals be consigned to roles limited by sexual designations rather than being allowed to develop fully their unique and varied capabilities?

Human beings are not predestined or controlled by instincts as are the lower animals. Even studies of the higher anthropoids (apes and chimpanzees) show that their behavior is less determined by instinct and more by learning.[10] Scientists debate whether humans should be said to have *any* truly instinctual behavior. But all agree that even if we do have instinctual drives to eat, socialize, mate, survive, etc., these instincts do not determine actual behavior which could be labeled "masculine" or "feminine."

CULTURE

The meaning and content of these labels "masculine" and "feminine" in terms of behavior and temperament are totally determined by culture.

Classic illustration for that statement is found in Margaret Mead's *Sex and Temperament in Three Primitive Societies* in New Guinea. Among the Arapesh both sexes are mild-mannered, gentle, cooperative people concerned primarily with nurturing the lives of their children, animals, and crops. Mundugumor men and women are ruthless, aggressive individuals devoted to fierce and sometimes violent competition in which maternal, cherishing aspects of personality have little place. In Tchambuli society women are energetic, dominant, impersonal, unadorned managers while the men, less responsible and emotionally dependent, indulge in catty gossip, wear curls, and perfect their dancing.

Many other cultures offer similar illustrations. In Iran women are expected to be practical and cool while men are emotional, sensitive, intuitive. The Tutsi of Africa consider women "naturally" stronger. Among the Navaho and Hopi Indian tribes, one considers weaving men's work and pottery making only for women while the other tribe declares the reverse to be "natural." As Mead concludes, if those temperamental attributes which we as Americans have traditionally regarded as "feminine" can so easily be declared "masculine" in one group and totally outlawed for the majority of both men and women in another society, then "many, if not all, of the personality traits which we have called masculine or feminine are as lightly linked to sex as are the clothing, the manners, and the form of head-dress that a society at a given period assigns to either sex." [11]

Human nature is unbelievably malleable, capable of taking a variety of directions. What we become is the result of cultural conditioning, enculturation, socialization. Individuals acquire a sexual identity from a very early age through the process of psychosexual development. It is learned through identification with the parent of one's own sex, interaction with the other parent, and imitation of one's peer group. After age five identity is merely reinforced by mastering and testing role behavior outlined by society.

In our society we have no ideal for "personhood." All aspects of life—emotional, intellectual, vocational, even spiritual—have been arbitrarily divided into two categories labeled "masculine" and "feminine." Persons are given access to one or the other of these realms usually depending solely on whether they possess male or female external genitalia at birth.

The pervasive influence of this initial decision is incredible. As the baby is pulled from the womb, the obstetrician takes one look and promptly has the child color-coded with a bracelet. Parents accordingly choose a name which is hopefully unambiguously "boy" or "girl." Relatives bring gifts in either blue or pink. After all, it is embarrassing if we remark, "Doesn't the baby have a cute face!" when we are supposed to say, "My, he looks like a potential football star!"

Purpose of the color-coding is to apprise everyone of the category into which they are to begin to enculturate this newborn member of society. And there are radical, far-reaching differences. From birth girl babies are hugged, kissed, coddled, and controlled, while their brothers are touched less, left alone in their cribs longer, and encouraged to venture out away from their mothers.[12] Girls are taught to be affectionate with friends; boys are encouraged to shake hands, shadowbox, and wrestle.

At play girls are expected to be quiet, cooperative, cautious, and close by. Boys are allowed to be tough, rough, daring, and venture-some. Boys are given the building blocks, chemistry sets, trucks, and rockets they will presumably deal with as adults. Girls are offered doll babies, miniature houses, and toy stoves. In one set of picture books[13] on the question of "What will you be when you grow up?" girls are given such choices as stewardess, model, movie star, secretary, or nurse "with white uniforms to wear." For boys the suggestions include fireman, policeman, farmer, pilot, or doctor to "help save people's lives." As a finale, the girl says, "I may even be a housewife some day when I am grown. . . . I'd love to be a mother with some children of my own." For boys, however, the book never mentions marriage or children. Instead their ultimate goal is being an astronaut or President!

The church condones and encourages society's divisions, adding to them the stamp of God's approval. A child in church notices immediately that most, if not all, of the major services are con-ducted by men. A study of Sunday school curricula for three-year-olds (!) found all ministers portrayed as men (in a denomination which does ordain women), all teachers women, all men in exciting vocations, all mothers in the home, none of the girls helping their fathers, most of the girls working around the house. Little girls were portrayed as timid, fearful, unhappy, needing help, waiting, victims of their emotions. The boys in the stories were adventurous, independent, self-sufficient, sociable, and happy.[14]

Formal education merely continues the process. Americans take pride in the fact that we offer equal education for all, yet this is far from true in many areas and is a relatively recent innovation for women. Girls initially do well in school because they have already been extensively socialized into behavior which teachers reward—sitting still, listening, and following orders. Because their mothers talk to them more from birth, they have the edge over boys in verbal skills. Boys have been pointed toward scientific, mechanical, and mathematical skills. Primary education concen-trates on learning verbal skills and gradually boys close the gap. Girls, however, are not given such compensatory study in the scientific areas and so they eventually fall behind.

Despite the fact that boys and girls show no significant differ-ences on intelligence tests or college entrance exams and girls generally have higher grade point averages at all levels, women have been systematically discriminated against in education. Skills courses and vocational programs have been largely sex-segregated. This means in some cities high schools which not only offer impor-tant vocational training but also often the best college preparation available are off limits to girls. In higher education women have been discriminated against in college admission, financial aid, classroom participation, athletic opportunities, internship programs, teaching assistantships, research grants.[15] The problem again is not biological or intellectual; it is simply cultural. As one woman law student commented, "When your advisor insists on addressing you as 'Sweetie' you know something is wrong!"

Outside the classroom, sex role stereotypes are reinforced by the media. Advertising portrays a woman as unable to cope with daily living without help from men to tell her how to wax her floor, clean her dishes, or wrap leftovers. A woman's major concerns seem to be white teeth, clean hair, dry underarms, and an uplifting bra. Her goal is sufficient sex appeal to attract a man.

The inordinate stress which our society places on feminine beauty is contrary to the biblical emphasis on inner grace. As William Law said long ago:

> It is therefore much to be lamented, that this sex, on whom so much depends, who have the first forming both of our bodies and our minds, are not only educated in pride, but in the silliest and most contemptible part of it.
> They are not indeed suffered to dispute with us the proud prizes of arts and sciences, of learning and eloquence, in which I have much suspicion they would often prove our superiors; but we turn them over to the study of beauty and dress, and the whole world conspires to make them think of nothing else. Fathers and mothers, friends and relations, seem to have no other wish towards the little girl, but that she may have fair skin, a fine shape, dress well, and dance to admiration.[16]

The Bible, however, stresses not outward adorning but "reverent and chaste behavior," "the hidden person of the heart with the imperishable jewel of a gentle and quiet spirit" (1 Pet. 3:2, 4). The Christian woman's goal in life is not to be beautiful but to serve God.

In his teen-age years, a boy is involved in essentially one task: deciding on a vocation and training for it. Finding a wife and establishing a family are of secondary importance and will presumably fit into and enhance his career aspirations. The teen-age girl, on the other hand, is torn by conflict. In school she is expected to work hard, develop her gifts, and prepare for a career too. But from all sides she is getting the message: what do grades and degrees matter if you don't get married? Having a date for the high school prom and a diamond ring for college graduation are the important accomplishments. Higher grades than one's current boyfriend must be shamefully hidden. Counselors suggest only such "feminine" professions as teaching and nursing; if a girl prefers auto mechanics or physics they discourage and ridicule her.[17] Parents take more pride in a girl's beauty and dates than in her grades and honors. As one girl put it, "When I turned out to be a mathematical genius, my mother said, 'Put on some lipstick and see if you can find a boyfriend.'"

Thus the bright young woman is caught on the blade of a two-edged sword. In achievement-oriented situations in school and career, she wants to succeed, to live up to her potential, to fulfill her talents. Yet society tells her that such achievement requires a loss of femininity. Men are the achievers in our world. To succeed in a man's world means that one must become masculine, or so it has been defined. A woman caught in this situation fears both failure and success—if she fails, she has not been true to herself; if she succeeds, she is going against society's expectations.[18]

PSYCHOLOGY

These expectations which permeate popular thinking have also been woven into all of our "official" psychologies. The "father" of modern psychology, Sigmund Freud, declared "anatomy is destiny." He was sure that all women felt themselves to be castrated males, envied the male's penis, and were incapable of cultural achievement. Their only hope was to accept their inferior role and have babies as a penis substitute. Feminist Kate Millett has effectively answered many of his assertions.[19] Freud confused biology and culture, anatomy and status. Confronted everywhere by evidence of the male's superior status, women do not envy the penis but only what that organ gives one social pretensions to. In many cultures men have similarly envied women's ability to bring forth human life.

Other schools of psychology also regard the cultural sex roles as innate. Erik Erikson sees in small children evidence that boys are concerned with "outer space" (exploring and interacting with the world around) while girls are only concerned with "inner space" (subjective and interpersonal experience). Thus the originator of the "identity crisis" declares that "much of a young woman's identity is already defined in her kind of attractiveness and in the selectivity of her search for the man (or men) by whom she wishes to be sought." He defines her maturity in terms of the view that a woman's "somatic design harbors an 'inner space' destined to bear the offspring of chosen men, and with it, a biological, psychological, and ethical commitment to take care of human infancy." [20] No one would dream of defining adult male identity and maturity in terms of attractiveness to women and their destined fatherhood!

Cumulatively these influences add up to very well-defined and rigid personality types and behavior models. The "mentally healthy male," according to a 1968 survey of mental health professionals by Donald and Inge Broverman, is aggressive, independent, unemotional, logical, direct, adventurous, self-confident, ambitious. The "mentally healthy female" is passive, emotional, dependent, less competitive, nonobjective, submissive, vain, easily influenced, religious, and in need of security.[21]

Basically these role definitions have been made by and for the convenience of men. Men are relatively comfortable with their identity because it is shaped by their own needs and desires. Women's identity is also shaped by men's needs and desires. If a woman is not built like Miss America, she must diet or pad. Whatever her intelligence and talent, she must make them appear less than her male companions'. Even Christian organizations tell female workers that their ministry is to be of encouragement and service to the men staff members, that they should channel any ideas through the men. All of this encourages women in the conniving, cajoling, and coercion better known as the use of "feminine wiles."

All social and civic functions are masculine; women participate in "feminine" functions. In order to narrow the competition, men have relegated women to an entirely different ball game. And despite all the camouflage, women's realm is clearly secondary, different, inferior. Men hold all the important positions of leadership, creativity, and responsibility. Women's work is unimportant, unspecialized, and often unpaid.

Male personality traits and behavior are defined as "adult" and "healthy" while those defined as "female" by society are still regarded as childish and even neurotic. The Brovermans discovered this by asking psychologists to list the traits of a "mentally healthy adult." It conformed exactly to the list previously drawn for a male but contrasted sharply with that for a female. A woman who exhibits "male" traits of aggressiveness and rationality is labeled "masculine," "neurotic," even "lesbian." If she conforms to female stereotypes, she is not a healthy adult; if she does not conform, she is sick. It is a no-win option.

Not only are our masculine cultural stereotypes defined as adult, healthy, and superior, but also God-like and God-ordained. God is creator, initiator, self-sufficient, all-powerful. And he created men in his image. Thus ours is obviously the "natural," "normal," "God-ordained" way of ordering society. Women who exhibit "masculine traits" must simply be defective in creation; those who would seek roles outside what is prescribed for them are simply rebelling against God's decrees. Although cultural expressions are entirely relative, each society seeks to absolutize its ways and to invoke divine sanction. We try to make God in our image.

And so women do conform to the stereotypes. Any group told repeatedly and forcefully that it is inferior, incapable of certain accomplishments, will soon begin to believe it and act accordingly. A woman teacher once told her all-girl class that of course their text pictured a male chef because "everybody knows" that men make the best cooks, dress designers, hairdressers, and even laundry workers. Constant repression kills ambition. Only a woman with extraordinary strength of character and an exceptional home background would have the courage and stamina it takes to fight her way into a "male" profession—thus the stereotype that women cannot succeed in certain fields and thus the fact that younger women have no role models to follow. Drifting with the tide is much more comfortable and much less difficult than fighting it. Women take the easy way out: they conform. They either accept the image men have outlined, or escape any identity crisis by becoming "Bill's wife" and "Beth's mommy."

At least they have in the past. Today women are asking more and more for the opportunity to define themselves. They are increasingly more willing to accept the challenge and responsibility of their own lives. Christian women are claiming the right to seek God's will for their individual lives and to act on his direction rather than simply confining themselves to what society decrees as "feminine."

THE DANGERS OF CHANGE

To call sexual identity and traditional sex roles into question, however, is like "picking up the ground on which we stand and shaking it," as Rosemary Ruether once commented.[22] Isolated from other cultures by our conviction that Western civilization is vastly superior, and schooled to see all other cultures through glasses tinted by our own role stereotypes, we have very few models for change. Women in particular have no feminine heroes, no *heras,* to emulate—women have been systematically excluded from our history. Women's accomplishments have been minimized or attributed to men. Only pagan idolaters or heretics believe that there is any feminine component in the divine.

And so, many people opt for the status quo. It is comfortable (particularly if you are male, middle class, and married). It has a long historical and theological tradition to undergird it. Yet the so-called status quo is no longer an option—it has been slowly disintegrating ever since the Protestant Reformation, the American Revolution, and the Civil War. With the growing belief in the equal dignity of all persons, we have jettisoned belief in the infallibility of the Papacy, the divine right of kings, and the superiority of the white race. If we really believed our myths of male dominance, we would have to take away women's right to be educated, to vote, and to work outside the home. Few would opt for such radical retrogression. To implement rigorously the implications of our supposed sex role concepts would clearly waste too many gifts of both men and women.

But if we are to change society, in which direction shall we go?

Some fear that the goal of women's liberation is the reversal of the traditional roles. Psychologists say that this fear of women taking over society is a fantasy based on ruling class ego and guilt. Men assume that women want to imitate them and when given power will inflict on men the oppression they have received. However, women do not want all the power—they simply want the power of choice in their own lives and to share in the decisions which shape *our* society.

An alternative to the status quo or role reversal would be to have only one pattern for both sexes. Often labeled "unisex," this alternative raises many questions. Most often expressed is the fear of homosexuality. The thinking seems to be that if society did away with sexually distinctive ways of acting, dressing, working, etc., no one could tell the difference and would end up falling in love with people of their own sex.

Interestingly anthropological research has contradicted this impression. Mead found no homosexuality whatever among any of the tribes she studied which made one set of personality traits mandatory for all. In fact psychosexual identity is much more secure in such societies because one who deviates from the "normal personality" is not labeled as acting like the other sex but like a person from another tribe or area. In such a culture a child displaying aberrant behavior will be told, *"People* don't do that!" While slightly different behavior may be expected from the sexes, this fact is never invoked. Thus the child's sense of membership in its own sex is never challenged.[23]

Societies with rigidly defined sex roles like our own generate anxiety because the threat of failing to behave like a member of one's own sex colors almost every detail of life from nursery routine to ways of sitting and walking, patterns for expressing emotions, even ways of speaking. All of us know ourselves to be human beings with a full range of possible thought, emotion, behavior. Yet we are taught to recognize only half of that potentiality as "masculine" or "feminine." Thus we strive to exhibit all the "correct" behavior and to inhibit all other feelings lest our sexual identity be questioned.

Actually homosexuality has been historically most widespread in cultures with the most pronounced sexual segregation. When men and women are seen as radically different kinds of beings who relate to each other only biologically for procreation, those who seek deep, personal, intimate relationships with like-minded persons often turn to homosexuality. The idea was so pervasive in the ancient world that Augustine believed that if God had intended intellectual and spiritual companionship for Adam rather than sexual mating he would have created a second man.

Homosexuals today express similar feelings. Said one female member of "gay lib": "I didn't like the roles society said men and women are supposed to have—which meant I couldn't be myself. I just couldn't accept society's prescribed role for women— sweetness, submissiveness, and no possibility for equality in a relationship with men. So I turned to women, and there I find good relationships." A Christian homosexual, seeking to change, also feels the same difficulty: "On the emotional level it is a man who has given me more than I could ever imagine a woman giving. . . . I could never imagine a relationship with a woman like the relationship I already know." [24] Men understand each other; women can empathize with each other. But the two sexes are said to be totally different—and thus the major problem in marriage is communication.

Not only do our current exclusive roles breed sexual identity problems for our adolescents and relational problems for adults, but they breed problems for the next generation. Psychologist Matthew Besdine suggests that limiting some women totally to the motherhood role can cause severe stresses and perhaps homosexuality in their children. The "Jocasta mother," as Besdine describes her, is a brilliant woman with great talents who is forced by traditional categories to pour all of her creative energies into her child. The result is a genius, but one who is psychologically and psychosexually troubled. [25]

Actually as we will see in our chapters on marriage, breaking down stereotypes between male and female and moving toward more egalitarian marriages can strengthen the marital bonds and actually enhance sex life. Communion is possible only between those who are the same—that is the message of creation and the Incarnation.

Another fear expressed is that changes in sex roles will destroy

the male ego. This depends on one's definition of that mystical
entity. Are men so fragile that they will be shattered if they can
no longer rule the roost because they wear male plummage, if they
have to compete not only with other races for their jobs but also
with another sex, if women no longer let them win at chess and
bowling? That "ego" is based on pride and oppression. It deserves
to be destroyed. Why should a person's sex organs be any more
relevant to his holding power than his skin color, his ethnic origin,
or his religious affiliation? On the other hand, both men's and
women's egos will be supported and nourished by a society that
encourages all people to achieve full potential. After all, women
need self-esteem, recognition, and inspiration too.

The real danger in a unisex society is not sexual aberration
but the same old limiting of potential found in traditional Western
society. If we were to try to impose any arbitrary pattern on everyone, we would sacrifice complexity, further cripple the deviant,
and limit the full range of the extraordinarily gifted.

A better alternative would be a society which recognizes and
encourages the widest possible variety in individual behavior and
temperament. Each person would be accepted as fully human
and helped to develop all inner potential. This is exactly what
women's liberation is asking for: the chance for every woman to
develop and test her inner capabilities without having someone say,
"That isn't ladylike!"

CHRISTLIKENESS

Christians should be the least threatened by such visions of
liberation. We of all people should have a historical, transcultural
perspective. We serve the Creator of all cultures who is creatively
at work in every culture. We are only pilgrims here; we seek a
city in which we have been told that sexual polarities will be
irrelevant. Our goal in life has never been to conform to the stereotypes of this world but to be transformed into Christlikeness.

Christ came into a world dominated by ascribed roles, positions
decreed by birth. Only a Jew, a son of Abraham, was one of the
chosen people. Only a Levite could be a priest. Only a male could
receive circumcision. Only a Roman citizen was protected by Roman
law. Only privileged aristocrats were allowed in the Roman senate.

But the Good News was that *achieved* roles were what counted
in the kingdom of God. "Believe in the Lord Jesus, and you will be
saved" (Acts 16:31). "There is no distinction between Jew and
Greek; the same Lord is Lord of all and bestows his riches upon all
who call upon him" (Rom. 10:12). In Christ we are no longer

servants and children but friends and heirs (John 15:15; Gal. 4:7).

Jesus did not endorse the patriarchal attitudes of his culture. He never once exhorted women to be good wives and mothers. He did not shoo Mary back into the kitchen but reprimanded Martha for getting too involved in it. He commended the gutsiness of the Canaanite woman who would not take no for an answer (Matt. 15:21–28) and the widow who would not let a corrupt judge ignore her plea (Luke 18:1–8).

Nor did he encourage the *machismo* attitudes of his male contemporaries. He criticized their casual attitude toward divorce that considered wives as servants who could be dismissed for trivial mistakes (Mark 10:2–9). He punctured their pride in thinking that they could view women as sex objects as long as they did nothing about their fantasies (Matt. 5:27–28; Luke 7:37–50). He called their bluff when they exercised a double standard in bringing to him a woman taken in adultery while letting her male companion go (John 8:1–11). He condemned their worship motivated by ego and assertiveness (Mark 12:41–44; Luke 18:9–14). He observed that the rational and clever did not understand his teachings as well as the simple did (Matt. 11:25).

Power and dominance were foreign to Jesus' teaching and practice. When the disciples wanted to call down fire from heaven to "get even" with the Samaritans, Jesus rebuked them (Luke 9:51–55). He commanded Peter to put away his sword (John 18:11) and told Pilate, "If my kingship were of this world, my servants would fight . . . but my kingship is not from the world" (John 18:36). Jesus scolded the disciples for their competitive, grasping spirit and scramble for power and position (Matt. 20:25–28). While he acknowledged that the gospel would bring division, it was never between the sexes (Luke 12:53).

Christ himself did not conform to cultural sex roles. He never felt compelled to prove his masculinity in marriage and fatherhood. He was not afraid to be tender and loving with men, women, and children. He was gentle, meek, generally unassertive. He wept publicly on more than one occasion. His paradoxes often confounded the logic of his critics.

But he was also strong and resolute in the face of temptation and death. His righteous anger drove the money changers from the temple. He decisively debated and sometimes bluntly denounced the scribes and Pharisees. He declared the demands of justice and righteousness forthrightly.

He is our example, our paradigm. We are not told in Scripture to seek what it means to be a "man" or a "woman" in our society, but what it means to be Christlike. He calls us to mature personhood in his image (Eph. 4:13). And he offers us the Holy Spirit's help in that transformation.

The fruit of the Holy Spirit's work (Gal. 5:22–23) cannot be pigeonholed under "masculine" or "feminine" but only categorized as "imago Dei." According to the New Testament, the Christlike person exhibits the best in human qualities: love, joy, peace, patience, kindness, goodness, faithfulness, gentleness, self-control, humility, integrity, meekness, sensitivity, empathy, purity, submissiveness, confidence, courage, strength, zeal, determination, compassion, common sense, generosity, self-sacrifice.

Against such there should be no law for any person in any culture.

8. Love, Honor, and ———?

> If workable marriages are to exist in this latter part of the twentieth century, the artificially determined roles of male and female . . . must be discarded and replaced. The rigid, male-dictated marital structure . . . cannot function in today's environment. Neither can the extreme feminist dream of female domination. Modern marriage requires equality, just as world history indicates a trend toward equality among people regardless of sex, race, or creed.
>
> *The Mirages of Marriage*[1]

MANY CHRISTIANS consider the inclusion of the word "obey" in the marriage vows almost as a badge of orthodoxy. They are alarmed that many modern wedding ceremonies omit this wifely pledge. "Father is no longer given his rightful place!" worried pastors lament. There are dire predictions of the demise of the family, the emasculation of husbands, the delinquency of children, and the horrible specter of a society dominated by power-hungry women.

Christian publications and sermons plead with husbands to assert their leadership. Wives are told that godly submission to their husbands is their duty, that the Divine Order requires a woman's position in marriage to be one of subordination. Women who refuse to accept this role are told they will miss out on the joy of living in God's will. In this view, patriarchy—not partnership—is the unquestioned biblical standard for marriage.

This teaching has been so widespread that few have dared to question or challenge it. Yet it bothers many young couples contemplating marriage, just as it disturbs some who are already married and who were untroubled by questions of "Who's boss?" until they heard a sermon or read a book that insisted that equalitarian marriages are contrary to God's plan.

"But why is it so wrong for persons to stand on equal footing in a relationship of love?" some are wondering. "Why must there be a hierarchy of superior inferior, a dictatorship instead of a democracy, an insistence that one person must lead in all practical and spiritual matters—regardless of abilities—simply because of having been born a member of a certain sex?" The answer they usually hear is that God has simply designed things that way, that

woman was created to meet man's needs, and that to complain
that it's an unfair setup is to rebel against God himself.

A traditional view of marriage stressed such matters as respect,
duty, authority, obedience, and role differentiation. Today another
ideology emphasizes the importance of companionship, affection,
self-actualization, growth, and equalitarianism. In such marriages,
the partners recognize each other as unique individuals rather than
as roles or sex stereotypes. Each has needs, abilities, and special
personal assets to contribute to the marital unit. This leaves room
for creativity, flexibility, and imagination in family life-style. Each
spouse has maximum freedom to explore his or her own particular
talents and interests, without being cramped by traditional re-
straints resulting from role stereotyping.

Although examples of egalitarian marriages seem to have been
rare in history, the idea itself is not new. Priscilla and Aquila
provide a biblical example, which we will discuss in the next chapter. John Stuart Mill, writing in the last century, also spoke of
such an ideal, as did John Milton in the seventeenth century. Each
envisioned the richness that could be possible in a marriage based
on true soul-companionship. Mill spoke of a marriage between
a man and woman of similar education, opinions, and purposes
"between whom there exists that best kind of equality, similarity
of powers and capacities with reciprocal superiority in them—so
that each can enjoy the luxury of looking up to the other, and
can have alternately the pleasure of leading and of being led in the
path of development." [2] Milton wrote, "It is not the joining of
another body [that] will remove loneliness, but the uniting of another compliable mind." [3]

Yet many Christians are suspicious of attempts to promote
equality between the sexes because they think such a notion is
contrary to the Bible. "Scriptures declare unequivocally that the
sexes are *not* equal," announced an editorial in an evangelical
periodical. [4] With such an understanding of the Bible, it isn't surprising that a religious publisher turned down a manuscript on
Christian sex ethics that it had commissioned, because the manuscript emphasized equality and the positive implications of such
equality for dating and marriage. "It is unnecessary to make
woman equal to man, even at the dating level," said the publisher.

Some Christian young men quickly latch on to the notion that
women were made for men. One coed at a Christian college told
us of her first date with a fellow student. He suggested they have
a time of devotions before going out, and she gladly assented. But
immediately he whipped out his pocket Testament and read aloud
Ephesians 5, beginning with verse 22, "Wives, be subject to your

husbands, as to the Lord." He paused and said, "See what that says? It means you're supposed to *obey* me." "Obey you?" the girl countered. "Why, I hardly know you, and we've never been out together before—and I'm certainly not married to you! What makes you think I have to obey you?" She said as far as she was concerned, it was "Goodby, Charlie!" She never dated him again.

HUSBAND-WIFE AUTHORITY RELATIONS

Why are so many Christians afraid of equalitarianism in marriage? There seem to be two main reasons: a fear that the Bible will be disobeyed and a fear of anarchy or disorder.

First, there is a strong conviction that the Bible upholds the patriarchal ideal as the divine pattern for marriage in all cultures and in all ages. To question this is tantamount to questioning the plan and Word of God himself. Furthermore, some argue, if one abrogates the principles of male authority and female submission, might there not be other biblical teachings that could also be questioned, argued away, or set aside? Doesn't that undermine the total authority of the Scriptures?

Again, we must refer to the principles of hermeneutics discussed in chapter 2. The man-woman question must be raised in the spirit of theological interpretation. Otherwise, we are merely playing games by tossing isolated biblical proof texts at one another, while all the time failing to grasp the basic principles of what it means to be fellow-citizens of the kingdom of God, of what it means to walk anew as children of God pulsating with new life through Jesus Christ. In short, we need to learn what it means to be Christians —Christians who demonstrate that both men and women are Christ's disciples. How? By the love we have toward one another, regardless of differences of age, race, sex, or social class. And we need to learn how to exhibit the fruit of the Spirit and the signs of Christian maturity in all of life's relationships—including marriage.

But in addition to the worries over biblical authority, many people express a second fear about viewing marriage as egalitarian rather than patriarchal. Might not chaos and anarchy result in the absence of a clearly spelled-out chain of command? The equalitarian marriage ideal is thus rejected on the grounds that the Bible insists upon a *hierarchical* ordering of society.

Interestingly, the same argument was once used to keep the "common people" from having a say in government. Subjects were told that it was God's will that they submit to the higher authorities on the basis of such passages as Romans 13 and Hebrews

13:17. Kings were persuaded that they ruled by "divine right," and they made no apologies for tyrannizing over their subjects.

Similarly, the issue of slavery was defended by those who twisted Paul's analogy of the church as a body (1 Cor. 12). They contended that this was a picture of God's will for society, with some persons ordained to lower spheres and some to higher, yet each having a part to play. "The feet are as indispensable to the head as the head to the feet," wrote slavery defender James Henley Thornwell, who went on to point out that if the "feet" ever desired to be anything but feet all society would be plunged into "irretrievable confusion." [5] Slaves must be treated kindly, but clearly kept in their place, said Thornwell. And they must be taught that their position was God's will.

Christians convinced of a God-ordained, iron-clad arrangement for all society for all time understandably have difficulty thinking in equalitarian terms. They see an order or chain of command based on rank (masters-slaves, rulers-subjects, men-women, parents-children). The idea of two mature human beings relating to one another as equals within the marriage relationship strikes them as absurd. Therefore, they emphasize that the husband is to be the head of the home, and if the wife wants to be equal—well, that would mean there would be two heads. And doesn't everybody know that a two-headed monstrosity could never function well?

There are other commonly used illustrations intended to make the same point. Some argue that two riders wouldn't ride side by side on a horse, but rather one would be seated in front of the other. (However, two riders might sit side by side in a carriage with the horse pulling them—and two Christians might sit side by side in a marriage with the Lord leading them, too. Or we might ask, even if one horseman does ride at the front of the horse and the other behind, who's to say the two wouldn't occasionally change places? The illustration doesn't stand up well.)

Then there is the illustration borrowed from government. Some say marriage requires the husband as the final authority because otherwise it would be as confusing as if a country chose two heads of state with equal powers. It is alleged that this could never work. Yet, such a plan *did* work in ancient Rome during the long period of the Republic. Keenly sensitive to the problems of unlimited powers in government, the Romans worked out a detailed system of checks and balances. Heading the government were two annually elected consuls or "presidents" of equal rank (so that power would be restricted by sharing). In case of conflict, the negative right to veto took precedence over the colleague's positive right. In practice, however, as we shall see in a later section, the consuls largely avoided conflicts in ways that might be paralleled in marriage. (No, it was *not* this dually shared leadership that caused the "fall of Rome"! The western empire crumbled centuries later under a government of one-man rule.)

However, such arguments can end in a dead-end street. We need to see that God intended marriage to be a relationship—a companionship, a covenant (see Mal. 2:13–16). Marriage is not a body needing a head (the man) and a heart (the woman) in order to function. It is not a ride on a horse, nor a government needing a king. It is a relationship between two human beings who willingly join themselves together, each investing all that he or she is and has in the new social unit being formed.

Husbands and wives are two made one. But that "one" is not the husband, with the wife's identity lost and merged into his (as so many laws and customs suggest—such as the practice of changing a woman's name to Mrs. William Jones, which means "the mistress of William Jones").[6] Rather, the two form a new unit and can think of themselves as *partners*—just as two business partners can join together to form a business in which each has an equal share and voice. We are not speaking here of a president and vice-president arrangement, or a pilot and copilot setup, but of a fully equal partnership. John Stuart Mill argued that such an arrangement can and does work in the business world.[7] It is foolish for Christians to insist that there must always be one person in any voluntary association who has final authority in all matters. If two persons have made equal investments in a business partnership, they should have equal say about all matters concerning their mutual venture. The same thing holds for marriage.

Yet, the traditional Christian position has been opposed to the equalitarian marriage ideal. Over the ages, Christians have generally interpreted Scripture to favor male headship.

PATRIARCHY OR PARTNERSHIP—WHAT DOES THE BIBLE SAY?

In the Old Testament, there is no question about who is the head of the household. The patriarchal structure of Israelite society regarded the husband as both possessor and master. His will was the will of the house; he was the center of the family. All members of the household were expected to look up to him and obey him, no matter what the cost. Pedersen points out that a wife was supposed to be willing to sacrifice herself for her husband "because his life is always more valuable than hers."[8] A husband could arbitrarily and unilaterally divorce his wife, sending her out from his house, whereupon she was called *gerushah,* meaning "expelled." [9]

Marriage meant that a woman was *ba'al-taken* by her husband, that is, she came under his ownership. Both Genesis 20:3 and Deuteronomy 22:22 speak of a married woman as *be'ulat ba'al* which means "a wife owned by her husband." A wife called her husband *ba'al* or "master" or else *'adon,* which means "lord." Thus, as Roland de Vaux points out, a woman addressed her husband "as a slave addressed his master, or a subject his king." [10]

This patriarchal agreement was common among other peoples, as well. Esther became the bride of a Persian king who had divorced his former wife for refusing to obey him. Queen Vashti's failure to bow to her husband's command upset the men of the king's court. Perhaps all the women of Persia and Media would follow the queen's "bad example"! They enjoined him not only to replace his wife with a new queen but also to send out a decree that " 'all women will give honor to their husbands, high and low.' . . . that every man be lord in his own house" (Est. 1:20–22).

The Apocrypha says, "Do not leave a leaky cistern to drip or allow a bad wife to say what she likes. If she does not accept your control, divorce her and send her away" (Ecclus. 25:25–26, NEB). In the Hebrew culture, even if a wife were above her husband in social status, she was supposed to consider him above her. The Midrash tells the story of a certain woman of wealth and noble birth. She married a poor beggar who never masked his delight in his masculine prerogative of lording it over her. One day he went to the sages carrying a golden candelabrum on top of which he had placed an earthen lamp. This he said was a fulfillment of Genesis 3:16, illustrating that he who was so much lower in birth and social standing than his wife nevertheless ruled over her by virtue of being a male.

Daughters of Sarah—1 Peter 3

Moving to the New Testament, it again seems at first glance that husband-wife authority relations are weighted in favor of the man. However, the passage instructing wives to obey husbands in 1 Peter 3:1–6 deals with a special situation. These were wives with unbelieving husbands who hoped to win them to Christ. Instead of preaching or nagging, they were to follow the Old Testament pattern of modesty, submissive behavior, and a meek and gentle spirit. Such an evangelistic strategy would be the most persuasive for these men, accustomed as they were to patriarchal arrangements in the home. This instruction is counterbalanced by a message to husbands who were already Christians, appealing to

them to treat their wives considerately, recognizing them as
"joint heirs of the grace of life." To fail to show such consideration
could result in ineffective prayers (1 Pet. 3:7).

Yet, many Christians see a great deal more in this passage, laying much stress on verses 5 and 6: "So once the holy women who
hoped in God used to adorn themselves and were submissive to
their husbands, as Sarah obeyed Abraham, calling him lord. And you
are now her children if you do right and let nothing terrify you."

Some Christian writers (both men and women) find it highly
significant that *Sarah* has been chosen as a model of wifely obedience here. One writer suggests that this example settles the question of how far wives must go in their submission—especially as
questions arise about obedience to husbands who are cruel or heavy
drinkers and the like. He writes:

> Both Paul and Peter state the command to submission without
> qualifications. Peter's use of Sarah as an illustration of obedience
> is notable since Abraham *twice* in order to protect his own life,
> denied that Sarah was his wife and allowed her to be taken into a
> ruler's harem (Gen. 12:10–20; 20:1–18). The implication is not
> that a wife should allow her husband to sell her into prostitution
> if he wishes. But by stating the case absolutely, both Peter and
> Paul forestall capriciousness in the matter of submission.[11]

Another author calls our attention to the same passage, but from
a slightly different angle. She praises Sarah's quiet submission to
her husband's plan, even though it showed that Abraham regarded
his own life more highly than his wife's, and draws the lesson that
just as God protected Sarah because of her obedience in such a
difficult situation he will also bless and protect wives who follow
her example of submissiveness today.[12]

But what was Sarah really like? Does Genesis present her as
the quiet, passive, obedient wife that some have inferred from
1 Peter 3? Decidedly not! Sarah was by no means a dull, colorless,
subservient person, but rather displayed real spirit and voiced her
own opinions. And Abraham did not rule with an iron hand, making
decisions unilaterally, while paying no attention to his wife. In fact,
perhaps he would have been better off had he *not* given into her
wishes in one instance (Gen. 16:2), for it was Sarah's idea that
Abraham should have a child by her maidservant Hagar rather than
waiting for God's time and plan. But later, when Sarah demanded
the expulsion of Ishmael (son of Abraham's union with the maidservant), and Abraham disagreed, it was *God* who told Abraham
to obey his wife! "Whatever Sarah says to you, do as she tells
you, for through Isaac shall your descendants be named" (Gen.
21:12).

Sarah was a woman of strong personality—a real partner to Abraham. God included her by name in his plan. It wasn't enough that Abraham should have a son; it must be a son *by Sarah*. And she would be blessed by God and the mother of nations (Gen. 17: 15 ff.).

Genesis 18 records an incident that might be called "reverently humorous," for it includes some friendly banter between the Lord and Sarah. In a theophany, the Lord and two angels visited Abraham's tent. While Sarah was preparing a meal for them, she overheard the announcement that she would bear a son in her old age. She laughed to herself. The very thought seemed so utterly fantastic! God knew she had laughed in her heart and rebuked her, saying nothing is too hard for him. Then "Sarah denied, saying, 'I did not laugh'; for she was afraid. He said, 'No, but you did laugh'" (Gen. 18:15). Her laughter, like Abraham's (Gen. 17: 17), wasn't a laughter of scorn or mockery, but was an expression of surprise and incredulity. No doubt when she and her husband named their little son *Isaac* (a word meaning "laughter") as God had instructed them, they looked back on this sharing of laughter with God—almost as though it were a private little joke between the three of them. Now it was laughter of gratitude and delight. Sarah said, "God has made laughter for me; every one who hears will laugh over me. . . . Who would have said to Abraham that Sarah would suckle children? Yet I have borne him a son in his old age" (Gen. 21:6–7).

In the two incidents telling of Abraham's denial that Sarah was his wife (out of fear that powerful rulers would kill him in order to possess his beautiful wife), Abraham didn't suddenly decide to tell an untruth at Sarah's expense when danger confronted him. He had talked it over with her in advance, and she had agreed to go along with his plan (Gen. 12:11–13; 20:5, 13). Perhaps they had rationalized the whole matter and decided it was only a half-truth and not a bold, outright lie to claim they were brother and sister. They actually had been born of the same father, though of different mothers (Gen. 20:12).

Obedience to God or Man?

The marriage of Abraham and Sarah, then, doesn't really provide the kind of authority model that some Christians assume; nor is the biblical picture of Sarah one of weakness, meekness, and subservience. But there is an additional lesson here: Sarah's example does *not* warrant a wife's unquestioning obedience in cases where a husband asks her to violate God's law.

Abraham and Sarah were newly emerged from paganism. Man-

kind was in a kind of spiritual infancy and only gradually learning the revelation of the one true God. (Even so, although the Ten
Commandments had not yet been given, there was evidently common knowledge that God considered adultery sin in his sight, according to Genesis 20:3–6.) Perhaps we can excuse the conduct of
Abraham and Sarah as the actions of those whose moral sensitivi-
ties were not yet fully developed. But we cannot draw the conclusion that a Christian woman today, enlightened and indwelt by
the Holy Spirit, should obediently follow her husband's wishes
if they are contrary to God's will. (Incidentally, it's possible that
Sarah agreed to lie and risk the possibility of adultery not so
much out of *obedience* to her husband as out of *love* for him and
a genuine desire to preserve his life.)

However, to argue that a woman is responsible to submit to
her husband under all circumstances—even if it violates a command
of God or the wife's own conscience (and sermons have been
preached to that effect)[13]—goes totally against the spirit of the
New Testament. "We must obey God rather than men" (Acts 5:29).
Each Christian, male or female, married or unmarried, is responsible to God.

This point comes through clearly in the story of Ananias and
Sapphira (Acts 5). With his wife's knowledge and cooperation,
Ananias had kept back an amount of money that had been pledged
to the Christian community. The apostle Peter rebuked him for
lying not to men but to God, and Ananias died suddenly in a way
that convinced the church of God's judgment. Three hours later,
Sapphira (not knowing what had happened to her husband) came
in and was asked about the money obtained from the property sale.
She told the same falsehood that her husband had told. "How is it
that you have agreed together to tempt the Spirit of the Lord?"
said Peter just before Sapphira too was overtaken by sudden death.

It is noteworthy that the apostles did not excuse Sapphira by
saying, "Well, after all, wives must obey. She just dutifully did
what her husband said; she had to submit. Therefore, the responsibility for sinning against God was entirely her husband's." Quite
the contrary. Wives are accountable to *God*.

Susannah Wesley—A Case Study

Another question arises with regard to the 1 Peter passage. If
Sarah is taken as an exemplary wife because of how she addressed
her husband, is it the writer's intention that Christian wives should
actually call their husbands "lord"? (Gen. 18:12, to which 1 Peter
3:6 alludes, is obscured in modern translations which usually use
the term "husband.")

Earlier we noted the custom of ancient Israel where wives *did* call husbands "master" or "lord." And there have been some Christian women who have taken 1 Peter 3:6 as a literal command to do likewise (although it would seem the writer was calling attention to Sarah's respect for her husband as revealed in her thoughts in Genesis 18, rather than ordering Christian women to address their husbands in a prescribed manner). However, ascribing such titles to one's husband by no means always indicates that a spiritless, passive, submissive wife is on the scene. Susannah Wesley is a case in point.

Often referred to in sermons and articles as the ideal pattern of Christian wifehood and motherhood, Susannah Wesley in truth outwardly showed submission to her proud and hot-tempered clergyman husband. All the days of their married life, she called him "my master," and "sir." But since most of the burden of rearing their large family fell to her, she and her husband often clashed over matters concerning the children, and Mrs. Wesley did not hesitate to express her opinion that her approach to discipline was best. Disagreements were common in the Wesley household, and after thirty-five years of marriage, she confessed in a letter to her son John that their home knew much unhappiness because husband and wife so seldom thought alike.

Frequently, through what is generally called "female tact," Mrs. Wesley was able to have her own way without giving any indication that she wasn't being submissive and obedient to her husband. But one notable exception brought such a strong reaction from him that the world came close to being denied John and Charles Wesley!

After family prayers one day, Mr. Wesley noticed that his wife had not said "Amen" to his prayer for King William (whom Susannah regarded as a usurper without any right to the throne). Samuel Wesley called her into the study and asked why she hadn't said "Amen" as was her custom after his other prayers. She explained her honest feelings. Then her angry husband knelt down and called God's vengeance upon him and his posterity if he should ever come near Susannah or get into a bed with her again—unless she asked for God's and her husband's forgiveness for not praying for the king.

When the king died shortly afterwards, the Reverend Mr. Wesley changed neither his mind nor his vow. He threatened to apply for a chaplaincy on a ship and set off for London, resolving never to see his wife again. Deeply distressed about whether to obey him or stay true to her conscience, Susannah Wesley sought the advice and comfort of two close friends, a woman and a noted divine, whose encouragement sustained her during the uncertain months of separation from her husband. Eventually Samuel Wesley, moved by news of a fire in the rectory and the counsel of a fellow minister, forgot his stubborn pride and rash vow and returned to Susannah. John Wesley, called by one writer, "the child of their reconciliation," was born a year later.[14]

Ephesians 5

Perhaps even more than the 1 Peter passage, it is the fifth chapter of Ephesians that many Christians feel insures for all time the divine right of husbands.

> Be subject to one another out of reverence for Christ. Wives, be subject to your husbands, as to the Lord. For the husband is the head of the wife as Christ is the head of the church, his body, and is himself its Savior. As the church is subject to Christ, so let wives also be subject in everything to their husbands. Husbands, love your wives, as Christ loved the church and gave himself up for her (Eph. 5:21–25).

On the basis of this passage, many religious leaders say the uniqueness of Christian marriage is clearly set forth, namely, the subjection of the wife and the headship of the husband. Couples are told that a marriage ceremony which includes the bride's vow to *obey* can be a real "testimony," instructing wedding guests in the way that Christian marriage is marked off from all other conceptions of marriage.

However, a view of marriage that considers the husband dominant and the wife submissive is *not at all unique!* In the Roman culture of that time, the *paterfamilias* ("father of a family") ruled over the entire household (wife, children, grandchildren, and slaves). He controlled the property, decided whom his children would marry, and had the final say in matters concerning everyone under him. The Romans spoke of the *patria potestas*—"the power or authority of the father."

We have seen that this view of marriage prevailed in ancient Israel and in other nations during Old Testament times. It has been the pattern in other religions throughout history. The Hindu Law of Manu demanded that "a virtuous wife must constantly revere her husband as a god"—even if he had no good qualities whatsoever and even if he were infatuated with another woman. A fifteenth-century Confucian marriage manual tells a wife to look up to her husband as her lord, never disobeying his instructions, giving him reverence and service, and looking on him as if he were heaven itself. Why? Because a wife's lifelong duty is obedience.

Social customs and religious traditions the world over have long presented this outlook on marriage. Mark it well: There is nothing either unique or Christian about insisting that wives obey and subject themselves to their husbands.

What *is* unique in Ephesians 5 is groundwork for an altogether new ideal of marriage. The key lies in an understanding of marriage as a picture of the relationship between Christ and his church. (Similar imagery is also found in 2 Cor. 11:2; John 3:28–30, and Rev. 19:7 ff.) In this analogy, the New Testament writers are following the tradition of the Old Testament where the relationship of God and his people is frequently spoken of in terms of marriage (cf. the book of Hosea; Ezekiel 16; Isaiah 62:5*b*; 54:5–8; also the entire Song of Solomon if it is interpreted allegorically).

Although the instructions for wives and husbands in Colossians 3:18–19 and Ephesians 5:21 ff. again appear at first glance to make the husband the unquestioned head of the house with the wife required to give unconditional obedience, we find upon looking closer that there is a real difference between these instructions and the Old Testament patriarchal tradition. There a woman was to sacrifice herself for her husband because she was of less value than he. In Ephesians 5, we read that a husband is to love his wife to the extent of Christ's sacrificial love for the church—even to the point of giving himself up for her! Husbands are told to love their wives as their very own flesh. *Both* husbands and wives are told to be submissive to one another in the realization that *all* Christians should be subject to one another (Eph. 5:21). Such attitudes, if put into practice, can't help but set up a climate where there is no need to battle about authority rights. The teaching of Ephesians 5 provides the atmosphere in which a new and thoroughly Christian ideal of marriage can grow.

But isn't the main emphasis on the wife's subjection to her husband? No, it is not. A close look at these verses shows that much more space is given to requirements for the husband's conduct (although articles and sermons seldom present the passage in this way). The reason for this focus is that the passage is primarily presenting the deep, spiritual truth (the "great mystery") of Christ's love for the church. Practical implications for the human marriage relationship are interwoven with this.

A New Pattern Set in Motion

Ephesians 5 allows for an "evolution" or development of the ideal of marriage as God intends it. This is often overlooked, because we get sidetracked by the words "head" and "subject" and their usual connotations. Most speakers put the emphasis on

"Wives, be subject to your husbands," and "The husband is the head of the wife." Often they don't quote the remaining parts of these verses at all. But as we have seen, such a message wasn't at all new or unique. New believers certainly needed no such instructions, because the dominant-husband submissive-wife model of marriage was the norm in the societies of that time. There would have been no reason to tell wives to submit to their husbands, or to tell husbands they were the heads.

What *was* new in these instructions of Ephesians 5 was the *way* husbands and wives were now supposed to relate to each other. The headship subjection pattern was transformed. Now wives were to submit in a totally new way—not out of fear or grudging duty, but "as to the Lord." That means a response of love, joy, and delight. We yearn to please Christ and serve him and love him. Why? Because he has given his all for us and spares nothing on our behalf. From this, the husband takes his cue as to how he is to be the "head" of his wife—a way so startlingly different from older ideas of male headship that the first husbands who read this epistle must have been astonished. Who had ever heard of such a thing? To follow Christ's example meant that a husband must spare nothing—not even his own life if need be—in his concern and care for his wife. He must think of her as part of him, his very own flesh, and "no man ever hates his own flesh, but nourishes and cherishes it, as Christ does the church" (Eph. 5:29). As we saw in chapter 3 of this book, Christ's headship over the church refers to his being the source of its life, making it an organic, living unity that is fed and nourished by his constant giving.

If we think of the term "head" in the sense of *archē* (beginning, origin, source), we are again reminded of the *interdependence* of the sexes, each drawing life from the other. In the creation story of Genesis 2, where the origin of marriage was described, we saw that God took from man and made the woman. But ever since, as Paul reminds us, man has come from woman. That is why he stressed that "in the Lord woman is not independent of man nor man of woman" (1 Cor. 11:11). And the head or source of all things is God himself (1 Cor. 11:12). Christ is the head of the two made one flesh.

The wife, according to the pattern of Ephesians 5, can't help but respond to her husband with a fervent desire to show her love to him, just as he has expressed his love to her. The cycle goes on and on, each giving to the other and receiving in turn.

In such an ideal (and Ephesians 5 pointed toward that ideal, even though it had to begin where the people were and didn't spell

out all the details and implications), marriage is not something
fixed and static, with rigid roles, clearly designated duties, and
"places" in which each spouse must "stay put." Rather, Christian
marriage should be something alive and exciting and on the move,
as each gives and receives from the other in a continuous exchange
of Christ's kind of love. The reciprocity of mutual respect, self-
sacrificing concern, and deep affection serves as the dynamic that
invigorates and energizes the exhilarating adventure God wants
marriage to be. It's an adventure of growth together.[15]

Misusing Ephesians 5

Those who think in terms of duties, roles, and hierarchy (rather
than in personalistic terms) often twist the meaning of Ephesians
5. Their stress is always on the wife's subordination. And if the
husband isn't loving her after Christ's example—well, then it's the
wife's fault, not the husband's! Such reasoning is an insult to the
love of Christ, yet it is common in Christian circles. The following
excerpt from an article in a Christian magazine illustrates this type
of thinking:

> Do not forget that your husband spends the better part of his
> day with people who are not only interested in his work but who
> are often well-informed and stimulating. Furthermore, women he
> meets or works with in the business world make a consistent effort
> to be neat and attractive. How then is he to be excited about lov-
> ing you as Christ loves the Church if he comes home to find you
> with your hair in curlers and so taken up with the household
> affairs that the most interesting part of your conversation has to
> do with enzyme active detergents or baby food? [16]

"How then is he to be excited about loving you as Christ loves
the Church?"—as though Christ's love for us depends upon how
"attractive" we make ourselves to him! Where would any of us be
if such were the case? What would be the meaning of the book of
Hosea or passages like Romans 5:8 and 1 John 4:10? We are not
saying that wives shouldn't try to look attractive for their husbands (or husbands for their wives), but rather that Ephesians 5
is speaking of an unconditional love that accepts, overlooks, for-
gives, and loves—even when the other person seems unlovable.

All too many sermons and articles interpret Ephesians 5 and related passages in ways that are decidedly one-sided. They seem to
support the old idea that "a man's home is his castle and his wife
is his janitor," implying that this is the divine order. The wife
must subordinate her interests to those of her husband; all the
privileges and rights are weighted in his favor. True, such articles
usually end with a reminder that a husband should imitate Christ

and be willing to die for his wife—but that's a lot easier for men to take than being asked to do the dishes for her, since the former situation isn't likely to arise very often! Grudgingly, some rights are conceded wives however, but usually in a spirit of condescension (such as the article suggesting that it might be a good idea for Christian husbands to give their wives a small allowance with no questions asked, even though the husband could assume that his wife "would probably spend it foolishly").

The picture of Christian marriage usually given is one of an autocrat lording it over a docile child-wife who has no mind of her own, no interests but those of her husband and children, and little inclination toward personal growth. It is dangerous teaching and can only work against the Christian principles of unselfishness, love, and striving toward Christian maturity—principles that God asks of all believers, whether male or female. As Sidney Callahan points out, God desires free persons who have "grown up into Christ, not crushed automatons without freedom, without identity." She goes on to say that it is unfortunate that some women "have made too many of the wrong sacrifices; they have been guilty of a suicide of personality. For too long Christians and Christian women have confused free sacrifice, service, and obedience with passivity, servility, and self-destructive acquiescence." [17]

The usual way of teaching Ephesians 5 suggests that it is the wife who must make the self-sacrifices (just the opposite of what the text says) and unwittingly encourages the husband to be selfish, egocentric, convinced of his right to have his own way, and filled with pride and a heady sense of power. That is why the usual interpretation is so harmful. No person can remain unspoiled by the corrupting effect of power when he is told he holds by divine right a position of superiority in which others are dutybound to subject themselves to him.

If the husband's example is Christ, we must remind ourselves of how Christ regards and relates to the believer. He never compels us against our wills; he never forces or coerces. There really is no basis for insisting that wives obey husbands even if it goes against their own better judgment. One minister gave the illustration that a situation may arise in which a husband and wife disagree over which physician to call when their child suddenly becomes ill. In such a case, he said, they must call the one the husband chooses. And even if the child should die, the wife must never suggest that her choice of a doctor might have saved his life. [18]

In such sermons and articles, wives are always told to adapt and adjust to their husbands. If wives don't trim their own interests and fit into their husbands' plans, it is said the marriage will be out of balance and contrary to the divine pattern. But why shouldn't husbands do some of the adjusting? Because, such speakers and writers claim, God ordained that the wife should adjust and not vice versa. "The woman was made for the man" and thus she should center her entire life around her husband's plans, interests, problems, work, and needs.

To prove this point, one Christian counselor told a troubled wife to submit to her husband's wishes because the Bible makes clear that the wife should always be interested in "how [she may] please her husband" (1 Cor. 7:34). He used this verse as a proof text while completely ignoring the preceding verse which describes the married man as one who is concerned about "how to please his wife." The verses are the same, except for the mention of husband in one and wife in the other. (And even at that, their intent wasn't to spell out marital duties so much as to show that married persons sometimes find that the energy, time, and responsibilities of family life conflict with service for God.) At any rate, an equal and mutual desire of the spouses to please one another is described as the normal situation in marriage. That a counselor would quote only the verse about wives is just one more indication of the bias characterizing much Christian teaching, thereby giving the impression that wives must always be the ones to defer to their spouses' wishes.

Self-actualization for women is discouraged in much Christian writing. Somehow women are supposed to be different from men, being able to live through someone else (husband, children) and to find their fulfillment through self-effacement and vicarious experiences rather than through direct participation in the world. When women complain about this and ask to be able to achieve as men do, they're called "selfish" and are told they are rebelling against God. Some religious leaders still seem to think in terms of the Old Testament era when wives were considered possessions. One writer speaks of what he calls "the spiritual terms that God has laid down" for a woman in which "with delight she learns the joy of knowing it is her husband's house, his home; the children are his; she is his wife." [19]

Missing in such discussions is an effort to learn what it really *means* when husbands are told to love their wives as Christ loves the church. Christ's spirit of self-sacrifice is what is emphasized in Ephesians 5. Jesus said he came not to be ministered unto, but to minister; not to be served, but to serve. He criticized the disciples for arguing about who would be the greatest, emphasizing that the first shall be last and the last shall be first. If anyone really wants to have the privileged position and stand in first place,

he said, that person must be willing to be a slave—a servant rather
than a ruler. The seeking of power, prestige, privilege, and position is the world's way, not God's way (cf. Matt. 20:25-28).

In spite of such clear admonitions, Christian marriage is still
considered to be modeled after the pattern Jesus condemned—
lording it over, seeking privilege and power, exercising authority.
If a husband doesn't have natural abilities for such a position of
authority and leadership—well, then the situation calls for dissimu-
lation. Books, articles, and sermons tell wives to *pretend* husbands
are the ones who are always right, who always know best. If a
wife is more gifted, intelligent, and shows better judgment than
her husband, she must never let on. She must arrange things so
that her ideas are subtly accepted without her husband's awareness
that they were not his own ideas. And husbands must always get
the real credit. Christian leaders sometimes seem totally unaware
of the inconsistencies in what they are saying. One woman, for
example, tried to illustrate her conviction that the husband should
be the head of the family by pointing to her own childhood when
everyone looked up to her father. "If Papa said it, it was just as
though God had said it." But in the same breath she said, "Papa
did the work, and Mama ran Papa without Papa knowing it, and it
was a beautiful situation." [20]

Christian articles point out that "behind every great man is a
woman," but are quick to add, "yet, she is always behind and never
out in front." The "masculine ego" is said to be very fragile and
can be damaged severely if a wife doesn't constantly bolster it.
(Could "masculine ego" be another name for "pride"?) Training
for this begins early in life when girls are told to hide their intelligence if they want boys to be interested in them. Never mind
the hypocrisy; it's part of the male-female game (and isn't Christian at all). In one Christian organization, wives (and women in
general) were told never to say to a man, "I *think* thus and so
about such and such a matter," but rather to say, "I *feel* thus
and so."

The idea that Christian husbands fulfill the instructions of Ephesians 5 by requiring their wives to be immature, nonthinking
servants to be ordered about and to minister constantly to husbands' comforts misinterprets Christ's attitude toward his church.
In John 15, Jesus made clear to his disciples that they had reached
a point where he regarded them not as servants but as friends—
those with whom he could share totally all that he had received
from the Father (John 15:15). His ministry had been directed toward bringing them to that point. He had no desire to keep them
in a subservient position so that he could lord it over them and

build up his ego at their expense. The aim was toward true friendship which requires a relationship of equals.

Similarly in Ephesians 4:13–16, the emphasis is on the growth of the body of Christ, the church, toward spiritual maturity—true adulthood. The husband who follows Christ's example will likewise do all in his power to help his wife in her spiritual and mental growth. He will encourage her to be a mature, fulfilled, fully developed personality. Such a husband will not force his wife into a mold that stifles her gifts, her spirit, her personhood. Unless he has such an attitude of deep concern for his wife's freedom and growth, he is *not* loving her as Christ loves the church.

9. Living in Partnership

> There are three sights which warm my heart
> and are beautiful in the eyes of the Lord and of
>   men:
> concord among brothers, friendship among
>   neighbors,
> and a man and wife who are inseparable.
> —Ecclesiasticus 25:1, NEB

LOVE, IN THE full-orbed biblical sense, must determine the conduct of both husband and wife within the marriage relationship. Unfortunately, some Christians like to say that the Bible instructs only husbands to love, while its message for wives is submission. But Jesus told *all* Christians—male and female—that love is the badge of discipleship. We are to love each other as Christ has loved us. And Christ has loved us as the Father loves him—which means that Christians are supposed to love each other in the same manner and to the same extent that God the Father loves God the Son! (See John 13:34–35; 15:9–13; 17:26). This is the kind of love that a husband is asked to show his wife. And this is the kind of love that a wife is asked to show her husband.

What will such a concept of marriage mean to a couple? For one thing it will eliminate the desire to dominate, exploit, or manipulate the partner in any way. Neither spouse will consider it a right to demand his or her own way. And such a concept will mean that each one will do as much as possible to help the other develop fully as God intends. This will mean sacrifices on the part of both husband and wife. Rather than viewing marriage as a functional arrangement with rigid roles and fixed duties assigned on the basis of sex, the couple will look upon marriage as a living relationship between two equal partners, "each for the other and both for the Lord," as an old marriage motto puts it.

But would such an equalitarian ideal destroy the model in Ephesians 5 in which the Christ-church relationship is presented as a paradigm? After all, Christ and the believer, though united in love, are not equals. Again, we must emphasize that the marriage ideal presented was not intended to exalt husbands to the position of gods or kings, but rather draws our attention to the *way* Christ loved the church. The pattern, if allowed to work itself out over history, with mutual love and delight and self-sacrifice on the part of both husband and wife, could not help but move in the direction of egalitarianism and democracy in the home.

In other words, the New Testament writers did not call for *immediate* social change in most areas. This would have only caused societal disruption, confused the issues of the gospel, and brought Christians into conflict with the civil government as subversives and revolutionaries. Yet certain teachings when put into practice could not help but lay the groundwork for the outworking of justice and love in social institutions.

Paul, for example, sent back a runaway slave to Philemon. But as we saw in our chapter on the early church, he asked Philemon to receive this new convert as a brother in Christ and as one of value "both in the flesh and in the Lord" (Philem. 16). In other words, the fugitive was to be appreciated both as a person, a fellow human being, and also as a Christian. It isn't difficult to see the implications of this teaching. Once Christian masters would begin viewing slaves as persons valuable in God's sight and as fellow members of Christ's family, an atmosphere would be created for recognizing an *equality* of personhood and rights.

The same principle applies to marriage. Once Christian husbands would see that they were called to emulate Christ in his love for the church, an atmosphere would be created for raising the position of women in marriage instead of "keeping them in their place." If a wife is an equal heir of grace, she is surely not intended to be treated as a servant without any rights except to fulfill her husband's demands and wishes.

To insist that marriage must be maintained as a hierarchy because otherwise the Christ-church analogy breaks down is like saying that all nations must have a monarchy because other forms of government fail to reproduce the picture of God's kingship over all the earth. Or to say that slavery must be maintained in order to keep us aware of what it means to be bondservants of Jesus Christ. We are not so rigid about other models in Scripture; why should we insist on such rigidity in the institution of marriage? It is the spirit of love—self-expending love—that is the main point of Ephesians 5.

Such love means that often the wife will give in to her husband's wishes and lay aside her own interests and desires in order to assist, encourage, and build him up in every way possible. But it also means that just as often the husband will put aside his rights, privileges, and personal convenience in order to aid his wife. And often they will both have to make sacrifices for the sake of the children. This will mean constant adjustments from which neither partner is exempt—and many of these adjustments will be difficult.

DECISION-MAKING IN MARRIAGE

But won't there be utter chaos (or a "hung jury") if two persons haven't determined in advance to settle matters according to the wishes of one who is in final authority (in traditional thought, the husband)? Not necessarily. We spoke earlier of the two equal business partners in John Stuart Mill's example. Such partners work out solutions to disagreements through discussion and compromise until they can settle on an agreeable position.

There was also the example of the Roman consuls who had the power of a negative vote so that, in the case of a disagreement, the one who said "no" prevailed. In other words, *nothing* would be done on a certain issue until both agreed. This could also work in marriage with regard to issues on which the couple is deadlocked. Or the couple might work out a compromise. Or they might decide to delegate the decision to either one—perhaps the one for whom the particular matter is most salient in a given situation.

In the Roman Republic, there were three main ways that conflicts were avoided under two-man rulership. There was the method of *cooperation* in which there was joint action taken by the two working together in harmony. There was also the method of *alternation of duty periods,* with one man serving as leader one month, the other the next month, and so on. Or thirdly, they sometimes used the method of assigning *different spheres of action*—for example, one consul might be off on the battlefields running a war, while the other consul remained at home presiding over the affairs of state.

It's easy to see how similar ways of avoiding conflicts might be used in an equalitarian marriage situation. Many couples today are trying to work out ways to divide up tasks according to abilities and interests rather than roles and traditions, or to take turns in taking leadership and responsibility in certain areas, as well as looking for ways they can grow together through cooperative ventures rather than seeing all of life rigidly marked with labels of "his" and "hers." They would prefer to see the totality of marriage labeled "ours."

DIVISION OF LABOR

A marriage of equal partners requires flexibility. It will mean taking a new look at traditional patterns with a view toward change. No longer is there a clear-cut demarcation between "woman's work" and "man's work." No longer can it be asserted that "woman's place is in the home" or that "God has ordained the man to be the breadwinner." To rethink such matters demands openness and maturity. Both imagining and implementing the many possibilities that may arise is not an easy matter; it may even seem quite costly in many cases.

Many persons will also find such views threatening. Aren't we tampering with God's plan? Doesn't the Bible tell women to bear children while men labor for bread by the sweat of their brows (Gen. 3:16–19)? And in Titus 2:5, young women are told to be "keepers at home" or "domestic." Aren't careers, child-care centers, and fulfillment outside the home contrary to God's plan for women?

However, if we look closely at the Scriptures, we see that what is usually thought of as a divinely ordained division of labor occurred only after sin entered the world (Genesis 3). Earlier we saw that Genesis 1 makes clear that at creation God intended both parenthood and the outside occupational realm to be the shared responsibilities of both sexes. Similarly, the Book of Proverbs and other Scriptures make it clear that mothers and fathers alike have an obligation under God for the rearing of their children. Babies, growing youngsters, and teenagers all need interaction from *both* Mom and Dad. All family members need to be lovingly involved with one another, enriching and strengthening one another's lives. Children need to (and long to) know and enjoy both parents as persons, as unique individuals—not as rigid role-performers operating in fixed, frozen spheres.

Both parents and children are apt to find that family life takes on a new sparkle and zest when sex role stereotypes are broken down. Dinner conversation may include Mom's anecdotes about her day on the job, just as it includes accounts of the children's school adventures and Dad's latest news about his work life, too. If a son feels like stirring up a batch of brownies or sewing a necktie, he won't feel that he's being a "sissy" doing "woman's work." If a daughter dislikes cooking and sewing, but enjoys using power tools and building furniture, she needn't feel she's being "unfeminine." The children grow up accepting it as completely natural that Dad helps with the laundry or does the vacuuming, or that Mom stays up late at night studying for the courses she's taking at the university. All in all, every family member is a distinct individual, an interesting person in his or her own right. And all feel they have a responsibility to share in the smooth-running of the household, rather than pushing off everything onto one person.

Passages like Titus 2:4–5 and 1 Timothy 5:14 must be read in context. Women in the situations described, lacking in educational opportunities and often emerging from paganism, needed to be taught what it meant to be Christian wives and mothers. They were told to center their interests in building Christian homes so that criticism by enemies of the faith could be avoided and "the word of God may not be discredited" (Titus 2:5). In other words, the sanctity of marriage must be upheld in the midst of charges that Christianity was a sect that would undermine the home. And new converts had to learn of their great responsibilities in Christian parenthood and in other social roles. This was the reason for the *Haustafeln* (lists of household duties for persons in various positions: husbands/wives; parents/children; slaves/masters), which are provided in various epistles (e.g., Eph. 5:21–6:9; Col. 3:18–4:1; 1 Tim. 6:1–2; Titus 2:1–10, etc.). However, to interpret these verses to mean that God's will for all women in all times requires confinement to the home is a mistake with unfortunate consequences.

A new look at male-female roles, division of labor, and spheres of activity distresses many. They prefer to think in terms of "complementarity"—the old "separate but equal" idea. Many Christians thus speak of a wife's being equal to her husband in personhood, but subordinate in function. However, this is just playing word games and is a contradiction in terms. Equality and subordination are contradictions. But evidently some writers and speakers are motivated by good intentions, hoping to soften a bit of the harshness and injustice of traditional teachings on wifely subjection. Therefore, "equality" is elevated to the spiritual realm; and on the practical, functional level of running the home, subordination becomes the rule "for the sake of order." But regardless of terminology used, this pattern cannot indicate an equalitarian marriage. True egalitarianism must be characterized by what sociologists call "role-interchangeability." Both spouses can fulfill the roles of breadwinner, housekeeper, encourager, career-achiever, child-trainer, and so on. Specialization according to sex disappears.

However, hard decisions may be required—for example, both husband and wife have career commitments and one of them is asked to make a move to another geographical location. Whose career will determine the place of residence? Or should they live separately and commute on weekends? Yet, for a husband and wife who love each other and love God, and who sincerely desire to make decisions with a view toward pleasing and honoring him at the same time that they are genuinely concerned with finding what is best for each other and for their children, difficult decisions can be worked out.

New ways of family living can emerge. New approaches to the

most menial household tasks may come about, with everyone pitching in to help as much as possible. If Jesus could pick up a towel and wash the disciples' feet, why can't a Christian husband in imitation of Christ's love pick up a towel and wipe the dishes? Or cook a meal as the Risen Lord did on the Galilean beach? And wives can learn to handle money matters wisely as did the woman in Proverbs 31 (an asset now and an absolute necessity should one's husband die, as so many widows have found out belatedly). The clinging-vine, dependency image can be cast off, as wives pursue new ways of aiding their families—without fears of losing femininity or damaging husbands' egos.

In all of this, a balance must be sought. *Neither* husband nor wife must get so busy that the family as a whole is neglected —spiritually, emotionally, or physically. Traditionally, the woman has been expected to be the warm center to which all family members can retreat from the hard knocks of life. If she too is out in the hubbub of the world, who will provide the refuge that makes home a place of calm and refreshment? Who will be the binder of wounds, the healer of hurts, the ego-builder, the one who always understands and has a word of comfort and encouragement? Such concerns are part of what Dr. Jessie Bernard calls "the stroking or supportive function," and a woman is expected to excel at it and specialize in it, often at a tremendous cost to herself.[1] Women, too, need emotional support, appreciation of achievement, encouragement, and so on. There's no reason why husbands and wives cannot perform the stroking function for one another, rather than expecting it to be one-sided. Even the children can develop a sensitivity to the needs of other family members and learn to minister to one another. Certainly this is consistent with Christian principles (cf. 1 Cor. 12:25–26; Gal. 6:2; Rom. 1:12).

THE HUSBAND AND WIFE AS LOVERS

Companionship

Many people today talk about a search for warmth, intimacy, and meaningful relationships. Yet there is a suspicion that such deep soul-comradeship cannot exist within the institution of marriage, that somehow its possibilities are destroyed once a relationship is confirmed by ceremonies and legal papers. To some young people, marriage is a societal regulation that insists on rights, duties, roles, and restrictions, forcing couples into the mold of "the establishment." They therefore conclude that relationships have more possibilities for freedom and growth in living-together-out-of-wedlock arrangements. Other young adults drift into conventional marriage patterns based on notions of "romantic love" that in time evaporate, leaving the couple with only a working relationship and little experience of deep friendship between the spouses. Yet, it is true companionship that is the sought-after ideal today. And sometimes it is found. Strangely, some people think this ideal is contrary to the Bible! One writer suggested that the Apostle Paul would have been offended by the modern idea that a wife should be her husband's best friend.

Such an allegation has no real foundation. Two of Paul's dearest friends were Priscilla and Aquila—a husband and wife team who were united not only in their love for each other and their devotion to Christ, but also worked together in an active Christian ministry and labored side by side in a common trade (tentmaking) as business partners. Paul regarded this gifted couple fondly and was grateful to God for their companionship as fellow workers in Christ's kingdom (Acts 18:1–4, 24–28; Rom. 16:3–5; 1 Cor. 16:19). Perhaps Paul knew of other such marriages among Christian workers; he mentions that some of the apostles had wives who traveled with them on their missionary journeys (1 Cor. 9:5).

The biblical conception of marriage is a partnership, a covenant. It is an agreement freely entered in which each gives himself or herself to the other. "My beloved is mine and I am his" (Song of Sol. 2:16). The theme that sings its way through the entirety of the Song of Solomon is the utter delight of husband and wife in one another. Mutual joy, mutual love, mutual enthusiasm and pleasure spring out of every paragraph. There is a blending of spirit with spirit and body with body within the marital union.

In a marriage where the worth and dignity of each partner is recognized, there is the possibility of the highest type of companionship. There can be a sharing of common interests, an enjoyment of common pursuits, and a desire to be informed of one another's individual interests as well. Likewise, there can be a drawing upon one another's resources, advice, and help in a reciprocal manner. A couple who enjoy one another as friends can find great delight in just being together and talking, walking, reading, or listening to music, as well as in going places together. The simple things of life take on deep meaning when they are shared with a dearly loved friend—and so it should be (and can be) in the husband-wife relationship.

If both partners in such a relationship are devoted to Christ, they can know the joys of sharing together their service for him and their faith in him. The intellectual, emotional, and physical aspects of marriage become permeated with spiritual awareness and the vitality that grows out of a deep relationship with God. The sharing of our relationship with God with someone else who is dear can be a rich and wonderful experience. At one Christian wedding, a friend of the bride told her, "What I envy most about you is that now you'll have permanent Christian fellowship wherever you go."

Such a marriage must be worked at; it doesn't just happen. Both spouses must steer clear of manipulation and domination, each instead seeking the other's good and prayerfully striving to put into effect the principles of 1 Corinthians 13. They must also strive to avoid falling into the stifling trap of sex-role stereotyping, which stresses differences and separate spheres, driving men and women apart rather than drawing them together. Christian marriage should be the kind of relationship that encourages both spouses to grow in Christ and to exhibit the fruit of the Spirit (Gal. 5: 22–26). That kind of partnership can't help but enrich the lives of both husband and wife, their children, and the lives of others with whom they come into contact day by day.

Sex and the Christian Wife

"Do most housewives and mothers really enjoy their sex life? Or is it just something they put up with?" The question came from a listener to a radio call-in program.[2] The guest psychiatrist replied that this depended upon the maturity of the individual, because the close intimate relationship of which sex is a part is for mature individuals (as opposed to selfish, immature, ego-centered persons). This, he said, determines enjoyment—not whether a person happens to be a housewife or mother or whatever. At this point, the program's hostess interrupted. "But doesn't it depend on whether a person is a man or a woman?" she asked. Without hesitation, the psychiatrist replied, "I don't think that has anything to do with it."

Yet, most people seem to think that has a lot to do with it. And indeed it does in many cases. This isn't due to natural, biological differences between the sexes, however, but rather stems from cultural conditioning. Many wives have grown up with the notion that "good" women shouldn't find pleasure in sex. They've accepted the idea that while husbands enjoy it, wives only endure it. During the Victorian era, even medical books emphasized that high sexual drives in a woman indicated that something was wrong with her. If a wife showed too much eagerness for coitus or very much enjoyment of it, husbands often became suspicious. What kind of woman was she? The myth was that only "loose" women and prostitutes liked sex, whereas women in general considered sex to be dirty, shameful, and disgusting. Seeking to correct such ideas, Marie Stopes in 1918 wrote a book entitled *Married Love* in which she attempted to show a wife's right to experience sensual enjoyment through sexual intercourse with her husband. A pioneer effort, her book was published in Great Britain but long banned in the United States.[3]

Fear and shame are still associated with sex, even in our supposedly enlightened and emancipated age. When an evangelical magazine had a cover photo of a young husband and his pregnant wife strolling arm in arm along a beach, readers wrote in to express shock and threatened to cancel subscriptions. And if the cover was considered "suggestive," the accompanying article was criticized even more because it emphasized the joyous aspects of sex as a gift of God. When another magazine described a major denomination's report on sexuality, which included an affirmation that sex is fun, a woman wrote in to imply that it was virtual blasphemy to call sex "fun" when God meant it to be "sacred."

Somehow, it seems that many Christian wives actually do think of sex as an unpleasant duty, something required "as part of one's submissiveness to one's husband." They wouldn't want to call sex *evil*, because after all God created it; but to call it *joy* is too much for them. Therefore, they settle on the word "sacred," at the same time giving the impression that it is something highly undesirable, a hush-hush subject one doesn't think or talk about.

Other Christian wives are more frank about showing their distaste. One put it this way: "I can't see how my husband and I can get up from our knees after talking to God together and then crawl into bed to engage in such an animal act. It defiles the sacred atmosphere." Another said, "I'm always so glad when it's over with."

Still others say they would like to correct their lack of interest and their failure to respond to their husbands. They wish there would be more discussion among Christian wives about how such problems may be dealt with. A minister's wife said that she thinks a woman in her position has even greater problems than others— mainly because so many people have the mistaken idea that Christian workers aren't supposed to have such problems. Hence, there is the loneliness of having no one to talk such matters over with. Another woman has asked, "Why did God create men and women with such differences in sex needs and desires if he intended sexual harmony in marriage?"

Recent research indicates that there are not such differences as were once supposed. In particular, the Masters and Johnson research has exploded the myth of the vaginal orgasm and has shown woman's tremendous capacity for sexual pleasure through clitoral stimulation.[4] Women have been shown to be capable of multiple orgasms within a short space of time—much more so than men because of their physiological make-up.

Furthermore, although the principal disagreement among married couples with regard to sex continues to be disagreement over frequency, we may no longer simply assume that a husband desires intercourse more often than his wife. Increasing numbers of women have reported to marriage counselors (and in research surveys) that they would prefer to engage in coitus more often than their husbands desire. Cross-cultural studies also confirm the fact that it is not "female nature" to be passive, disinterested, and incapable of sexual enjoyment. Where women have negative attitudes toward sex, those attitudes are learned—not innate.

Some women think that their negative ideas about sex stem from the Bible, but a close look at what the Scriptures really say will correct this. The overall message of the biblical writers is that God created sex and pronounced it very good (Gen. 1:27–28, 31), and marriage in all its aspects is to be regarded as a gift from God to be received with thanksgiving and sanctified by the word of God and prayer (1 Tim. 4:1–5; Heb. 13:4).

God intended sex to be pleasurable for both husband and wife. Wives can be freed from many of their fears and hang-ups about sex by meditating on all the implications of that statement. Proverbs 5:18–19 speaks of the tremendous ecstasy possible in the sexual relationship of two persons united in marriage. The idea of sex play, sex pleasure, and sexual thrill is not an idea foreign to the Bible or forbidden by it. Rather, it is encouraged.

The Song of Solomon presents a beautiful picture of a husband and wife who utterly delight in each other, and who are filled with awe and wonder at the marvelous pleasure they experience in the sexual expression of their love. There is no sense of shame as they adore and explore one another's naked bodies, but rather feelings of deep delight in this gift of beauty God has created. And they don't hesitate to verbalize those feelings. (Notice the husband's adoration in Song of Solomon 4 and 7, and the bride's praise for her beloved in 5:10 ff., for example).[5]

A Christian wife who can look upon sex in this way will find she is no longer a passive "object" acted upon, but is rather a happy participant in a creative, dynamic, beautiful adventure with her husband. Sex doesn't have to be dull, one-sided, or in a rut; it can be an exhilarating experience. It is a way of acting out physically the inner unity of two made one flesh. It is a way of sharing oneself with the beloved, of being fused together in union and communion. All this can take place in an atmosphere of ecstatic delight in one another and with feelings of gratitude to the Creator for providing this marvelous means of expressing marital love.

Even the Apostle Paul (so often thought to be negative about marriage and sex) saw an equality in the sexual relationship of a husband and wife. 1 Corinthians 7:3–5 clearly points out that both husband and wife are expected to have sexual desire and that the body of each spouse belongs to the other. (In other words, Paul didn't lay the stress on the woman's body as her husband's possession. He spoke of reciprocity and equality.)

What are some implications of the teachings in these verses? For one thing, we see that there is nothing indecorous or immodest about a wife's approaching her husband to initiate sex relations. Whether she does this by words or gestures, she is offering herself and her love to the man she loves and who is a part of her; and she is asking for his love to be expressed in return.

Similarly, she shouldn't be afraid to explore her own body and determine the areas that bring the most pleasure, and she should feel free to tell her husband so that he can better express his love in the ways most pleasurable to her. Likewise, she should feel perfectly free and uninhibited in caressing her husband's body and learning what is most pleasing to him.

It's important for both spouses to maintain an openness of communication and not be afraid or ashamed to tell one another what they like and don't like about their sex life. This can be handled tactfully and lovingly without tearing the other person down. Many couples participate bodily in the intimacies of sex and yet feel strangely embarrassed and ill at ease about discussing it verbally with one another. So many difficulties could be overcome, and so many new joys and thrills could be experienced, if couples could only cultivate the habit of talking things over together and sharing deeply and honestly their innermost feelings.

Experimentation and imagination likewise have their place in the marriage bed. There is no one and only "right" way or "correct" technique or "proper" position. Many couples hesitate to be innovative in sex play because of misconceptions that new techniques may indicate abnormality or are "perversions." But most marriage counselors today tell couples that anything that is pleasurable to both partners and is neither emotionally nor physically harmful or offensive to either one may be engaged in without guilt or shame.

The playfulness and joy of the married couple in the Song of

Solomon certainly suggest that time was allowed for full bodily pleasure; there was no hurry. All five senses came into use in savoring the experience together. There was the fragrance of spices and perfumes, the sweetness of kisses, the pleasure of caresses, the hearing of endearments, the beauty of one another's bodies—all combined to bring delight in the giving and receiving of married love.

Even where such attitudes are held, however, occasional problems arise. Difficulties in the sexual side of wedded life are not unusual and shouldn't be looked upon as indications of failure. Sometimes, for example, fatigue or worry may cause one of the partners to feel like declining the other's request for a time of loving. But this can be talked over in a mature manner and shouldn't be taken as a personal affront.

A good idea is immediately to plan together a "date" for another time—the next morning or evening, for example—and arrange schedules with that in mind. It can be made something to look forward to and planned in ways designed to create a special, romantic atmosphere. For example, they might play mood music on the stereo and the wife put on her loveliest, filmy negligee. They might dim the lamps or use candles to provide a subdued lighting effect. They might take a bath or shower together or make love in a different room or before the fireplace if possible—the possibilities can extend as far as the couple's imagination. That way the "postponed" time can take on a unique aura rather than merely being a "make-up session" to hurry through in compensation for an earlier refusal.

Another problem is often the problem of privacy—particularly as the children grow older. Again, with planning, imagination, and careful arranging of schedules, couples can work out times to be alone, uninterrupted, and totally uninhibited with one another. This may mean making love at rather unusual times on occasion, but this can add zest and excitement. Innovation and flexibility are crucial in keeping the sexual side of marriage from settling into a dull, predictable routine, in which many couples complain of boredom but aren't quite sure what to do about it.

The Christian wife shouldn't hesitate to discuss any problems about sex with her husband, or with an understanding counselor if she needs further help. Husbands and wives can pray about their sex life together, just as they feel free to pray about any other area of life in which they sense a need for God's guidance and aid. Sex isn't a set-apart area of life, unrelated to one's Christian faith. It is something God has given and about which he cares.

Occasionally, one hears a fear expressed that the sex life of a couple will deteriorate if there is an equalitarian marriage. Such a fear has no basis in fact. Actually, evidence indicates quite the opposite. Some studies (particularly those of Maslow [6]) have shown that the self-actualizing wife—the wife who is allowed to be a total, fulfilled person in her own right—enjoys sex more and is a better sex partner than is the wife who regards sex as a duty and thinks women ought to be passive. Sex, after all, was not intended by God to be an act of conquest (on the part of men) and surrender (on the part of women). There is no reason for men to feel threatened by the idea of equal sexual desires and rights for women. The marriage bed isn't a battleground, a power struggle, a place to prove oneself in some sort of performance. In fact, it's not so much an *act* at all (at least ideally) but is rather a relationship—an enactment of an inner union of spirits.

If wives are self-actualizing and active with regard to sex, it doesn't mean they are being "aggressive." Rather, it can mean they are *expressive,* desiring to give as well as receive love. This can be delightfully pleasant for husbands, surprising them with new blissful thrills, instead of being considered as a threat to their *machismo.* This egalitarian approach to marital sex is supported by the biblical pictures we saw earlier. There we did not see only one person bringing something to the sexual relationship (or taking something from it), but rather two whole persons, free to be themselves, and free to share themselves completely with one another in order to experience the total joys of the one-flesh relationship.

10. Womb-Man

> If I am asked for what purpose it behooved man to be given this help [woman], no other occurs to me as likely than the procreation of children. . . . I do not see in what way it could be said that woman was made for a help for man, if the work of childbearing be excluded.
>
> —AUGUSTINE[1]

> The feminine situation is only established . . . if the wish for a penis is replaced by one for a baby, if, that is, a baby takes the place of a penis in accordance with an ancient symbolic equivalence.
>
> —SIGMUND FREUD[2]

> People say I shouldn't have so many kids— especially us being so poor and all. But they just don't understand. My babies are what I live for. I never was able to get much education, and there ain't much I feel like I can do for the world— except have babies. Every time I have a new baby I get such a good, happy feeling—like I've done something really important!
>
> —Pregnant mother of seven to social worker

IN WESTERN EUROPE, among tools and art objects dating from the Upper Paleolithic Era, archaeologists have discovered an abundance of sculptured figures of pregnant women. The bodies are rotund, with enormous breasts and greatly swollen abdomens. Each head is a mere sphere, lacking eyes, ears, nose, mouth, and hair. Sociologist Gerhard Lenski comments: "Most scholars think it is no coincidence that the artist ignored the facial features and devoted all of his attention to the symbols of fertility." [3]

Modern feminists can't help but bristle at such a notion. These fertility figurines symbolize so well what the "woman problem" is all about. Women are viewed as "sex objects"—faceless creatures (or at least, mindless ones) whose one function in life is to mate and bear children.

Yet, the ancients didn't see this as degrading at all. They thought woman's reproductive capabilities marked her off as possessing special *mana* (supernatural power). A mixture of awe and fear characterized their feelings about the birth process. A tiny, living human being could come out of a woman; surely she must be linked with magic forces!

How did such veneration of woman-as-reproducer affect woman's actual status in society? Opinions vary. Some writers cite evidence indicating deep reverence for women as "priestesses of nature" equipped with special ability to affect agricultural productivity. The fertility cults worshiped female deities and had women as well as men who performed priestly functions. John Langdon-Davies suggests that mother-goddess worship is "the logical outcome of woman's chief claim to power, of her one gift which no man can share with her." [4]

Since woman's childbearing powers were thought to influence productivity of fields, woodlands, and livestock, she was given the task of cultivating the land. To ancient man, "Mother Earth" was the cosmic model that human mothers mirrored. Out of the earth's fecund womb sprang life-sustaining food, but sometimes that womb was closed and the people suffered. Women understood such things. They seemed to be at one with the earth; surely they would be able to coax fruitfulness from its stubborn, barren soil. Therefore, for magico-religious reasons (not because men were forcing them to become drudges), women took over horticultural tasks. In societies that stress this close connection between women and agriculture, matriarchal systems of social organization are not uncommon.[5]

Historically, then, woman's function as life-bearer has resulted in female goddesses, fertility priestesses, and women in the farm fields. Whether any of this is a point on the women's liberation scoreboard probably depends on one's personal value system. And as with anything else, there's another side to be examined.

Some authors argue that although woman's procreative functions call forth male awe and worship, these same powers may make men resentful and envious. Langdon-Davies refers to the theory that men seek to compensate for their inability to bear children by being creative in other ways—by becoming "pregnant in soul" and bearing "children of the mind," giving birth to ideas, as stated for example in Plato's *Symposium*.[6]

A like view is presented by psychoanalyst Karen Horney who suggests that "our entire culture bears the masculine imprint" because man, filled with admiration for woman's reproductive capabilities, has set about to create in other ways to make up for the childbearing powers denied him. Thus, he has produced government, religion, art, and science.[7]

Reasoning along similar lines, Ashley Montagu goes so far as to suggest that male jealousy led ancient man to mimic female bodily functions at the cost of great suffering. Among some nonliterate peoples, men go through ceremonies that seem to imitate pregnancy, childbirth, and even menstruation. Some tribes require boys at puberty to enter some type of artificial womb from which they emerge as "new-born" *men*. In other tribes, men go aside to be ceremonially delivered of stones. Subincision (cutting the under-side of the penis) and periodically induced bleeding are practiced by some tribes, and Montagu sees this as an imitation of female menstruation. For him, even taboos imposed on women are rooted in male envy. Jealous over women's ability to have monthly periods and babies, men have reacted by forcing women into ceremonial regulations that are both handicaps and punishments.[8]

Taking issue with such views is H. R. Hays, whose studies in anthropology and social psychology cause him to doubt men's alleged envy of women's reproductive functions. Disagreeing with Montagu, Hays points out that periodic bloodletting occurs in only a few cultures, whereas the idea that menstrual blood is dangerous and to be avoided by men seems almost universal.[9]

Margaret Mead provides a balanced viewpoint by showing that either sex may envy the other. In Western cultures, man's achievements are praised and woman's role is depreciated. Anthropologists, however, have discovered other societies where woman's role is the one revered, envied, and imitated.[10] But where the role of woman is extolled, it is always her role as life-bearer that is meant.

WOMEN AND REPRODUCTION IN THE OLD TESTAMENT

In many respects, Hebrew customs surrounding women's sexual functions did not differ markedly from those of neighboring cultures. As Max Weber pointed out, marriage was viewed as a means of producing children and of providing economic security for women.[11]

However, Israel stood apart from other nations in that it had no fertility rites. There were times in the nation's history when it did slip into such practices and had to be called to repentance, but the people knew that Yahweh was a jealous God who would not tolerate idolatry. God commanded the Israelites to have nothing to do with "the gods of the peoples . . . round about" (Deut. 6:13–14). Who were these forbidden deities? Gods and goddesses common to agricultural societies where fruitfulness of fields, flocks, and the human womb is desired above all else. Thus, phallic cults flourished, images of genital organs were set up, and ritual prostitution and ceremonial orgies were incorporated into pagan worship. But Israel stood apart. There were lapses to be sure; yet at the heart of Israel's belief, God was not viewed as a male deity with a female consort requiring sexual rites in imitation of the divine marriage.

Motherhood Extolled

If fertility religions revere woman as the giver of new life, what about Israel where such worship was forbidden? Was a woman's child-bearing ability viewed with wonder and appreciation here too? Very definitely. Large families were considered blessings from God (Ps. 127:3–5). To give birth meant honor and rejoicing for the mother. As Leah announced upon Zebulun's birth, "Now my husband will treat me in princely style, because I have borne him six sons" (Gen. 30:20, NEB). An abundance of children signified God's approval (Ps. 128:3–4). Conversely, sterility was seen as a disgrace—a sign that God had withheld his favor. Therefore, when a woman conceived after long years of barrenness, she was apt to exclaim joyfully, "The Lord has taken away my reproach among men!" (e.g., see Gen. 30:23; Luke 1:25).

Yet, woman's procreative abilities were not linked with strange, mystical female powers, as in the minds of fertility worshipers. Israel looked to God alone as the giver of life. Only he could bring the increase of "the fruit of your body, and the fruit of your ground, and the fruit of your beasts" (Deut. 28:4). God alone was trusted for bountiful harvests and flourishing fields (Ps. 104:14). It was to him that prayers were uttered for the fecundity of animals (Ps. 144:13–14). And it was God alone who could affect fertility in women. "He gives the barren woman a home, making her the joyous mother of children. Praise the Lord!" (Ps. 113:9).

Thus, when Rachel echoed the cry of longing common to all Israelite wives, "Give me children, or I shall die!" her husband Jacob was understandably disturbed. "Am I in the place of God, who has withheld from you the fruit of the womb?" he replied (Gen. 30:1–2). Jacob himself and his twin brother Esau had been born in answer to their father Isaac's prayer for his barren wife (Gen. 25:21), even as Isaac too had been the child of God's promise, born to Abraham and Sarah in their old age.

Understanding of Reproductive Processes

Knowledge of the facts of reproduction were necessarily limited during this stage of human history. Yet, the Israelites did not think that women brought forth children magically through their own powers, nor were they unaware of the association between sexual intercourse and pregnancy. A man *knew* his wife (had sex relations with her), and she conceived and brought forth a child. (Some writers have suggested that many ancient peoples did not see this connection, and this explains their awesome respect for the mystery of woman's fertility.)

On the other hand, there is no evidence that the Hebrew people thought of the child as the product of the father alone. This contrasted with the widespread ancient belief that a baby was engendered exclusively by the male, the wife's body being merely the "field" in which the husband planted his seed so that in time *his* child would be produced. Such a notion is seen in the sacred writings of Hinduism ("This woman has come like living soil: sow seed in her, ye men!" [12]) and in Islam ("Your women are as fields for you" [13]).

Ancient Greek authors expressed the same idea. Sophocles describes the anguish of Oedipus upon discovering that he had unknowingly married his own mother. He cries out in horror about "this mother's womb, this field of double sowing whence I sprang and where I sowed my children!" [14] And in Aeschylus's *The Eumenides,* when Orestes is brought to trial for avenging his father's death by murdering his mother, the god Apollo tells the jury that matricide is not so terrible a crime as they may think. Why? Because only the father is the actual parent; the mother is "but the nurse of the new-planted seed that grows." [15]

In Hebrew tradition, however, mothers were not viewed as mere incubators. There are references to *seed* to be sure, and in Genesis 38:9 the meaning is clearly semen. But the usual meaning of the word is offspring, children, descendants. There is no clear-cut agricultural analogy here as in the examples from other cultures; and while most of the Scripture references speak of seed with regard to the father (since lineage through the male was emphasized in a patriarchal society), Genesis 3:15 speaks of the seed of the woman. There are references to woman's "conceiving seed" (Num. 5:28, KJV) and to the "godly seed" of both husband and wife (Mal. 2:15, KJV). Israelite children were expected to give equal honor to both parents. Indeed, as the commandment is recorded in Leviticus 19:3, the mother is mentioned first.

God, in his covenant with Abraham, said, "I will make you exceedingly fruitful; and I will make nations of you, and kings shall come forth from you" (Gen. 17:6). But Sarah's part was equally important, for God said, "I will bless her, . . . and she shall be a mother of nations; kings of peoples shall come from her" (Gen. 17:16). Eventually, there developed the tradition in Judaism that a child is not a Jew unless he has a Jewish mother, thus placing the primary stress on the mother's role in reproduction.

Commenting on Genesis 4:1, a rabbi of the last century describes how Eve might have felt when Cain was born. No doubt other Israelite women had similar feelings upon giving birth.

And she said, I have gotten a man from the Lord. I have gotten a
child *with* God. God Himself created us, but now I and my husband have also a share in the child; for *three* have a part in a
child; the father, the mother, and God, He gives the soul.[16]

The writers of the Old Testament did not understand the science
of embryology, but they never ceased to wonder at the way a child
was formed in the uterus. "As you do not know how the spirit comes
to the bones in the womb of a woman with child, so you do not know
the work of God who makes everything" (Eccles. 11:5). "For thou
didst form my inward parts, thou didst knit me together in my
mother's womb. I praise thee, for thou art fearful and wonderful.
Wonderful are thy works!" (Ps. 139:13–14).

Taboos Associated with Woman's Sexual Functions

If a woman's status and worth were measured by her ability to
bear children (cf. 1 Sam. 1:2, 6), and if childbirth was so highly
regarded in ancient Israel, why then did such strict taboos, cleansing ceremonies, and sacrifices surround a woman's sexual functions?

We must keep in mind that the Israelite conception of ceremonial
defilement was related to *cultic worship*, which in the words of
de Vaux refers to "all those acts by which communities or individuals give outward expression to their religious life, by which they
seek and achieve contact with God." [17] Cultic worship involved
fixed rules, regulations, and rituals, and a rigid division between
what was considered to be "clean" and "unclean."

If the God of Israel was a *holy* God, he must be approached in
just the right way. To come before him while ritually unclean would
be viewed as an affront to his majesty and purity. Therefore, a
person in a condition of defilement was cut off from the life of the
cult and not permitted to participate in its worship until he or she
underwent the prescribed rites of purification. Again, as de Vaux
makes clear, ceremonial impurity should not be thought of as
physical or moral defilement. It is rather a "state" or "condition"
out of which a person must emerge in order to reenter the normal
life of the religious community.[18]

Such ritual impurity was considered contagious and able to be
transferred to anyone or anything the affected person touched. It
is interesting to note the states that were considered unclean:
childbirth (Leviticus 12), leprosy (Leviticus 13 and 14), discharges
from the sexual organs of both males and females, including normal
menstruation (Leviticus 15), and touching a dead body (Numbers
19). Some Christian commentators see here an association with the
idea of original sin and the fall of man, since the states of ceremonial
uncleanness relate to the propagation of human life in a sinful

world, the ordeal of suffering and disease, and man's greatest enemy death—all of which could imply a connection with Genesis 3:16–19. Other scholars consider such interdicts to be vestiges of primitive beliefs and customs common to many ancient cultures.

Menstruation

Notice that two of the states of ceremonial pollution affected only women. Certain persons were forced to be set apart periodically simply because they had been born female. Every woman from the age of puberty onward would be considered unclean for at least seven days out of every twenty-eight (Lev. 15:19, 25, 28)—unless she were pregnant, in which case an even longer period of ceremonial uncleanness followed the birth of the child.

William Graham Cole warns against calling this discrimination against women, since an issue of semen from a man rendered him unclean also. A male, however, was considered unclean for only one day, whereas female contamination lasted a full week. Why the disparity? The simplest explanation would seem to be the difference in duration of the two discharges. However, Cole suggests other possible reasons: (1) a patriarchal society's bias which would assign greater impurity to the sexual discharges of a female's body than those of a male, (2) the general awe, fear, and reverence of the Hebrews with regard to blood, or (3) a simple economic factor because a man couldn't afford to give so much of his time to purification rites.[19]

One might wonder how a woman could afford such time either! Probably she had a large family to look after. Yet, not only was *she* considered unclean all week, but so was anyone who touched her (even the tiny toddler clutching at her skirt?), as well as anything on which she had lain or sat. If someone happened to touch her bed or something on which she had sat, that person was required to wash his clothes, take a bath, and even then was considered ritually unclean the rest of the day. (Similar rules were in effect for men who had certain kinds of discharges that were evidently infectious—Lev. 15:1–15.)

Why did these customs regarding menstruation become part of Israel's religion? What was their significance? Were they mere superstitions similar to those of other peoples? Or did they mean something quite different? There are no easy answers, and opinions vary.

The phenomenon of periodic bleeding in women has been a source of wonder and mystery throughout history. In fact, even though the process is now well understood, there are still elements of "mystery" surrounding menstruation; and some physiologists are at present questioning its value—even going so far as to call it a "biologic failure." [20] By this they mean that the reproductive processes of many animals are accomplished in a way similar to those of human females, yet without menstruation. Only among humans, monkeys, and apes is menstruation found.

Be that as it may, women *do* menstruate. This has given rise to numerous beliefs and customs in different cultures. Some primitive groups associated menstruation with the moon's phases and the ebb and flow of the tides, even suggesting that the moon was female and was "having her sickness" when she waned. Many groups keep women totally isolated during menstruation. The ancient *Natural History of Pliny* attributes the blighting of crops, the rusting of iron, and the killing of bees to the presence of menstruating women. Some cultures forbid a menstruating woman to handle food, believing that her cooking would make food spoil and milk turn sour. Certain tribes associate menstruation with evil spirits.

The ancient Greeks took the idea of "uncleanness" literally and thought a woman's body needed periodic purging to be rid of impurities and poisons. They called the menstrual period "the katharsis." Similar ideas are found in the traditions of India.

No such beliefs surrounded Hebrew customs regarding menstruation. No explanation was suggested for this female bodily process; it was simply accepted as a given. The Talmud, however, does associate it with the curse upon Eve,[21] and the euphemism, "the curse," is still applied to menstruation by many women. *Why* God should demand the rituals surrounding this natural function is likewise not explained in the Bible. There is no indication of an association between these rites and notions of fertility, as in Hindu traditions where the ten days after menstruation began were viewed as the woman's *rtu* (fertile period) and therefore called for sexual intercourse to take place immediately upon the cessation of the flow.[22]

Nor are the ceremonies of Leviticus 15 considered "magic cures" of some sort, as in other religions. Rather, purification ceremonies were performed *after* the unclean condition had ceased.

The Israelite taboo regarding menstruation seems to have been bound up with ideas of ceremonial purity as demanded by God and the concepts of holiness that he required. Anthropologist Mary Douglas suggests that the levitical laws about pollution, taboo, and purification make little sense unless we try to grasp how the Hebrew mind conceived of holiness.[23] It meant much more than justice and moral goodness in this society. Kind and humane treatment of one's fellow man may have formed part of the notion of holiness, but the concept embraced a great deal more.

Although at its root holiness means "to be set apart for God," it also referred to wholeness—to the idea of physical perfection, completion. Sacrificial animals had to be blemish-free. Men with physical defects could not serve as priests. Even in the social sphere, completeness was important; tasks and schemes had to be finished so that a new totality could come into being.

In addition to holiness as *set-apartness* and *wholeness,* Douglas mentions a third aspect—*right order*. Certain classes of things must not be confused or co-mingled; there must be separation (cf. Deut. 22:9–11). Right order, for example, is seen in the rules for sexual morality which prohibit bestiality, incest, adultery, and homosexual practices (Lev. 18:6–23).

Therefore, any deviation from wholeness or perfection, and anything that deviated from right order fell into the category of "unclean." Defilement required separation; otherwise God's blessing would be withheld. However, when wholeness was restored, the separation ended. Special ceremonies reinstated the person into the religious community.

If we accept the Douglas explanation of the rituals of Leviticus, it may be that a woman's periodic isolation symbolized that her body was temporarily not whole and therefore could not properly mirror the holy. Blood flowing from her vagina seemed to signify something out of place, out of order.

Another possible key to understanding Israelite menstrual taboos lies in the Hebrew attitude toward blood. Other nations, in connection with fertility rites, ate and drank blood; Israel was expressly forbidden to do so. Israel was a separated people, and separation from blood—except in the sacred context of the sacrifice where it was sprinkled upon the altar of God—was one of the marks of such separation. Not that blood was considered vile and evil. It was viewed with awe and wonder as the source of life and the means of atonement (Lev. 17:11). Therefore, special taboos surrounded blood.

By extension, special taboos began to surround women. In later Judaism, for example, there arose a prohibition about touching women. If a merchant counted out money into a woman's palm he must be especially cautious. She just might be having her period and her contamination would pass on to him, making him ceremonially defiled.

Sexual intercourse during the menstrual period was especially singled out for condemnation under Israel's ceremonial law. Perhaps the mildest denunciation is given in Leviticus 15:24, where the man "defiled" by the woman's impurity must, like her, observe seven days of uncleanness. The message of Leviticus 20:18 is much stronger: "If a man lies with a woman having her sickness . . . he has made naked her fountain, and she has uncovered the fountain of

her blood; both of them shall be cut off from among their people"
(implying exile, possibly even death, according to some Bible
scholars). In Ezekiel 18:5, one of the indications of a righteous man
was his avoidance of a woman "in her time of impurity." (These
ceremonial rules do not imply that intercourse during menstruation
and the specified days thereafter is inherently evil in God's sight.
They must be viewed in connection with other Israelite rituals given
for a specific nation and time. This particular rule may have even
involved humane considerations, allowing Israelite women the freedom to say no to their husbands at a time of discomfort.)

Although blood upon the altar was revered, blood upon a menstrual cloth was despised. Again, perhaps there is the thought of
something out of place and the idea that losing this blood signifies
a body not in a state of "wholeness" (and therefore "holiness"). At
any rate, the ceremonial uncleanness of menstruation became a
favorite analogy for the pollution of sin—especially in the
prophetic writings. Thus we read, "Ye shall defile also the covering
of thy graven images of silver, and the ornament of thy molten
images of gold: thou shalt cast them away as a mentruous cloth;
thou shalt say unto it, Get thee hence" (Isa. 30:22, KJV).

Similar imagery occurs in Isaiah 64:6, although the English
translations are usually less vivid ("All our righteousnesses are as
filthy rags"—KJV—or "like a polluted garment"—RSV). The defilement of a menstruous woman was used to portray the revolting
vileness of a sinful condition in God's sight. Ezekiel describes God's
judgment on Israel: "Their conduct before me was like the uncleanness of a woman in her impurity" (Ezek. 36:17). In Jeremiah's
lamentation over fallen Jerusalem, he describes the city as "a
menstruous woman" (Lam. 1:17, KJV), with the idea being that of
something "filthy" (RSV).

Modern women who think of menstruation as a normal body process are understandably disturbed in reading such passages. But we
must remember what the Israelites were expected to learn from
their ceremonial regulations, namely that God is holy and expects his
people to be holy. They were taught through object lessons which
emphasized completeness or perfection. A sinful nation that turned
from God was like a diseased body—unwell, not whole. Isaiah described God's people as a sick and wounded human body in need of
healing and cleansing (Isa. 1:5 ff.). The nation could not know God's
blessing unless it was in a state of health. (Our own word "health"
comes from the Old English word *hale* which means "whole.")

Each time a woman menstruated and was required to go through
the prescribed ceremonies, she was symbolizing this concept of
holiness. The taboos meant a great deal of bother and inconvenience

and were probably just as annoying to the Hebrew women as they are today in tribes with similar regulations, where women complain that the rules disrupt life and slow down work schedules terribly.[24]

Childbirth

Leviticus 12 describes regulations surrounding the second condition of ceremonial uncleanness for women, childbirth. Upon reading the chapter, we can't help but ask two questions: Why did having a baby make a woman "unclean" and require a sacrificial offering? And why did giving birth to a *daughter* demand a double period of purification?

PURIFICATION FOR MOTHERS

Scholars have suggested many possible reasons for the placement of a postparturient woman in the category of uncleanness. Since the baby is not said to be unclean, but only the mother, the purification requirement may have been associated with the bodily discharges associated with childbirth and a short time afterward. The taboos related to blood and the general cultic significance of ceremonial purity once again offer the most plausible explanation. The woman's body needed time to be restored to wholeness; until then, the state of ceremonial uncleanness prevailed.

Others have suggested that the long period of being set apart was simply out of consideration for the new mother's health—similar to the "lying-in period" for maternity cases which persisted in our own culture until comparatively recent times. However, the emphasis on not touching any hallowed thing and the prohibition against entering the sanctuary indicate that the reasons behind the ritual were primarily religious rather than hygienic.

Some commentators see something more here than ceremonial taboos connected with bodily discharges. They point out that the woman was commanded to bring a burnt offering and a sin offering (Lev. 12:6–8) and conclude that this refers to the doctrine of original sin. In this view, the sacrifice is necessary because a woman "has brought another sinner into the world." However, such offerings were also required in cases other than childbirth where bodily health was somehow not in a normal state (see Lev. 14:10–32; 15:13–15; 15:25–30).

In Genesis 3:16, God told the woman, "I will greatly multiply your pain in childbearing; in pain you shall bring forth children." The Talmud interprets this to mean that ten curses came upon Eve, menstruation and the travail of childbirth being two of them.[25] Rabbis explained the requirement of sacrificial offerings by saying

that a woman was likely to sin in a specific way while bearing an infant, and this must be atoned for. What "specific way" did they have
in mind? The regrets a woman might voice during the pangs of
labor—perhaps similar to Rebekah's anguished cry when her twins
were to be born (Gen. 25:22). In particular, argued the rabbis, a
woman on the birthstool might swear impetuously that she would
never again have intercourse with her husband if this is what comes
of it! Thus, she would have to make a sacrifice for having spoken
such a foolish vow.[26]

Among Christians who have interpreted Leviticus 12 to relate to
the taint of mankind's ongoing sinfulness, transmitted through birth,
was S. H. Kellogg, who wrote in *The Expositor's Bible:* "The extreme evil of the state of sin into which the first woman, by that
first sin, brought all womanhood, is seen most of all in this, that now
woman, by means of those powers given her for good and blessing,
can bring into the world only a child of sin." [27] He goes on to say
that apparently childbirth shows the operation of the curse in its
most conspicuous form, and thus women had to be barred from the
tabernacle worship for an extended period.

There is one final interpretation sometimes suggested to explain
the childbirth offerings. Could these sacrifices have been offered in
thanksgiving to God for a safe delivery and for the gift of the
child? Such a notion was incorporated into the old custom of certain segments of Christendom where "the churching of women"
was required after childbirth, bringing women back into the fellowship of the church. (However, even the "churching" custom may
merely reflect a later development of ancient taboos of restoration
to community following a condition of uncleanness.)

DOUBLE PURIFICATION FOR GIRL BABIES

If a woman gave birth to a daughter, the purification period was
twice as long as when a son was born. In a rather misogynistic
statement, S. H. Kellogg again sees the explanation to lie in original
sin:

> [The ritual] teaches us that not only has the curse thus fallen on
> the woman, but that, because she is herself a sinful creature, she
> can only bring forth another sinful creature like herself; and if a
> daughter, then a daughter inheriting all her own peculiar infirmi-
> ties and disabilities.[28]

The implication is that by bringing another female into the world
she has increased the likelihood of the continuation of the curse, because this child too will one day bear the uncleanness of menstruation and childbirth. "Because 'first in the transgression,'" Kellogg

writes, "[woman] is under special pains and penalties in virtue of her sex."

Others feel that the prolonged uncleanness after a daughter's birth was more a matter of social custom than of theology. Cole calls it "the prejudice of a patriarchal society." [29] And Hays points out that the longer period of purification after the birth of a female was a practice by no means confined to the Israelites. Such a custom has been practiced in India, New Guinea, within West African tribes, and among the Cree Indians of North America.[30]

Sons were clearly more highly valued and desired than daughters in Hebrew culture. As de Vaux points out, sons were wanted to "perpetuate the family line and fortune and to preserve the ancestral inheritance." [31] Girls, on the other hand, grew up, married, and joined their husbands' families. The strength of a household was measured by the number of sons.

The Apocrypha provides further clues to the Israelite preference for boys. Daughters seemed to be just too much bother!

A daughter is a secret anxiety to her father,
and the worry of her keeps him awake at night;
when she is young, for fear she may grow too old to marry,
and when she is married, for fear she may lose her husband's love;
when she is a virgin, for fear she may be seduced
and become pregnant in her father's house,
when she has a husband, for fear she may misbehave,
and after marriage, for fear she may be barren (Ecclus. 42:9–10, NEB).

The passage goes on to warn fathers that "headstrong" daughters could put the family to shame, and therefore girls must be closely watched. Added to the inconvenience of keeping daughters "in line" was the notion that females were inherently evil as compared to males. "Better a man's wickedness than a woman's goodness; it is woman who brings shame and disgrace" (Ecclus. 42:14, NEB).

No wonder the Talmud explains the prolonged period of purification for female births by referring again to a woman's probable rash vow to avoid future sex relations with her husband! The rabbis wrote: "On the birth of a male with whom all rejoice she regrets her oath after seven days, but on the birth of a female about whom everybody is upset, she regrets her oath after fourteen days." [32]

In addition to the *theological* reasons suggested for this custom (in particular, the idea of a woman's part in perpetuating original sin), and *cultural* reasons (the preference for sons in a patriarchal society), there was a third category—attempted *physiological* explanations.

According to one ancient notion, a greater physical derangement occurred within a woman's reproductive system if she gave birth to a girl, and the effects of this disorder took longer to pass away. Along this same line of thought, the Talmud suggests that the "fashioning" of a female occurred after eighty days in the uterus, whereas the male body was formed forty days after conception; the periods of uncleanness corresponded to this.[33]

Some rabbis also advanced a rather fascinating theory of obstetrics. They said that the mother's pain was much worse when giving birth to a female child. Why? Because "the female emerges in the position she assumes during intercourse and the male emerges in the position he assumes during intercourse. The former, therefore, turns her face upwards [the turning intensifying the pains of the mother] while the latter need not turn his face." [34]

Bardis refers to an old Israelite belief that girls were inferior because they were thought to originate in the supposedly weaker and smaller left testicle, whereas boys were thought to come from the right one.[35] However, the Midrash indicates a belief that a child was produced by both parents, the infant's sex being determined by the parent of the opposite sex. "If the woman provides the seed," wrote the rabbis, "she bears a manchild. A female, on the other hand, is formed from the seed of the male." [36]

Modern medical science, of course, explodes these attempted physiological explanations. We are left then with the harshly misogynistic implications of the theological view that emphasizes female nature as the carrier of original sin—so that girl babies are seen as little Pandoras or tiny Eves who will bring more trouble to the world and must be "welcomed" with a longer period of ceremonial defilement. Or else we must simply accept the likelihood that boys were more desired in the patriarchy of Israel, and therefore the time of purification was cut in half out of joy that a woman had brought a manchild into the world.

Before leaving the subject of how the Old Testament viewed woman-as-childbearer, we must remind ourselves that despite many of the "negative" practices discussed, there was a real sense of wonder at the phenomenon of birth and a high estimate of motherhood. The overall picture of woman as the bringer of new life into the world is not one of degradation, but rather of appreciation. Despite the difficult and discriminatory passages examined (and there is the possibility that many of these customs, laws, and taboos originally reflected awe and reverence for woman's special place rather than attempts to "put her down"), it seems clear that the command to "be fruitful and multiply" was taken seriously in Old Testament times. The designation of Eve as "the mother of all living" (Gen. 3:20) was not considered an insult but a term of high esteem. To be a mother of many children was the highest honor known to the Old Testament woman. Reproduction, with all its attendant joys and sorrows, was regarded as her destiny simply by having been born a member of the female sex. In the culture of Israel, motherhood was both a divine duty and a happy privilege. It was the barren woman who was to be pitied, for she had no children to "rise up and call her blessed" (Prov. 31:28).

NEW TESTAMENT ATTITUDES TOWARD MOTHERHOOD

There is a shift in attitudes when we reach the New Testament. Some theologians explain it by the fact that The Child—the Savior, Redeemer, Messiah, the one whom Jewish mothers had hoped to bear—had already come. The seed of the woman had already entered the world to crush the serpent's head (Gen. 3:15).

At any rate, there was a gradual move away from the implication that reproduction is a woman's most important contribution to the world. A woman's status and self-worth no longer depended upon the number of children she produced. The emphasis changes from physical birth to spiritual birth—entrance into the family of God through faith in Jesus Christ. Membership in God's household, the church or community of believers, was valued above human family ties. Even singleness for the sake of the kingdom of God was highly regarded. This had special significance for women because, under traditional Israelite cultural norms, to be unmarried (or married but childless) was a deep misfortune if not an actual disgrace.[37]

Thus, the New Testament has little to say about woman as womb-man. There is neither the awe nor the mixture of both revulsion and reverence observed in portions of the Old Testament as well as other cultures. This aspect of woman's life is largely ignored in the New Testament, with but a few exceptions.

Perhaps the verse with the most difficulties is 1 Timothy 2:15. "Yet woman will be saved through bearing children, if she continues in faith and love and holiness, with modesty." The un-Pauline view of salvation here (by childbearing rather than through faith) is one reason some Bible scholars conclude that this epistle was not written by Paul but by his later followers. Even if one attempts interpretations other than the idea that having babies is efficacious for securing eternal salvation, the passage continues to be obscure and puzzling.

Some Christians interpret the verse to mean that a woman is saved "through *the* Childbearing," that is, the Savior's entrance into the world through a woman (Gal. 4:4). To others, the verse means that a faithful Christian woman will be delivered through the ordeal of giving birth to children, despite the effects of the curse pronounced upon Eve. One problem with this last view has to do with the committed Christian woman who dies in childbirth. Is the verse implying that she has not continued "in faith, love, holiness, and modesty"? Should others conclude that God has "punished" her by failing to deliver her through the anguish of giving birth? Such a notion hardly fits with New Testament theology and would offer little comfort to the grieving husband.

Another passage in the same epistle (1 Tim. 5:14) also stresses childbearing as a worthy activity for women, with the context in this case hinting that having babies would keep troublesome, meddlesome women at home and out of mischief.

Interestingly, in discussions of the marriage bed (Heb. 13:4) and sexual relations between husband and wife (1 Cor. 7:3-4), there is no reference to procreation. There is, of course, no negation of the Jewish idea that children should be regarded as gifts of God. And the New Testament epistles provide exhortations on nurturing children in the fear and discipline of the Lord, instructing them in the faith (e.g., Eph. 6:1-4). Children born of a "mixed marriage" (between a Christian and a nonbeliever) were not considered "unclean," but holy, by virtue of the believing partner (cf. 1 Cor. 7:14). Spiritual analogies to childbirth and child care are made in the New Testament, just as in the Old Testament (e.g., Gal. 4:19; 1 Thess. 2:7).

The Gospels record the births of John the Baptizer and Jesus, and the customs and attitudes of Old Testament Judaism are seen in their mothers. Elizabeth speaks of God's goodness in "removing her reproach" (childlessness). The cousins visit together during pregnancy and exult in the joy of their approaching motherhood (Luke 1:39 ff.). Neighbors and kinsfolk gather to celebrate John's birth, circumcision, and naming (Luke 1:57 ff.). Mary, the mother of Jesus, fulfills the Levitical law of purification after childbirth, bringing the sacrifices of a family able to afford only the simple offering required of those in poverty (Luke 2:22-24; cf. Lev. 12:8).

Although Jesus certainly honored his mother and cared about her welfare (even as he was dying on the cross), he was never sentimental about the virtues of childbearing. When a woman yelled out from one of the crowds, "Blessed is the womb that bore you, and the breasts that you sucked!" (Luke 11:27), Jesus did not seize upon the occasion as a unique opportunity for a Mother's Day sermon. Instead, he showed that a woman is not honored in God's sight according to her possession and use of reproductive equipment, but rather by her performance of the will of God.

A similar thought is expressed in Matthew 12:46 ff. There, when

Jesus is told that his mother and brothers are seeking him (presumably because of spreading rumors that he had taken leave of his senses), Jesus replies that his *followers* are his family. Again, the shift is away from the human family unit to the larger family of God.

Jesus empathized with mothers, having deep compassion for those who would be pregnant or nursing infants at their breasts during the prophesied destruction of Jerusalem (Matt. 24:19). And as he walked the painful steps of the Via Dolorosa, he turned to the weeping women who watched and said, "Daughters of Jerusalem, do not weep for me, but weep for yourselves and for your children. For behold, the days are coming when they will say, 'Blessed are the barren, and the wombs that never bore, and the breasts that never gave suck!' " (Luke 23:28–29).

Jesus loved children, and when mothers brought them to him he welcomed them warmly. But the many unmarried women who followed him were just as warmly appreciated and honored.

Earlier in this book, we looked at Christ's compassion and concern for the woman who by faith touched his garment, believing he could heal her from the vaginal bleeding that had plagued her for twelve years. It took courage for her to disregard the fact that the Levitical law called her unclean. Yet Jesus did not shrink from her, as would have been the normal reaction of the rabbis of that day. The entrance of Jesus Christ into the world brought an end to the ceremonial laws that applied to women, just as his coming brought about the end of dietary laws, other rules, and the rituals of animal sacrifice (Heb. 9:9–11; 10:1, 9).

A concluding indication of Jesus' attitude toward the childbearing function of women is seen in John 16:21. There Jesus used the analogy of childbirth in speaking of his disciples' sorrow in view of his coming departure. He wanted them to know that their sadness would give way to greater joy than ever before, for they would see him again as the risen Lord! "When a woman is in travail she has sorrow," Jesus said, "because her hour has come; but when she is delivered of the child, she no longer remembers the anguish, for joy that a child is born into the world."

The statement is realistic (there *is* pain), but it is positive. No negative statements are made about the curse of Eve, the punishment that childbearing is supposed to be, the evil natures that women have, the awfulness of bringing new sinners into the world, and so on. Rather, there is a note of great joy.

Interestingly, the Greek word for child used in the last part of the verse (in some Bible versions translated "man") is *anthropos,* meaning "a human being." It is not a designation of a person of

the male sex. Thus, Jesus is speaking of the thrill of bringing into
the world a new *person*—a human being, whether son or daughter,
with all the potential that little child may have as a member of the
family of God and a disciple of Christ. Nothing is said here to
indicate a preference for boys or a longer purification period for
daughters. Only joy is mentioned. Joy over the birth of any baby,
regardless of its sex.

Children are equally valued by Christ as human beings made in
the image of God—and so are their mothers.

11. Reproduction and the Modern Woman

In 1972 . . . the birth and fertility rates fell to the lowest levels ever observed in the United States.[1] Whether such low rates continue into the future depends upon the extent to which this decline represents delays in childbearing that will be made up later, and the extent to which it represents a reduction in the total number of children ever born.

—ARTHUR A. CAMPBELL [2]

I came to terms with motherhood when one of my plainspoken daughters asked me the ultimate question. . . . *No one* was paying attention to her. When would *somebody* have time to play with her? . . . I had an article deadline to meet and would be at my desk all afternoon with the door closed. . . . That was when she asked, "Did you ever wish you never had us in the first place?" I think I became partially paralyzed. Guilt flooded my cheeks with blood . . . I've scarred her, I thought: I've made her feel like a burden—unwanted, unloved, rejected. . . . I sorted my ragged thoughts and took her onto my lap. Gentleness wrapped around us like a fog. "Sometimes my life is a little too full because I have you children," I said. "But, for me, it would be much too empty if I didn't."

LETTY COTTIN POGREBIN [3]

AT ONE TIME in our society, motherhood seemed sacrosanct. Politicians supported popular issues because not to do so would "be like coming out against apple pie, the flag, or motherhood." Women who gave birth to large numbers of children were praised highly and presented with "Mother of the Year" awards. Children and grandchildren made a woman's life seem worthwhile. Why should she worry about personal aspirations when she could bask in the reflected glory of her offspring's achievements? Her son the statesman or the doctor would one day pat her wrinkled hand and say, "Everything I am today I owe to my dear mother who sacrificed everything for me." She could end her days with a warm, contented feeling, knowing she had contributed something important to the world—children. She had performed the task society expected of her. And society was well pleased.

But things are changing. The population explosion throughout the world has caused politicians to wonder if it might not be wise to come out against motherhood after all! Some have proposed changes in income tax laws to discourage having large families. Abortion laws have been liberalized. Research on better contraceptive methods continues, and efforts at wider dissemination of birth control information are being made. The notion of planned parenthood and limited family size is, with few exceptions, accepted with little debate in contemporary American society.

HOW WOMEN ARE AFFECTED

At this stage in history, as never before, a woman need not accept the life-bearing role that was once considered her natural and inevitable destiny. She may choose to have only one or two children—or none at all. Modern contraceptive technology makes this possible, and society's present mood makes it easier. At one time, a husband and wife were considered selfish if they chose not to have children; now it is not unusual to hear praise for such couples. Those now labeled "selfish" are couples who insist on having a large number of children, thereby aggravating societal problems because of population growth pressures. Bringing children into the world has come to be seen as a luxury rather than a duty or necessity.

Where does that leave woman? We have long since moved from the stage where agricultural prosperity was associated with woman's fertility, and quite likely that change of emphasis lowered woman's "self-image" long ago. Yet, there was still the sense of worth attached to woman's role as a baby-producer. Early societies longed for children to replace the many persons who died. In modern industrial societies, the worry is reversed. There are fears that too many new people will enter life upon a planet with limited resources and where the quality of human life could be severely affected by overcrowding. Today it is becoming as out of place to praise woman as a baby-producer as it is to praise her as a good-luck charm for fertile crops! Does the deemphasis on her childbearing role bring woman new freedom? Or does it threaten to take away her whole purpose for living? It can do either.

Traditionally, societal pressures have influenced women to believe that childbearing and childrearing should be the main focus of their lives. Marriage and motherhood *are* a woman's career, according to this viewpoint; why should she want any other career?

The church has reinforced this idea with its Mother's Day awards to women who have given birth to the largest number of children, as well as its sermons and religious writings about the unique contributions a woman can make by devoting her life to home and family. Seldom are awards given to women who have contributed to the church and society through their brains rather than through their biological makeup. Occasionally, of course, women missionaries are honored for spreading the gospel and alleviating human misery, but these are considered to be the exceptional women. Most Christian women, it is assumed, will serve God through motherhood. Clergymen tell women that the Bible teaches that this is God's will.

However, this is Old Testament thinking. Already we have observed the shift of emphasis as Christianity came upon the scene. In the New Testament, it is not the propagation of the race that matters so much as the propagation of the gospel message. Kinship ties—blood relationships—are valued less than spiritual ties. The tie that binds men and women together as brothers and sisters in Christ is their common membership in the community of faith, the family of God, the church. In this setting, virginity came to be seen as a positive good. A woman (or man) did not have to enter marriage and have children in order to experience God's blessing and a sense of usefulness.

By the same token, childlessness came to be viewed as not "sinful" or a social disgrace. Couples without any children or with small families could exhibit the virtues of Christian home life just as well as large ones. A shift from a material emphasis to a spiritual one also changed attitudes toward property. This affected attitudes toward having sons to perpetuate the family name and inherit the family wealth. The emphasis was no longer on laying up treasure for one's sons but on laying up treasure in heaven.

Seeing the total picture, rather than the Old Testament emphasis alone, can help the Christian woman rethink the matter of motherhood. She can come to see that being a physical life-bearer is not nearly so important as being a bearer of spiritual life—the kind of life-bearer Jesus was (see John 10:10). She can share herself, her energies, her service, her time in ways that heal and help and challenge and bring new life to mankind. She can learn that there are other gifts she can offer the world besides children, gifts that are every bit as important. No Christian woman should feel that being a member of the female sex somehow requires her to have many (or any) children, and that she will be displeasing to God and failing as a woman otherwise.

Most Protestant religious leaders encourage the use of birth control in our day so that children are planned for and wanted, spaced in ways most beneficial to the family, and limited in number. However, what is overlooked in most discussions of limited family size is woman's role and purpose. Often the same religious leaders who recommend small families are telling women at the same time that their destiny lies in wifehood and motherhood. Seldom are girls encouraged to think in terms of other goals.

Many Christians would quickly praise the following statement written by a young woman in a letter to a friend: "I've heard it said that everyone is put here upon this earth for a reason. . . . I like to feel (right or wrong) that my purpose is to be a good wife and mother. If I can help my children to grow into useful, responsible citizens, with a sense of duty to God, their fellow humans and their community, then, I will feel that I have completed my task."

While there is much to be commended in this attitude, the problem arises because the completion of that task comes upon a woman much sooner than she expects. Most women have their last child before reaching age thirty. That means that all her children will be in school by the time a woman is in her mid-thirties. It is then that many women begin finding that time is heavy on their hands. As the children grow older and develop other interests, and as her husband becomes more deeply immersed in his career, a woman who has invested herself totally in her family begins feeling less needed and less fulfilled. Thus, it isn't unusual at this stage for a woman to suggest to her husband that they have another baby. Once again, her life-bearing function seems to promise the most rewarding path to meaning, fulfillment, and an enhanced self-image.

A WOMAN'S CHOICE

Ideally, the time to be thinking about these matters is before marriage. Many young women today say they are learning to think about long-term goals and to plan their lives accordingly, just as men have always been encouraged to do.

All too often, marriage and children "just happen." Women who are serious about pursuing further education and commitment to a profession know they don't dare risk haphazard, indecisive, careless planning. And they realize that they must seriously and wisely face the issue of marriage and children. Otherwise, it will not be easy to arrange one's life with definite goals in mind—goals that will allow maximum utilization of talents and training.

Such women find themselves asking many hard questions: Should I marry at all? If so, when? What kind of man would I want for a husband? Would we want to have children? If so, would it be best for me to take out a few years from my career and have them early in the marriage, then go back to my profession when they reach school age? Or would it be better to have children later, after many years of getting established in my career? How do I feel about babysitters and child-care centers?

All of these questions and many more are of great import with regard to a woman's career aspirations as well as to her family life. They are the kinds of concerns she and her husband-to-be will want to discuss thoroughly before the wedding takes place. A woman seriously committed to a career may choose to have only one or two children. Some may choose to postpone parenthood for a number of years. Others may choose to remain childless in order to devote their total energies elsewhere. Christian women may prayerfully decide on any of these options, and they should not be judged by other Christians who can only see woman's role in terms of the childbearing function.

Many equalitarian couples feel that the outside careers of both husband and wife are equally important, but at the same time they do not want to deny themselves the experience of parenthood. They thus view it as a cooperative venture, determining that child-care should be the task of both partners in the marriage. Such couples can find ways to work this out so that neither family life nor career suffers. This takes planning, patience, and a willingness on the part of both spouses to make some sacrifices and pay some prices. Yet it can be well worth it.

CONTRACEPTION, ABORTION, AND STERILIZATION

In many ways, it's hard to believe that in this very century clergymen were denouncing birth control as sinful in the sight of God. Politicians were expressing fears of "race suicide." [4] States had laws banning the sale of contraceptives. Condoms were spoken of as "rubber articles of immoral use." Diaphragms for Margaret Sanger's birth control clinic were illegally imported from Germany via Canada and smuggled over the border in oil drums.[5] Abortion was a crime. Hospitals refused to perform sterilizations for other than "valid medical reasons." [6]

All of this has changed. The Pill, IUD, and other contraceptives are easily available. The 1973 Supreme Court decision on abortion overthrew restrictive state laws, leaving the matter of abortion up to the woman concerned and her physician; the state would only be permitted to step in with regulations regarding the later stages of pregnancy. And in 1970, the National Fertility Study was able to report the dramatic finding that voluntary sterilization had become the most popular contraceptive method used by older couples. One-fourth of couples in which the wife was in the thirty to forty-four age group had been surgically sterilized. Among these couples there was an almost equal division as to which of the partners had undergone the operation.[7]

Obviously, these matters relate directly to how a modern woman thinks about her reproductive capabilities. Other kindred matters both present and future are also difficult to evade—questions regarding artificial insemination, frozen sperm banks, fertilizations of a woman's ova by her husband's sperm which are carried out in a laboratory and then replaced in her uterus (in efforts to help couples with infertility problems), the possibility of growing babies in controlled conditions outside the uterus—from conception to full term, so that a woman might have her own baby without the necessity of giving birth. Then there are the experiments in "cloning," in which the nuclei of cells containing genetic material are transferred from one person to the ova of another. Resulting embryos would be expected to develop as genetic carbon copies of the donor. Another related issue is the possibility of one day choosing the sex of our offspring.

In view of such research, a statement by Dr. Richard Bube (in connection with other achievements of medical science) seems appropriate. He writes, "More and more, God is bringing man to the place where man must make the decisions that in previous years he felt justified in leaving in the hands of God." [8] This can be frightening, or we can accept it as a challenge—a further step in carrying out the creation mandate to subdue the earth and have dominion over the works of God's hands (Gen. 1:28; Ps. 8:6).

Controlling our own fertility seems to be one part of this great responsibility that God has placed in our hands. If we accept this responsibility with a sense of stewardship and accountability to God, we can surely trust him for wise guidance in the many decisions we must make.

Some of these decisions are easier than others. The method of birth control, for example, can be decided according to the individual couple's preferences, after discussion with a physician and studying the matter thoroughly with regard to effectiveness and health factors, such as safety, side effects, and so on.

The choice of permanent birth control by means of a vasectomy for the husband or a tubal ligation for the wife may be a bit more difficult to make. Christians who have elected voluntary sterilization emphasize the need for husbands and wives to talk the matter over thoroughly beforehand with each other, with physicians, and with trusted friends, and to be absolutely sure that they do not want more children. This includes facing the possibility of the death of a child or the death of a spouse and later remarriage. Once the decision has been made to go ahead, however, the couple should determine that there will be no regrets, assuring one another that they have made the *right* decision and need not feel guilt or remorse. Christian husbands and wives who believe God intended sex not only for procreation, but for communication and recreation as well, testify of the tremendous freedom they experience in their sexual relationship after sterilization. No longer fearful of an unwanted pregnancy, they are free to enjoy one another and express their love to each other with a new spontaneity that enhances their marital union often to a greater degree than ever before.

No doubt the hardest decisions related to reproduction concern abortion. Christians differ widely in their views on the subject, with some calling it nothing short of murder and others saying it can be a humane, merciful act fully in accord with Christian principles. There is no denying that questions about abortion are agonizing ones. Theologians have never settled the issue of when a fetus "receives a soul" or becomes a human being. Thus, perhaps the Supreme Court was wise not only with respect to a woman's right to privacy and leaving the choice with her, but in interpreting the Constitution to refer to postnatal life only with regard to the rights of individuals. "The unborn have never been recognized in the law as persons in the whole sense," wrote Justice Harry Blackmun in the majority opinion. In Genesis, man became a living soul when God breathed into him the breath of life. R. F. R. Gardner, who is both a practicing gynecologist and an ordained clergyman, writes, "My own view is that while the fetus is to be cherished increasingly as it develops, we should regard its first breath at birth as the moment when God gives it not only life, but the offer of Life." [9]

Even so, decisions about terminating a pregnancy are not to be taken lightly or casually. Yet, at the same time, is abortion entirely out of the question for a Christian couple faced with an unplanned pregnancy at a time when it would be detrimental to the whole family? Or what about an unmarried coed who was carried away in the emotion of a moment she later regrets? What about a Christian couple who learn through genetic counseling that tests show their baby will be a mongoloid, or the wife who contracts rubella early in her pregnancy and knows her child is likely to be malformed? Does Christian morality insist that these pregnancies be carried through, even though bringing the child into the world may cause extreme emotional distress and financial hardships for the family? We think not. A decision to have an abortion in such a case can free the couple to have another child, a healthy, normal child that might otherwise never be born.

It is one thing to discuss these matters theoretically; it is quite another to face them in "real life." Perhaps that is why the title of

Gardner's book is so apt—*Abortion: the Personal Dilemma.* This book and the Christian Medical Society's *Birth Control and the Christian*[10] are most helpful in thinking through these issues.

ADOPTION

Adoption is another subject related to a woman's life-bearing function. One can bring life to children in other ways than giving birth to them. Some couples today look upon adoption as an excellent way of giving their love to little children while at the same time having a small part in easing population pressures. Rather than bring a new child into the world, the reasoning goes, why not give love to some child already here? It would seem in keeping with the spirit of Christian teachings on self-expending love to take into our homes children who might otherwise never know the love of a family—especially children who are hard to place for adoption, such as handicapped children or children of racially mixed parentage. An unmarried woman can also experience the joys of motherhood in this way.

PARENTHOOD IN THE TOTAL SCHEME OF THINGS

We have seen that all through history woman has been praised, worshiped, feared, and criticized for her reproductive capabilities.[11] From her body new generations come forth. Because of her, life continues upon the earth.

Yet the body is not the woman; it is only part of her. And motherhood is only one aspect of a woman's life, just as fatherhood is but one aspect of a man's life. A woman is not a baby-machine. She is a total person, with mind, heart, will, and a multitude of talents and abilities. Never must she think that she has nothing to offer the world except the fruit of her womb. She can also bring to the world the fruit of the Spirit (Gal. 5:22–23) and the fruit of her mind. And if God calls her to motherhood, she can realize that it is quality more than quantity that matters. She can give her best to her family, trusting God for wisdom and strength to enable her and her husband as partners together to "train up a child in the way he should go" (Prov. 22:6).

Where motherhood is seen as drudgery, duty, and inevitable destiny, it can limit a woman's potential and cause feelings of restlessness and even resentment. But motherhood freely chosen and creatively implemented can be one of the most exciting and joyous experiences a woman can know.

12. The Single Woman

Denied love, denied self-respect, denied companionship, denied economic security, a single woman often begins to believe that there is something wrong with her, that she is a freak. Few females can look at singleness as a positive state; for most, it is the worst of all possible worlds.
—"A Woman Is a Sometime *Thing*" [1]

"WHO'S YOUR BOYFRIEND?" is the question a girl is asked from the time she is old enough to answer. If she manages to graduate from college with only a B.A. and no Mrs., the question becomes, "Aren't you married yet?" After she has worked for several years, the question turns to a pitying, "Why isn't a nice girl like you married?"

Our language has no polite word for an unmarried woman past twenty-five. We can be thankful that all but the most thoughtless have given up "old maid" which has usually connoted rigidity and wretchedness. Some use "bachelor girl" and "career girl," but who wants to be called a "girl" all her life? "Spinster" is making a comeback and still may prove acceptable, but at the moment "single woman" is about the best we can do. It serves as a constant reminder, however, that pairs are the norm.

As if another reminder of the "Noah's ark syndrome" were needed! At the supermarket everything comes in the "family size." At church one has a choice of the young marrieds' class or the old marrieds' class. At work a memo from the president concerning a company dinner offers the following options for reply: "Yes, my spouse and I will be able to attend. I can attend, but my spouse cannot. Sorry, we cannot attend." Ministers are notorious for their cruel "jokes" about single women missionaries. And a recent Christian book on marriage for teens puts it bluntly: "The plan of the Creator is *marriage,* not singleness. . . . The plan of God is marriage. Singleness for religious service is a cultural tradition and not the plan of God." [2]

Another essay describes the single life with equal frankness:

Every game has its losers. Every game has those who refuse to play. In short, some females never marry. For such a woman, there is the threat of a life of sheer hell. She faces ridicule and humiliation. If she is a virgin, she is called a dried up old prune. If she has affairs, she is a slut. . . . Everyone, every day, subtly

145

or bluntly, points out to her that her life is a failure, that she is unfulfilled, that she has lost out.[3]

With psychiatrists, ministers, media, and meddling acquaintances continually warning that life without marriage is meaningless, why are 16.5 million women over twenty-five in this country still unmarried? About 4.2 million of them have never married and another 12.3 million have ended up separated, widowed, or divorced.

WHY ARE SOME UNMARRIED?

Society's most stereotyped assumption is that the unmarried woman is sick, a misfit. Any woman who is single past thirty is suspected of being frigid, neurotically dependent on her parents, homosexual, or abnormal in some way. One woman working in a church was asked by a parishioner if she planned to get married. When she replied that it was not a priority item at the moment, he rebuked her, "Don't ever say that. Every normal woman wants to get married and the church wants normal women!" A bestseller by Dr. David Reuben titled *Any Woman Can!* perpetuates this image. His case studies "show" that any woman who is unmarried can be "cured" of her disability by his psychiatric help.

Yet psychological studies have found single women second in happiness only to married men (married women and single men were far less happy). Studies comparing personal and social adjustment of groups of married and never-married women found no significant differences. Several studies have found that single women have even less emotional problems than married women. Singles are also physically healthier (only ninety-one singles die of cirrhosis of the liver compared with one hundred married women; only sixty-one die of homicide compared to one hundred marrieds!).[4]

A second shibboleth is that the single person is afraid of marriage. She comes from a broken home, her parents had a loveless relationship, her father was a sadist, she was raped at an early age, or some such reason. Romantic explanations include the rumor that she was once jilted or her true love died in the war. Now she overeats, effects a "masculine" posture, or downgrades marriage in order to avoid it.

Unfortunately, some of these suggestions are true in some cases. Many young people today have been very disillusioned by the marriages they see around them and want no part of it. Others do have emotional problems that keep them from risking the commitment that marriage requires. In fact many people, single and married, have certain hang-ups which keep them from living a full, satisfying life. But getting rid of all one's neuroses is no insurance against singleness.

Another accusation which is often tossed at the single woman is "You're too choosy!" Popular wisdom has it that "anyone who really wants to can get married." The Census Bureau disputes that: they say there are currently only ninety-five men for every one hundred women in this country. For the woman of above average talents the marriage market is even more restricted. As Jessie Bernard outlines graphically, men tend to marry women less intelligent, educated, or socially prominent than themselves. Thus single women tend to be the "cream of the crop" while single men are the "bottom of the barrel" to use Bernard's terms. Single women tend to be highly educated, upwardly mobile, have a strong achievement motivation, and thus higher incomes. Particularly in older age groups the gap between them and the available men is "a veritable chasm." [5]

Feminist Germaine Greer has asked, "If men are content to spend their leisure time with their intellectual inferiors, why cannot women be so?" [6] But most women would rather be single than settle for less than the type of soul companionship described in our chapters on marriage. The Christian woman, particularly, searches for a man with whom she can truly share a one-flesh relationship that includes spiritual as well as physical and intellectual communion. Is waiting for God's best being choosy?

Despite some of society's misconceptions, what are some of the real reasons for singleness? Some women are only temporarily single. Most articles in the popular press and even in religious periodicals which talk about "singles" are really only referring to those under twenty-five who are still in college or working and waiting a couple of years before marriage. Many young women are now choosing to postpone marriage until later in favor of graduate school, a short-term mission project, a job in which they can test their skills and get to know themselves. Some divorced or widowed women will remarry though in the meantime they suffer all the trials of the single woman and sometimes a few more since they have known the joys of marriage and may have several children to support.

Some women have freely chosen singleness, though many people find this difficult to believe. Actress Arlene Dahl once commented: "Any woman who 'goes it alone' must be a victim of circumstances; or else—if she's really doing so by her own personal choice—in my view, she's a bit misguided. I'm delighted if there are some who claim to be perfectly happy. But I do think it's a little like saying you're enjoying a diet of skim milk and hard-boiled eggs—just slightly suspect." [7]

It is sadly ironic that the Protestant church in its revolt against medieval monasticism elevates marriage and denigrates celibacy, and yet almost requires singleness of women who wish to serve the church. Many women, however, do love God and want to serve him enough to make this sacrifice. Their names lead the honor rolls of missionary servants. They are also often the hidden backbone in the offices of Christian organizations.

During a discussion of marriage and divorce, Jesus' disciples concluded that it might be better not to marry. Jesus agreed but noted, "Not all men can receive this precept, but only those to whom it is given. For there are eunuchs who have been so from birth, and there are eunuchs who have been made eunuchs by men, and there are eunuchs who have made themselves eunuchs for the sake of the kingdom of heaven. He who is able to receive this, let him receive it" (Matt. 19:11–12). Paul declared, "To the unmarried and the widows I say that it is well for them to remain single as I do" (1 Cor. 7:8).

John and Mary Ryan, in their book *Love and Sexuality: A Christian Approach,* speak at length of those who are single "for the sake of the kingdom." Those who have this gift are able to grow in maturity as loving persons without the usual human aid provided by marriage. They are totally at God's disposal and devote their lives to serving him. It is one of the highest sacrifices that one can make and those who have made it should command respect rather than contempt.

Some women, though they have not chosen singleness, have been able to accept it. Born and reared on the mission field, one woman returned to the U.S. for college, enjoyed her education, and got on well with other students but never found a man who understood her background or shared her call to return to the field. So she accepted her single state and found fulfillment in her vocation.

A woman need not close the doors to marriage completely—some women do marry for the first time in their forties, fifties, or even later—but she should not go through life constantly mourning her "loss." No one is completely able to choose her life. Many who have been extremely happy in marriage have been suddenly widowed. We can never have total freedom and peace in Christ until we are ready to face the worst possible event which we can conceive and still know that our faith in God will sustain us. Hopefully we will never have to face that thing which is our personal dread— martyrdom, the loss of a mate, the death of a child, a lifetime of singleness. However, if one is to have a mature Christian faith, one must wrestle through such a possibility with God until like Christ in Gethsemane we can say, "Thy will be done." And receive that will with arms outstretched to accept God's gift of love in whatever form he chooses to give it.

Some women have not chosen singleness and have not accepted it. For various reasons both personal and social, some women simply never have the opportunity to marry. This can be very difficult even for a Christian to accept. In speaking of the gift of celibacy Christ says, "Let anyone accept this who can." It is a "gift" few people ask for and when it comes, one is usually tempted to cry, "Why me, God?" and return it marked, "No, thanks!" Many single people have prayed that God would either fulfill their longings or take them away, but he has done neither.

"God has a plan for your life. He has a mate for you. Just pray about it." So blithely we give such advice to our young people, but there comes a point in every single woman's life when this advice begins to wear thin. She has prayed for years, but God just does not seem to have a mate for her. And a "plan" that does not include one is not much of a bargain.

She is tempted to blame God for disappointing her. After all, had not the books and ministers all said marriage was part of God's will? Many single women go through at least a period, if not a lifetime, of bitterness and rebellion. And instead of understanding from the church that at least partly precipitated the problem, they only hear sermons about how dried up and selfish single people can get. Or homilies on such texts as "My God shall supply all your needs" and "Ask and ye shall receive."

The spiritual conflicts these teachings set up inside a single woman are devastating. How can a single woman believe that God wants the best for her when he has not given her what the church and society say is best? How can she believe he answers prayer when he has not answered this her most desperate cry? How can she believe in his goodness when he refuses to fulfill the urgent longings which he has planted within her? The easiest response is just to turn her back on the church and on God and try to forget such agonizing questions.

Another solution is to blame herself. Perhaps God is punishing her for some sin. Perhaps he has put a lifetime curse on her. What can she do to atone, to expiate her guilt, to find favor in his sight? She confesses all the sins she can think of and pleads forgiveness for those of which she is unconscious or forgetful. She devotes herself to serving God. And still he does not "reward" her with a husband.

So she turns away from God and looks inward. Maybe she is the problem. She begins to believe the myths of society. The church

must have been wrong with its teachings about "waiting on God"—
one must work out one's own salvation. So she enters a rat race of
self-improvement. She slavishly reads all the women's magazines
and follows their advice. She buys all the "How to Catch a Husband"
books she can find. She enters psychotherapy. She has plastic
surgery. She diets, buys a new wardrobe, changes jobs to somewhere that there are lots of men. She frequents singles' bars even
if she doesn't drink. She goes to "Parents Without Partners" when
her only dependent is a cat. (Ann Landers once reported on a sober
woman who joined Alcoholics Anonymous to meet men.) And still
she has no husband. Her self-esteem is shattered. She is a God-
forsaken failure.

Finally she settles into a life of fatalistic resignation. After all, it
is just more of the same numbing waiting she has been doing
since kindergarten when she was taught to sit quietly. During her
teens she learned to wait for the phone to ring, wait for a boy to ask
her out, wait for him to kiss her. So she waits—and drifts from
job to job or floats in the same low-level position. Or she tries to
escape through sexual promiscuity, drugs, alcohol, exhaustion.
After all, there's nothing else to do "until I get married." After a
while weariness and boredom set in and the stereotyped "old maid"
is born.

Is there a way out of this slough of despair? Many books and articles on singleness sound as if the writer has completely "solved" her
problem and is now joyfully alone—which often leaves the single
reader feeling even more of a failure because she isn't an equally
"victorious Christian." But like most of life's struggles, living the
single life is an on-going, up and down battle. The difficult process
could be made easier by friends who care and understand, but too
often Christians are part of the problem rather than the solution.

WHAT CAN BE SAID?

What solutions are there? The church could be most helpful by admitting that while God did create Eve to be a companion to Adam,
Jesus never married. Was he only half a person? He lived on this
earth well into sexual maturity and the pressures on him to marry
were at least as great as those today. He who was Love Incarnate
must have ached to share that love in the most intimate way. He who
left the oneness of the Godhead in heaven must have longed for the
totality of that relationship. We see him in life surrounded by sleep-
ing disciples in his most agonizing hour, abandoned by them and by
his own Father in death. Yet who would say his life was incom-
plete, his potential unfulfilled?

The church could also help singles by remembering more often that Paul spoke of marriage, not singleness, as a limitation to serving God. How many positive sermons have you heard on the text "To the unmarried and the widows I say that it is well for them to remain single as I do" (1 Cor. 7:8) or "an unmarried woman, like a young girl, can devote herself to the Lord's affairs; all she need worry about is being holy in body and spirit. The married woman, on the other hand, has to worry about the world's affairs and devote herself to pleasing her husband" (7:34, JB)? Preachers, depending on their inclination, explain these verses away by either saying they were only given because the early Christians thought that the Great Tribulation and Second Coming were at hand (2,000 years later they are farther away?) or that the author's thinking was tainted by body-denying gnosticism. Why can we not just admit that Paul, like Jesus, saw real virtue in devoting one's life to God without the encumbrances of family, pleasant as those may be?

Every person, single or married, must eventually come to terms with her life. It is impossible to change anything one does not first accept. No amount of crying, complaining, cursing, counseling, or camouflaging will alter the fact that at the moment a woman is single. So she might as well make the best of it. Contrary to popular myth, marriage is not what every woman needs to live a complete life. Her needs are the same as those of every person: loving relationships with other people and a purpose that makes living worthwhile. For some women establishing a marriage and rearing a family constitute that relationship and purpose. But having babies is not every woman's calling. Single women can find fulfillment in other relationships and purposes. Most everyone has sexual reproductive organs, but God has also given each person unique capabilities. Finding her own talents and developing them for God's use is every Christian's task. As Dorothy Payne says in *Women Without Men,* the single woman must "pick up her option to choose her own lifestyle." [8]

The maturing Christian can take responsibility for her own life. Confident in God's love and providence, she can rest in his leading, knowing that his will is always our best. She does not have to struggle incessantly to find a husband, or worry lest God would let her miss his chosen one. Sometimes she will have to wrestle with God to find answers to her needs and questions, but in her grappling she will feel his strong arms and see his working. Ultimately she will see the truth in my favorite motto: "To believe in God is to know that all the rules will be fair—and that there will be wonderful surprises."

The single life can be a joyous one. Its greatest asset is freedom—

freedom to do enormous things like quit one's job and go to Africa or back to graduate school; freedom to do little things like not wash dishes for a week or buy a new painting without being accused of embezzling the kids' lunch money. The single woman's time is her own. She can waste it feeling sorry for herself and accepting society's pity, or she can use it to find joy in the myriad ways God offers it.

The single life well lived, however, must be a creative life. Single persons have the same needs as married persons—for sex, touch, affirmation, and sharing—but satisfying those needs outside the structure that society persists in calling "normal" requires creative work.

SEXUAL NEEDS

Single women have the same sexual drives and needs that God put in all human beings. For some, admittedly, this is not as great a problem as for others. Their sexuality has not been fully aroused or desires have waned with age. For others, however, coping with their sexuality is a real and constant struggle. While true for many who have never married, it can be overwhelming for the divorced or widowed woman. Those who write about sexuality or who counsel women have often been steeped in the myth that women's sexual drives, particularly those of the unwed woman, are minor in comparison to men's. But Masters and Johnson have found in their research what many women have always known: female sexuality can be as strong or stronger than the average man's.

Contemporary culture exacerbates the problem. One can hardly find a magazine, book, TV program, or movie that does not talk about sex, often in graphic detail. Secular magazines assume that everyone, single or married, is participating in sexual experience. Most assume that the "liberated" single woman is on the Pill. About the only dissenting voice comes from some of the radical feminist groups who declare the so-called "sexual revolution" as just another con game to exploit women. Yet even they see sexual abstinence as only a very temporary thing.

The church's renewed interest in sexuality seldom helps the single person either. Thankfully the church has turned from denouncing all sexuality as earthy and evil and begun to affirm it as an aspect of God's goodness, but religious leaders offer little advice to help singles. Sexuality is to be totally confined to marriage—and they assume everyone will marry.

Those who don't are offered little more than the cliché, "God is sufficient." While it is true that God does enable us to endure whatever our life may hold, God himself suggested that Adam needed more than his companionship, that "it is not good that the man should be alone."

What is the single woman to do? She cannot hide from the evidences of sexuality in our society. Repression of her own inner needs and drives will only lead to emotional disturbance. Rather the Christian woman seeking liberation in this area must fully accept her sexuality and thank God for it. God created all of us as sexual beings and pronounced his creation good. As the Holy Spirit he dwells within our very bodies and shares completely every struggle. The single woman as well as the married woman should seek to fully understand her sexual nature and how it influences her life.

First she must define sexuality and sexual needs. Since marriage has been elevated in our society as the one and only relationship, what a single woman sometimes perceives as sexual needs may be desires for companionship, emotional security, concern, closeness, love. While these elements should all be found in a good marriage, they often are not. And they can just as easily be found in a deep friendship. "Sexuality" has been defined by those speaking from a Freudian perspective as including any "affective" relationship between two people from mother and infant to football teammates. To avoid such confusion, we are speaking of "sex" in much narrower terms, as genital feeling and/or contact. "Aha!" some will say, "then the single woman has no real 'sexual' problem—she may desire companionship, etc., but surely since she's not married, she has no genital sexual feelings." Yes, many do have such feelings. So what can she do about them?

Nothing, is what most discussions offer. Particularly the Christian woman is warned against touching herself or anyone else. She is warned against flirting with married men, against "getting involved" with anyone outside marriage. She is even warned against close friendships with other women. No wonder she sometimes feels totally cut off from the human race!

Society in general often views the woman without sexual experience as warped, unnatural, and probably "all cobwebs inside." *Cosmopolitan* once ran an article titled "I Was an Overage Virgin" and *Redbook* printed "A Young Woman's Story" on the topic "Virginity Was My Problem." Both stories detailed the dilemma of women who had reached twenty-five with their hymens intact. One writer said she resorted to wearing the same clothes to work two days in a row and yawning a lot to make her coworkers think she was liberated enough to have an affair! The contempt with which society views celibacy once led a woman to remark that the phrase "virgins and martyrs," in Christian liturgy is redundant.

"Chastity" and "virginity" are certainly unpopular terms in our day. Even Christian women sometimes feel a certain ambivalence about admitting to it. Yet the founder and the history of Christianity bear witness to the fact that the celibate life can have positive meaning. One can achieve a harmony of sex and self which is free to love and serve many people rather than just one. Sexual abstinence need not lead to psychic trauma or emotional withdrawal. The celibate person can find a wholeness of personality that is open and responsive to all.

Sublimation has been called "God's message to the unmarried" in answer to the question of how to integrate sexuality into one's life. It is usually defined as channeling one's sexual energies into other activities. For some sublimation works; for others such a suggestion is mockery. The capacity for sublimation is developed comparatively early in life and is largely an unconscious ability to tolerate the frustration of instincts and unconsciously redirect them. To say to a woman who did not develop this in childhood and who is now suffering from sexual need, "You must sublimate," as if she could do so on the spot, is futile.[9]

Some women have tried to take this advice. They have poured all their energies into, say, their job. They become compulsive, perfectionist, demanding because they are seeking to derive more satisfaction from work than it was ever intended to provide. As one artist commented, "The idea that creative work, such as painting or writing, is a substitute for sex is hogwash. It meets a different kind of need."

Sublimation cannot cope with genital feeling, the physical tensions which many women feel. Masturbation, the stimulation of one's own organs to the point of orgasm, is practiced by one-half to two-thirds of all women, single or married. Parents and teachers used to warn teen-agers that acne and insanity resulted from "self-abuse," but scientific research has found no substantiation of any ill effects. Freudians have warned that the woman who has learned to achieve orgasm through "childish" clitoral stimulation will not be able to switch in marriage to a "mature" experience of vaginal orgasm. But Masters and Johnson have proved that there is only one type of orgasm and physiologically it is produced in the same way whether one is participating in masturbation or intercourse.[10] The only harm caused by masturbation is guilt produced in those who have been taught it is wrong.

Christian writers have been taking a new look at the subject.[11] Some have argued that it is wrong because it is self-centered rather than other-centered, body-centered rather than person-centered. Some even agree with Thomas Aquinas who said that masturbation was worse than fornication because at least in the latter two people are involved as "God ordained." However, the Bible clearly condemns fornication (see 1 Cor. 6:9–7:2; 1 Thess. 4:1–8; Eph. 5:3–6), but says nothing of masturbation. Which leads others to say that it must at least be morally neutral. Because it offers a way of dealing with sexual tensions without "violating" another person (committing fornication) or "using" him (as sometimes in petting), some Christians approve the practice. As one says, it may well be "the wise provision of a very wise Creator" who "gave it to us because he knew we'd need it." [12] Particularly for the older single person (perhaps widowed or divorced) who is not just "waiting for marriage," masturbation can be accepted from God as a joyous release.

Many Christians do worry, however, that masturbation is linked with lust and that it can become a preoccupation. Just as sex is only one aspect within the total marriage relationship, so the single person must keep sex in perspective within her life. No one aspect— sex, work, hobby, or whatever—should become an "idol," a totally consuming passion. Jesus particularly warned about guarding one's sexual thought life (Matt. 5:28). Any fantasies that toy with the idea of sexual relations with any actual person to whom one is not married are wrong. But scientific studies have concluded that as many as half of all women who masturbate do so without fantasies of specific people in mind. With God's help, the Christian woman can avoid fantasies that corrupt existing relationships and confine her thoughts to imagining what her responses would be within an ideal and perhaps future marriage.

Sexual relationships with other people outside marriage can be very tempting for the single woman. Society, even in Christian circles, offers many opportunities for "body sex"—no commitment involved, no communion sought. "Everybody's doing it. Why not have some fun as long as nobody gets hurt?" goes the rationalization for participation. A Christian can sometimes even lead herself to believe that such opportunities are gifts from God. But such encounters do not satisfy one's deeper longings and each participant must live with the knowledge that they have exploited another person and been themselves exploited.

But what about more committed relationships? Can two people who have no intention of marrying yet offer each other freely and lovingly the physical pleasures which cuddling and petting bring? Can they enter into an affair? Some of the answers are clear-cut; others must be resolved through a personal grappling with God's Word. The single person cannot become involved in a sexual relationship with a married person—adultery is clearly forbidden by Scripture. For the single person to have sexual intercourse with anyone is fornication and that also is prohibited by Scripture. Relationships involving less than total union between single persons are not so explicitly covered by Scripture. To discern God's mind in this area involves constant prayer and reading of his Word as well as an honest knowledge of oneself and a fair evaluation of one's partner. Where does mutual affection end and exploitation begin? What will bring joy and what will produce guilt? The answers are not easy.

Another way of dealing with one's sexuality is to become involved in a lesbian relationship. Even a Christian woman, conscious of her own sexual needs and driven by a natural desire for an intimate relationship, may be caught up in such an arrangement. Embittered by the perverted state of many marriages today, some contemporary feminists even laud the lesbian life as an alternative to oppressive male-female relationships.

We must be careful to define homosexuality. The National Institute of Mental Health defines it as "physical contact between two individuals of the same gender which both recognize as being sexual in nature and which ordinarily results in sexual arousal." [13] Two women can have a very deep and close relationship, even living together for many years, without lesbianism ever entering the picture.

The Jews classed homosexuality, along with incest and other unnatural vices, as especially culpable practices. Leviticus 18:22 specifically says, "You shall not lie with a male as with a woman." To do so would be "unnatural" because God created male and female to "mirror" each other in a way that two individuals of the same gender cannot. Paul declared that homosexual activity was one of many foolish exchanges which men make: idolatry, philosophical confusion, and sexual sinfulness. They "exchanged the glory of the immortal God for images resembling mortal man or birds or animals or reptiles" (Rom. 1:23); "they exchanged the truth about God for a lie" (1:25); and "Their women exchanged natural relations for unnatural, and the men likewise gave up natural relations with women and were consumed with passion for one another" (1:26-27).

Neither Paul nor any other biblical writer speaks of a "homosexual orientation" or of an attraction for members of one's own sex. Nor do they confuse the issue in any way that would make deep friendships or Christian affection suspect. The engaging in actual homosexual acts is what the Bible considers sinful. As Christians we must never label others lightly. Sometimes women students are afraid to comfort each other with an embrace for fear that someone will report them to the dean as deviant. Young women experimenting with lesbian behavior at camp or college have been branded lesbian in such a way that they feel they must act out such a role for life. Compassion, rather than condemnation, should be our response. Many times even overt homosexual behavior is only a manifestation of a deeper psychological problem and a cry for help. As Christians we must heed that cry rather than cutting the person off from all communication.

The idea of "save yourself as a gift for your husband" has always been a part of Christianity's teaching on premarital chastity. But "hope deferred makes the heart sick" (Prov. 13:12). What has been a treasure turns to ashes when a woman has passed the "usual" age of marriage and still has not found a man with whom she can share herself. The temptation comes to give the gift anyway.

And sometimes she does and regrets it. She feels forever marked by sin, totally cut off from God. One young woman declared that she knew she would spend her life single because God was punishing her for involvement with a man some years ago. Yet Christianity has never taught that chastity was solely a physical condition that could be lost forever through one mistake. Chastity is purity of heart. God stands ready at all times to forgive those who confess their sins and seek his healing. Our sexuality was originally a gift from him and, single or married, the wise use of our sexuality is a gift we offer back to him.

Despite what our culture tells us, sexual union is not the goal of our existence. Marriage is only an image, an imperfect reflection, of the communion we will know with God and with each other in heaven. We call that communion "transparency." Paul says, "Now we are seeing a dim reflection in a mirror; but then we shall be seeing face to face. The knowledge that I have now is imperfect; but then I shall know as fully as I am known" (1 Cor. 13:12, JB). The Old Testament often uses the word "know" in discussing the marital union. Some have termed it simply a euphemism for intercourse, but the Bible is pointing toward a deeper relationship between two people involving openness, honesty, the "knowledge" of another person. The same word is used of our relationship with God. While a single woman may never share the delights of sexual intercourse with a man she loves, she can enjoy a "knowing" relationship, the essence of the marital communion, with God and with Christian friends.

TOUCH NEEDS

Our society, most unfortunately, has labeled all bodily contact as sexual. In many countries men hug and kiss each other upon meeting, women hold hands walking down the street, but we are taught to avoid such behavior as homosexual. We permit touch only under highly ritualized conditions. So men have invented all sorts of athletic mock-combat situations where it is perfectly acceptable to tackle one's opponent or put an arm around one's teammate. Unfortunately women do not usually get to participate in these games. The "average" woman satisfies her need for touch through the embrace of her husband and the hugs of her children.

Jesus often touched those he met—and his hands brought healing, both physical and spiritual. The early church laid hands on new members, on the sick, and on those sent out to minister as a sign of the Holy Spirit's presence and power. Christians were urged to greet one another with a holy kiss. Even today Eastern Orthodox churchmen retain this custom in the form of an embrace. Yet when liturgical reformers in this country sought a way to reinstate the "kiss of peace" into the communion service, they could barely get people in the pews to shake hands!

Yet we all need physical as well as verbal expressions that we are accepted, appreciated, valued. Researchers tell us that we have deep need for touching, stroking, caressing in addition to sexual need for orgasmic experience. They are not the same, though they are often confused. Psychologists call it "skin hunger." Husband and wife meet these needs for each other with a quick hug, a back rub, a supportive arm around the waist. The mother does not verbalize her love for her child at all times but cuddles him in her arms, strokes his head, or gives him a kiss.

The single woman observes these acts and feels very much left out. Dr. Marc Hollender, who has studied what he calls the need to be held, found that in some women (and men) the need for cuddling was even stronger than the desire for sex. One woman described it as "almost a physical feeling . . . an ache." [14] Cuddling represents security, protection, comfort, contentment, and love. Without it the women in Hollender's study became tense, let down, rejected, hurt, lonely. Many of them felt they must make sexual advances or give sexual responses in return for being held. Although some would wrap themselves in blankets or fuzzy sweaters or rock themselves as a substitute, none found satisfaction for their longings outside of actual holding.

The single woman who feels acutely this need for touch and holding often experiences misunderstanding when she tries to meet it. Men will invariably interpret most any reaching out on her part as a sexual advance and will either rebuff her sharply or respond sexually in a way she does not desire at all. Yet there are both men and women who do understand the single woman's needs and can respond. One Christian wife even encourages her husband, a very loving man, to occasionally hug a widow or give a single friend a backrub on their living room floor. I have several friends, both men and women, who are not afraid to greet me with a hug. For a woman alone, these can be very precious gestures.

Warmth and closeness can also be conveyed by eyes and voice. To some Christians the Holy Spirit seems to give this gift in abundance. In their presence one feels whole, accepted, loved. The single woman who cultivates this gift will be able to be honest and open with others—and she will in turn find others reaching out to her. Of course there will be times when she must reassess motives, check thoughts, evaluate responses. But the rewards of sharing oneself are enormous.

"Skin hunger" is primarily for the touch of another, but it can also be somewhat satisfied in solitude. The single woman should not underestimate the joys of bubble baths, silky robes, and soft linens. Her body needs to run, dance, sing, and shout. In our sedentary society she needs to find ways to unwind, to use her body fully. Bicycling, tennis, swimming, hiking, even doing exercises on the living room floor help. A pet offers an opportunity to stroke and to receive stroking—and long walks with a dog are excellent exercise.

Our bodies are meant to bring us all kinds of pleasures. The single woman need not be denied all of them.

AFFIRMATION NEEDS

In a society which equates love and marriage, the single woman often feels unloved and incapable of loving. As one woman commented in despair, "I mean nothing to anyone, therefore I am nothing." Or as another said, "Surely, God cannot exist in someone whom no one wants or loves?" [15] When no human being loves us, it is difficult to believe that God in heaven does. The single woman easily falls prey to self-pity here, but it does no good to play God to Elijah and remind her that her mother probably loved her or that she would certainly be missed by the friendly neighborhood service station attendant! Every person needs to feel worthwhile, valued as a person, accepted into the "family of man."

The church should be one place where a person can feel loved and accepted. After all, did not Jesus say, "Come to me, all who labor and are heavy laden, and I will give you rest" (Matt. 11:28)? Yet the single woman often feels most left out in church. "It's the place of my deepest loneliness," admitted one woman. Another explained, "I'm tired of singing in the choir or teaching a Sunday school class, but it's hard to always have to sit alone in the congregation amid all those families. There's just no place for us." Some single women just drop out of the church, particularly in the city where no one attempts to get to know her if she does attend, so no one misses her if she does not.

What could the church do to make single women feel more at home? Ministers could be more sensitive concerning the single person and avoid such statements as "only in marriage does one become a whole person" or filling their sermons with illustrations all taken from family life. Women could be encouraged to use their talents without discrimination. Why shouldn't a single woman serve on the church board if her job is in business or on the Christian education committee if she's a teacher? Study groups could be centered around topics and issues that would challenge all members, rather than always dealing with family life. Would you believe a newsletter from a suburban church which advertised a class with the stipulation "Limited to married people"? Since the topic was one that would interest few single people anyway, the prohibition stung like a deliberate slap in the face. Couples could be urged to attend separate classes and all participants encouraged to contribute to discussion. Many churches have also found enrichment through small groups meeting during the week for Bible study and deep sharing. If single persons are welcomed and accepted by such groups, both marrieds and singles would gain a great deal of understanding and empathy for one another. After all, the church is supposed to be the family of God.

With good programming and leadership, "youth groups" for single adults can have a real ministry—but they are usually aimed at the under 35s. After that a person is left out of church life until she is old enough to qualify for the senior citizens' club! Singles generally are not interested in a group aimed simply at matchmaking (a respectable version of the dating bar); but they do find participation rewarding in a group with worthwhile objectives like Bible study or a mission project.

Generally the single woman looks to her job as a source of personal satisfaction and affirmation of worth. Psychologically speaking, the single woman, even more than a married person, needs to develop as a person through meaningful work and activities which in one way or another give scope to her creative drives. To be frustrated in one's vocation obviously makes it far more difficult to see singleness as a meaningful and fulfilling way of life.[16]

Yet many single women are in depersonalizing and boring jobs. Locked into the lowest, most meaningless, least remunerative positions, they express their frustration in inefficiency, pettiness,

bickering. And society says, "Well, she's just a bitchy old maid."
Since her vocation is often the center of a single woman's life, she
must not allow herself to be trapped in a hopeless position. Part of
the panic of being single is being caught in a situation where
marriage looks like the only form of salvation. Getting married,
however, to "someone who will take me away from all this" is no
formula for success. This is where the single woman must take
responsibility for her own life, get up, and get out of her rut.

A single woman's future financial security and independence
rest solely on the development of her vocation skills. Younger
women are often counseled away from advancement programs
because "with a Ph.D. or as an executive, you'll never find a
husband." So she ends up thirty-five, without a husband anyway, and
still at the lowest level of her profession. Young women instead
should strive early to get all of the vocational training they are
capable of and desire. But it is never too late. The older single
woman will find it frighteningly risky to change jobs or cities or
even give up a job to return to school for further education, but
the sacrifices are worth the rewards in self-esteem and advancement. Unhampered by family, the single woman is free to take the
risk. She has no one to blame but herself if she is stuck at the
bottom. If she is discriminated against because she is a woman, she
can seek legal redress. Today as organizations become aware of
women's rights, she can often move ahead quickly if she has
attained the necessary credentials.

To anyone who piously asks if she should be striving for financial
reward, she can reply that her tithe will be larger. The single
woman must be concerned about insurance and retirement finances.
She has a tendency to drift through life, always thinking that some
day she will have a husband to make all those financial plans. If she
doesn't, she may well end up old and poor and alone, a very
difficult situation in our society. If she does marry later, her husband
will be happy to know his wife is solvent.

A single woman also need not be denied the comforts of home and
family if she desires them. Many Christians feel somehow that
having possessions is sinful, and they enjoy projecting this guilt
onto single people. They jealously eye the single person's new
car or good wardrobe. Christian organizations in particular feel that
women especially should work for significantly lower salaries and
effect a poverty level lifestyle. While a Christian should not be
covetously enslaved by possessions, Christ did once say that the
laborer is worthy of his hire. And this applies as well if the
laborer happens to be female and single. Since her job is the source

of her self-worth and worth is measured in our society in terms of pay, a decent salary for a single woman is very much a part of her affirmation.

The single woman who enjoys "pretty things" should not be denied them simply because she has never gone through a series of wedding showers to get them. Nor should she store up treasures in a "hope chest." She should purchase what she desires and use them for her own joy and to entertain others. One doesn't have to be married to exercise the gift of hospitality. If she longs for things like silver and china that usually come to the tune of wedding bells, she should select patterns and let family and friends purchase them for Christmas and birthdays. They will be happy to know that they are giving something she will really use and enjoy.

Wherever she lives can be "home" to the single woman. Thousands of urban women live in YWCAs or "hotels for women." Perhaps they are content in their 9 x 12 rooms, but there is no reason why they should not have a lovely apartment, condominium, or house. A single woman is tempted to think of her apartment as always temporary, simply some place to live "until I get married." Signing a long-term lease or buying furniture seems like an admission of defeat, yet it can be a source of joy. It takes real guts for a single woman to apply for and sign a twenty-year mortgage on a house, but it also represents security, permanence, "a home of my own" in which to settle down—to say nothing of equity and tax breaks!

And that home need not be devoid of children. A single woman has always been able to serve as a loving "aunt" to other people's children, but she has generally been denied children of her own. Today this is changing. Laws in most states allow single persons to adopt children or to become foster parents, particularly to kids with a handicap or mixed racial ancestry. Even one parent who really loves a child is much better than institutional care. There is also a growing trend for single women to intentionally bear a child. Some Christians are beginning to wonder if artificial insemination might be permissible for such single women who desperately want a child of their own but yet don't want to commit fornication.

Many single women have found that sharing their love with a child has brought new meaning and purpose to life. One woman who became guardian to her mentally retarded younger sister after the death of their mother commented, "I suppose some people pity me when they see us together, but they shouldn't. She gives me so much. The advantages far outweigh the disadvantages. I don't think I could love my own child more—in fact she seems like my own child now that Mother is gone. Although others in the family may spend more of the waking hours with her, she comes to me now as her authority and security. She's a bundle of sweetness in my life."

Several years ago an unmarried teacher took a seven-year-old girl from an orphanage to the zoo as part of a volunteer project. When the woman asked the child what she would like to call her, the child replied, "Mother." A year later a judge made it official. The fact that this affirmation grows out of choice and affection rather than simply the natural processes of biology, makes it a very special one.

SHARING NEEDS

Ask any single person what is the greatest problem of being single and they will undoubtedly say, "Loneliness." One side of the coin is the freedom not to have to consider anyone else in making one's decisions. The other side is the fact that no one else has to care about the single person. God said in the beginning that it was not good for man to be alone. A contemporary psychologist declares, "The deepest need of man is the need to overcome his separateness, to leave the prison of his aloneness." [17] One can break out of one's isolation, but it takes effort. And the single person gets very little help. Once we have discovered essentially who we are, we long to share that self in an intimate relationship with another. For many people this intimate relationship is marriage. Yet this is not automatic. Many marriages know no bonds of intimacy beyond physical coupling, while many single persons, aside from sexual union, have found the deepest sharing within friendship.

To avoid intimacy usually leads to a deep sense of isolation and self-absorption. Some single women become almost paralyzed by this sense of isolation; they just sit around in a "blue funk," a state of suspended animation, waiting for a man to somehow take them from the shelf and put them back into the center of "real life." Others try various ways to avoid loneliness through overindulgence in food, sleep, drugs, or alcohol. They develop hypochondria, they seek forgetfulness in a ceaseless round of meaningless activities, they bury themselves in overwork. Some, confusing bodily intimacy for true interpersonal relationship, enter all kinds of superficial, inappropriate, or destructive relationships. Some simply refuse to meet the challenge and retreat into infantile dependency on parents or relatives. Yet the problem remains, a gnawing hole in the middle of life.

How can the single person break out of her isolation? It is not easy to love without knowing that one is loved. As Christians we know theologically that God loves us, that through the death of Jesus Christ we are reconciled to communion with God. His is not a love that we can buy or that we must earn. He loves us freely, completely, steadfastly. He offers us daily, moment-by-moment, companionship. And he promises never to leave us.

Yet without the experience of concrete, interpersonal expressions of love, it is difficult sometimes for the single woman to realize the love of God existentially. Not having been loved and chosen by another human being, the single woman may have difficulty feeling that she is loved by God and that she can love herself. Society continually hammers away at the message that if she is unloved, she is unlovable.

We are taught to view love as a passive operation, a waiting to be loved.[18] We are taught to think of finding love in terms of being "attractive" enough—having the good looks, clothes, intelligence, winsome personality, money, social position, or prestige enough to draw others.[19] The single woman who adopts this philosophy, as we have seen, is caught on a frustrating treadmill of self-salvation.

Others see "love" in terms of either dependence, submission, and reliance on family stabilities, or domination, possessiveness, and the need for control. Parents sometimes involve their single children in this type relationship. For example, a woman once wrote "Dear Abby" to say her mother had made her promise never to marry but always to care for her. Now the daughter is sixty-five and her mother ninety, her life is spent and she deeply regrets what might have been if she had had the courage to break out of such a possessive relationship. Marriage can be an equally possessive relationship which cuts both partners off from outside friends. This places unnatural strains on the marital union and leaves single persons with few sources of friendship. It also leaves the widow defenseless.

A possessive relationship is first of all sinful because it allows another person to occupy the central place God wants to take in our love. Secondly, it is harmful to the other person in sapping her vitality, stifling her development. Thirdly, it is doomed to failure. Being human, such a friend will either fail to live up to our expectations or at least leave us in death. Only Christ has promised never to fail or forsake us—and only he has the power to fulfill that promise. He alone is our ultimate security, and our ultimate source of love.

Love is not to be found in being attractive, being dependent, or being in control. The "art of loving" is learning to express love, to exercise one's capacity to love. As Erich Fromm says, "Love is not primarily a relationship to a specific person; it is an attitude, an orientation of character which determines the relatedness of a person to the world as a whole, not toward one 'object' of love." [20] Loving is not something that goes on only between marriage partners or parents and children. Christ constantly encouraged his followers to love others as he had loved them. The early church was characterized by love for one another.

The source of our love, single or married, is God's love. "He who loves is born of God and knows God. . . . if God so loved us, we also ought to love one another. . . . if we love one another, God abides in us and his love is perfected in us" (1 John 4:7, 11–12). He calls us and enables us to love. The Christian single woman will find many God-given opportunities to perfect the art of loving.

God's love will radiate in her eyes and smile. One of the delightful things about children is that they will not flinch if one stares at them but often will return a steady look of curiosity that sometimes ends in a smile. It's sad that growing up often means that we learn to avert our eyes, to restrain the smile that might become the first bridge to friendship. A steady gaze, a warm smile can be ways of saying to another person that she is accepted, taken seriously, loved. Sometimes a single person needs to receive such reassurance before she is able to give it—but when God enables her to give first she often finds her openness rewarded.

In order to meet her needs to share her life, the single woman must reach out. She will find that even though she may not have one with whom to share everything, she can find many with whom she can share much. It's often easiest to find someone to share one's troubles because people need to feel needed. When my father first suffered a heart attack, I found it difficult to share my burden with my coworkers out of fear that they would not care or that they would be embarrassed by the necessity of responding. Yet when I was able to tell several, I found them eager to support me and my family in prayer and concern.

Surprisingly, it is more difficult to find someone with whom to share our joys. Yet when there is no one with whom to share a tribute, savor a compliment, or rejoice in a job completed, life seems empty and meaningless. If someone is in real difficulty, we will listen and help because it makes us feel important and superior. But if someone shares a small triumph, we immediately say, "How nice . . . but listen to what happened to me!" Or we make a perfunctory response and then find some way to deflate the other's joy. Why is it we are jealous of others' happiness or threatened by their advancement? A single woman particularly needs to know that what she is doing is worthwhile. She needs people who can share her joys and reinforce each contribution to her self-esteem. Paul speaks of the church as Christ's body in which "if one member suffers, all suffer together, if one member is honored, all rejoice together" (1 Cor. 12:26).

Single women often long to share at least part of their lives with men as well as women, but they are constantly warned of the dangers of cross-sex friendships. Some think them impossible: "God didn't build men's or women's emotional structure for prolonged male-female confidentials. Neither sex can ta:k of personal problems very long and keep their thoughts in objective focus." [21] True, many a single woman has learned to her regret that a favorite masculine "line" begins "My wife doesn't understand me any more."

Yet there are often male colleagues with whom one can cultivate enjoyable and helpful friendships in order to discuss those problems which are often a man's province in marriage—the car, the house, insurance, investments. And some men, married or single, can sustain a serious friendship with a single woman. Of course such relationships require honesty and vigilance to keep them on a proper moral plane. Sometimes this involves candid confrontation of sexual overtones that may develop. The Christian woman must take care that she does not become an "office wife," supplanting her colleague's wife. But a deep, mutual friendship can be cultivated which often extends into his home with the single woman becoming a friend also to his wife and children. A wife who is secure in her marriage and a single woman who is honest with God and herself need not be rivals.

In fact they can be the best of friends. The manuals which discourage the single woman from reaching out to married men, often go further and caution against friendships with those of her own sex. An otherwise excellent article on the single life in a Sunday school paper for teens contained an admonition against forming a "too-close friendship with someone of their own sex." While this was probably meant as a warning against homosexuality, the wording undoubtedly left teens with the message that any close friendship is wrong. The single person's only opportunity for intimacy is through genuine friendship.

German theologian Dietrich Bonhoeffer once said that true community is characterized by three gifts of God: sacrificing for one another in love, praying for each other, and forgiving one another's sins and lifting the burden of guilt.[22] As Protestants we are sometimes hesitant to exercise that final gift. We reject the idea of "absolution," yet it is really just the giving of a verbal reminder to the penitent that God is always here to forgive and heal. Confession is essential to human relationships. Deep love can never grow until we are willing to open our lives and get rid of the sins which we have kept hidden.[23]

There comes a point in any relationship where, if the two people are to go on to intimacy and communion, they must be ready to let each other see their faults and weaknesses as well as their virtues. Each must be ready to accept the other's faults and forgive his shortcomings. This involves great vulnerability and risk. Some have taken the risk and been hurt. Some have developed scar tissue so thick no one can get close to them again. But Christ can also dissolve that tissue and heal those scars if we are willing to let him. And we can find true community, even outside marriage.

Sometimes this involves living together. Single women continually debate whether one should or should not have a roommate. Ultimately it must be an individual decision based on desire and temperament. One should not live with someone just because one is afraid to be independent. A roommate should not be simply a financial convenience. Nor should one share an apartment just because parents warn that "you'll get so set in your ways you won't be able to adapt to a husband!" There's really not much sense in the idea of living with someone you don't like as preparation for marriage!

On the other hand, two women who are compatible should not be afraid to share an apartment just because it isn't considered the "liberated" thing to do or because people will "wonder." Many single women have found deep friendship and great companionship in living together. One of the most difficult things for the single person is to grow old alone. Banding together to form a home of their own has been the solution for many single women.

A more radical-sounding solution and yet a very old one being proposed repeatedly these days is the "commune"—it used to be called a "religious community." Some Christian communes include both single and married people. Some share all aspects of life; others have separate apartments in one building and come together for meals and worship. Groups of single women have also banded together in a communal life.[24]

Yet living together is not the essence of relationship. Communion can also develop over great distances. As we said in the Preface, Letha and I decided to write this book more or less as a business agreement. Yet before we ever met each other face to face, there developed in our correspondence an openness and honesty which laid the groundwork for intimate friendship. Since then we have had long hours of discussion at the typewriter or face to face; we have had deep disagreements and honest confrontations, times of confession and forgiveness, times of sharing triumph and tragedy.

Our love has grown constantly. Not a love that seeks to pour the other person into our mold or to possess and dominate the other person, but a love which accepts, encourages, fosters the other person's growth and good before our own.

Ours is a friendship of spirit and intellect, but also of day-to-day practical life. Though neither of us is generally the effusive type, we have learned the value of affection exchanged through embraces and backrubs. We've learned to rejoice together rather than envy the other's joys. We've each gained a much more realistic view of the other's life. Shopping, cooking, and cleaning for four, even if they are a much loved family, is just more work, not more fun. Children are a great joy, except when they are silly or cranky. A bustling household leaves little time for loneliness, but it also holds little room for solitude. Most of all, in each other we've found a friend to love, trust, confide in, and depend on.

A single woman is, after all, not a breed apart but simply another member of the family of God, a human being with all the gifts and needs of other human beings. She asks no more than any other person and she stands ready to give all that a person is capable of giving.

13. Wasting the Church's Gifts

Caller to radio talk show: "What do you think of Philip's four daughters who prophesied?"

Guest minister: "It just means they witnessed for Christ."

Caller: "But why can't women preach and teach?"

Minister: "That ministry is for men only and I can give you a very good reason: God made roosters to crow and hens to lay eggs." [1]

THIS STORY MAY ILLUSTRATE in more ways than one why the church today is in trouble! Christian poultry farmers tell us they keep roosters on their farms and call pastors to their local church to do a lot more than crow. Christian women tell us they want to do more for the church than bring children to Sunday school, warm the nursery nest, and fry eggs at pancake breakfasts.

Despite the varied ministries which women exercised in the early church, women have been systematically excluded from the ordained ministry and the power structure of the church. Today the issue is being raised in many churches, Protestant and Catholic, evangelical and liberal, but the response is still often akin to Archie Bunker's on television's "All in the Family." In a theological debate with his wife one night, he summarized the issue with his usual pungency: "Stifle yourself, Edith. God don't want to be defended by no dingbat!"

Most churches do permit women a variety of lay ministries—making pies for the church supper, doing macramé for the bazaar, redecorating the social hall, collecting clothes for missionaries, teaching the toddlers, and even leading a housewives' Bible study. But these ministries are usually limited to the domestic sphere and seldom integral to the church's mission to the world. For example, the church bulletin one Sunday advertised a "Men for Missions" breakfast coming up at a special restaurant. Men were also invited to visit a seminary in another state to discuss possible calls to the ministry with a leading theologian. A third announcement simply stated: "Women are needed to help make Raggedy Ann dolls for the nursery."

Women have been permitted a wider role, on a semi-clerical level, if they promise to do it elsewhere! Many women with leadership and evangelistic gifts have volunteered for missionary service overseas or in "underprivileged" areas of this country. One evangelical denomination which would not consider allowing a woman to pastor an established church has let an outstanding woman, and those women she has been able to draw around her, carry on a difficult work in Appalachia. Yet the work of these women is downgraded by repeated statements that God uses them only because men refuse to answer his call.

On the level of officially ordained clergy, women are scarce. Though some eighty Protestant denominations around the world do ordain women, not more than 5 percent of the ministers in these churches are women—though in every denomination more than half of the members are. And these denominations comprise a small minority of all Christians. The largest groups, which rely heavily on tradition—Roman Catholicism, Orthodoxy and the Anglican Communion—do not ordain women. Nor do many evangelical and fundamental groups.[2]

These churches' understanding of the ministry and the reasons they raise for denying ordination to women affect the role of women throughout the churches. In the Catholic tradition, priests are sacramentally commissioned to pronounce absolution and to celebrate the Eucharist. Their powers have been passed down from Christ and the apostles and they serve as dispensers of God's sacramental grace to his people. Protestant ministers are commissioned more as preachers, teachers, guides. Their essential function is the ability to publicly proclaim the gospel, to correctly interpret and teach the Word of God. Organizing and directing congregational activities are also important to their role. Why then are women generally excluded from the "ministry"?[3]

SCRIPTURAL PROHIBITIONS

Many people simply assume that "women should keep silence in the churches" (1 Cor. 14:34) and "I permit no woman to teach or to have authority over men" (1 Tim. 2:12) automatically rule out women pastors. As we have seen, and as the vast majority of denominational commissions which have analyzed these Scriptures have concluded, there is no basis here for denying women ordination.[4]

The issue is usually approached more broadly, if more bluntly. A contemporary Roman Catholic theologian put it this way: "The reason . . . for denying women the right to teach is a reason that is absolute and universal, based on the natural condition of inferiority and subjection that is the position of women." [5] The history of theology is strewn with such statements. Scriptural justification is usually sought in terms of "the order of creation" which we considered earlier. This is often buttressed by psychological arguments that women are by nature less apt at reasoning, less capable of handling doctrine objectively, more easily deceived, less assertive, less capable of public speaking. [6]

In Roman Catholic circles women have traditionally been told that they are incapable of receiving the "indelible character" which orders confer. This conjures up an image of paper or cloth so highly sized or glazed that God's indelible ink won't mark on it and simply washes off. Theologically this is not what the phrase means at all. The "character" of the priest is his spiritual power given by God at his ordination and used by him to perform the sacraments through which God acts. "Indelible" simply means that a sacrament cannot be repeated, that it is "once for all" (baptism and confirmation are also considered so). Thus, to say women are incapable of receiving "indelible character" is to say that first, God refuses to endow women with his power and second, that women are incapable of being validly baptized or confirmed either. [7]

Protestants speak more in terms of "the keys" or "ruling authority." They argue that "The New Testament evidence thus requires, in the present age, that the ruling-teaching office be restricted to the man and that the woman be restricted from it because she is a woman." Or as a Reformed pastor declared: "The whole of Scripture witnesses with one accord that to man is confided the heavy task of ruling, to woman the beautiful task of serving." [8]

The Orthodox variant on this theme reaches back into the Old Testament teachings on woman's periodic "impurity." [9] This comes close to pagan beliefs that women simply have "bad mana" and thus should not be allowed to participate in mystery or magic. In the Christian tradition women have been the ones most often labeled "witches." Yet if a woman was allowed the most intimate functions of bearing, nursing and nurturing the Son of God, should not women today be able to handle his body and blood?

Overall, it is clear that while many people feel they are arguing on the basis of scriptural prohibitions, they are simply standing on theological tradition based on cultural prejudices. What they are saying is that for one sex, half the human race, sexual differentiation is a handicap so crippling that no amount of personal talent, intelligence, piety, or even divine enabling can make them fit ministers of the gospel.

LACK OF SCRIPTURAL EXAMPLE

On the whole the Bible is a masculine book and reflects patriarchal cultures. God is spoken of in masculine terms; the Old Testament highlights patriarchs, priests, and male prophets; Jesus and
his apostles were males. These precedents are often used to bar
women from Christian leadership.

If God is male, then women cannot be ordained to represent
him.[10] As we have seen, the attribution of sexuality to God is a
misunderstanding of his nature. The Old Testament priesthood was
all male, based on patriarchal lineage, but its function was to represent the people to God. The Word of God to the people most often
came through the prophet. Throughout Scripture women were given
the gift of prophecy and used by God to convey his message. Christ
himself was outside the Old Testament priesthood, a member of the
tribe of Judah rather than Levi, "a priest for ever, after the order of
Melchizedek" (Heb. 5:6). His self-sacrifice was the culmination of
the old covenant and the termination of the priesthood.[11]

Jesus was a male. Few people would dispute that; the question is,
so what? We have discussed why Jesus came as a male and how
New Testament writers reacted to it. If his humanity did not in-
corporate all of us, then only half of us were redeemed by his sacrifice. Christ was both fully human and fully divine. If one of the
criteria for being able to represent Christ is to be like him (i.e.,
male), is this not elevating masculinity above divinity? Christ came
to be the Jewish Messiah, the sacrificial lamb to take away the sins
of the world, the king to reign on David's throne—for these reasons
he was male. But "the Christian priest is not ordained to be another
Christ and do again what only he could do and has done." [12]

A variant on this argument is a reference to Christ the Bridegroom, the church as his bride. The tacit assumption again is that
ministers represent Christ and thus only men can be bridegrooms.
Not only contrary to New Testament teaching, this is presumptuous!
In the Gospels Jesus speaks of himself as the bridegroom but his
disciples are the guests (Mark 2:19–20), at least some of whom
are women (Matt. 25:1 ff.). The priest or minister is always part of
the church, part of the bride, as are all Christian men and women.
We are also all the sons of God! [13]

Jesus' apostles were all men—and all Jewish. Which raises a
pertinent question: Why are we so selective about what in the New
Testament we emulate? As Krister Stendahl notes, Jesus ordered
his disciples to walk, staff in hand (Mark 6:8). Is that our biblical
paradigm for ministerial travel? Jesus himself said his disciples
were sent only to the lost sheep of Israel (Matt. 10:6). Is this norma-

tive today? [14] What was the point of Jesus' choosing twelve male apostles? He tells us that they represent the twelve tribes of Israel which they will judge in the kingdom (Matt. 19:28). If the New Testament church could make the radical innovation of allowing Gentiles to become leaders of the church and heirs to apostolic authority, could not the church today take the less radical step of ordaining women?

And while the Twelve all answered to masculine names, Jesus did commission and send out the Seventy (Luke 10:1–20). They were given the same instructions and powers. Women traveled with Jesus. Paul says some wives traveled with their apostle husbands (1 Cor. 9:5). So who is to say that pairs of women or married couples were not among the Seventy?

Were there any women at the Last Supper? If only men were there, theologians presume that only men can reenact the scene today. Several reasons can be offered as to why only men were there. Some say in Jesus' day women were never included at the Paschal meal. Others say they were present in family groups, but would not have been invited by a single man dining with male guests. Another suggestion is that Jesus knew of the imminence of his arrest and so did not include women. Jesus also ties it in with the New Israel (Luke 22:28–30).

And what about the meal referred to in Mark 14:1–2 and John 12:1–3? Many have suggested that Martha, Mary, and Lazarus were Essenes, a Jewish sect which followed a different calendar and celebrated the Passover earlier. This may well have been a ritual meal which included women.[15] And after all, if Jesus meant to set an example by not inviting women to the Last Supper, how did the church presume to do so?

Nowhere in the New Testament are any of these reasons used to prohibit women from ministry in the church. Paul did not allude to the Last Supper in his instructions to women even though he discussed it in the same context (1 Cor. 11–14). Paul, an apostle himself, never used his own example, or the Twelve, or Jesus as grounds that women could not hold office.

There is one rather cogent case that could be made from New Testament evidence—though we have yet to see theologians make it. Matthew and Mark clearly record that the Great Commission was given to the Twelve only (Matt. 28:16–20; Mark 16:14–15). If male theologians would like to absolve women of all responsibility for fulfilling this command, then perhaps women could simply devote themselves to other pursuits. All the evangelism and missionary sermons we have ever heard, however, leave the distinct impression that women too are under God's command to spread the gospel.

TRADITION

The church never has ordained women to leadership positions, it is often asserted, and therefore should not now. (Paul did not use a microphone either!) However, the case is not that clear-cut. For one thing, the New Testament is certainly not definitive about church order or we would not range from highly democratic congregations to strictly hierarchical churches all claiming scriptural basis. While some see clearly defined orders of bishop, priest, and deacon, others see nothing of the kind.

Secondly, despite their subordinate social status, some women were ordained in the early church, complete with the episcopal laying on of hands. Both the New Testament and historical evidence show women deacons until about the tenth century. Church history is a record of what women were successively stopped from doing. No one ever said they could not be martyrs but Tertullian told widows to stop teaching and baptizing. The Council of Laodicea in 381 said no more women presbyters could be appointed and women should henceforth not "approach the altar," indicating liturgical functions of some kind. The Synod of Orange in 441 forbade the ordination of women, but the second Council of Orleans in 533 still speaks of women deacons.[16]

Throughout history women have distinguished themselves in Christ's service. Paula (347–404), a wealthy Roman noblewoman, helped Jerome translate the Vulgate in addition to founding a monastery, convent, and hospice. Pulcheria (399–453), regent for her brother Theodosius and empress of the Eastern Empire for forty years, instructed her brother's bride Eudoxia in the faith and helped her in a poetical paraphrase of the first eight books of the Old Testament, plus Daniel and Zechariah. She attended the Council of Chalcedon and was influential in its defense of orthodoxy against several heresies. Other women founded religious orders and in the "Dark Ages" ruled as abbesses over huge double monasteries for both men and women. They held great authority (in tenth-century England four were peers) with the right to ban persons from their domain, send out knights, give judgment in court, mint coinage, and attend the imperial diet in Germany.

Despite its emphasis on the laity, the Reformation did little for women, but among the anabaptist groups women played a great part. Lysken Dirks, for example, was imprisoned for her faith in Antwerp in 1551. Monks questioning the pregnant woman asked why she was meddling with Scripture instead of sewing. She answered, "Christ commands us to search the Scriptures and Christ is to be obeyed rather than man." They drowned her. First Quaker missionary Elizabeth Hooten, on her second mission to America, was whipped at age sixty to "improve" her theology. Women in the nineteenth century helped found and fund the great missionary movement.[17]

To paraphrase John, there are also many other things which women have done in the church's history; were every one of them to be written, I suppose that the volumes would fill library shelves equal to those already devoted to the history of men's work in the church. Women have proven that God does call and empower them and that they are equal to the task. Their record has simply been ignored.

SOCIOLOGICAL CONSIDERATIONS

Deprived of scriptural and historical arguments, those opposing women's full ministry in the church often turn to cultural considerations. Women just could not combine the ministry as a career with marriage, critics warn. Only the Pope, however, raises this objection in regard to men. We laud male evangelists, missionaries, and denominational executives who spend a great deal of time away from their families. And yet we say families would disintegrate if women were to serve God outside the home.

From a biblical standpoint God did not seem too concerned that Deborah and Huldah were married when he chose them as prophets. Priscilla seems to have had a hand in every letter that is considered genuinely Pauline, probably having them copied and distributed to the churches, yet Paul apparently did not worry that it would hurt her marriage to Aquila. What about all the married women today who very successfully combine "secular" careers with marriage? And how does this argument apply at all to single women or widows seeking ordination?

A corollary is the assertion that a woman just could not handle some aspects of a pastor's job, like counseling, confession, certain visitation, etc. Men in the congregation just would not work with a woman pastor. The experience of ordained women in parishes has disproved all of these contentions. They find men do respond well to their leadership, that they can "shepherd the flock" in ways a man cannot. For any man who feels ill at ease counseling with or confessing to a woman, there have always been women who hesitate to discuss personal problems with male ministers. Women in secular counseling jobs have the same problems and have been able to successfully meet them.[18] Besides, not all people ordained are called to the local church—some serve as chaplains in the military, prisons, hospitals, colleges, etc.

Other foot-draggers note that seminaries are currently turning out more ministerial candidates than the churches can hire and that women entering the profession would drive men out. Which is to say that God does not know what he is doing, that he is calling too many people into his service. Perhaps it is the church which should have a broader vision.

"Society just isn't ready for women ministers" summarizes these arguments. The rapid changes in our society in the past decade already give the statement a dated ring. In this area society seems far ahead of the church in permitting women full development of their talents. And even if it were not, since when should the church wait to proclaim the truth until society is ready for it? Should the church cater to prejudices which society at large or its own members have?

IS ORDINATION RELEVANT?

Many people today, women among them, feel that the whole issue of ordination is passé. They argue that the church is moving into a new era when clergy-lay distinctions are being weakened, when the concept of ministry is changing from an authority figure to a serv- anthood model, when the priesthood of all believers is becoming more of a reality. True as that may be, Luther also said it four hun- dred years ago. And women are a bit suspicious when denomina- tional men's and women's boards are abolished in the name of egalitarian reform and the result is a new board with all male execu- tives and women administrators out of a job. As long as the church does maintain some sort of hierarchy and power structure, women should be admitted to it.

Ordination does have advantages. Whatever their theology, all churches consider ordination at least symbolic of God's empowering an individual for service. On a sociological level ordination is a sign that the recipient has been tested and found capable and worthy, just as a doctor's license certifies that he is trained and competent. A minister will be readily admitted into many areas of service such as hospitals and prisons where a lay Christian will not. Ordination is also a commitment by the church to stand behind and support its ministers, something which women need and deserve as much as men.

Ordination not only has advantages for the person ordained but also for those to whom she ministers. Refusal to ordain women has deprived thousands of Christians in remote areas of this country and on the mission fields of services which the church allows only or- dained men to perform. Women missionaries have not been allowed to baptize, confirm, perform marriages, or celebrate Holy Communion for their converts. Thus the church has willfully denied important aspects of the Christian life to these people just because of basic prejudices against women.

Ordination is relevant to women who feel called to the official ministry, and many women in all branches of the church do feel this call of God upon their lives. Can the church continue to deny them opportunity to respond to this call?

A TALENT BURIED

The Bible makes it clear that God has given each of us specific, unique gifts to be used to glorify him and to serve one another (1 Pet. 4:10). As members of the body of Christ we have a variety of gifts—wisdom, knowledge, faith, healing, miracle-working, prophecy, discerning of spirits, tongues, interpretations. We are equipped by the Holy Spirit for many tasks—to be apostles, prophets, evangelists, pastors, teachers, helpers, administrators, speakers (1 Cor. 12:4–31; Eph. 4:4–16).

None of these gifts is labeled "for men only." Scripture nowhere indicates that men alone are given the gifts of leadership and women those of following and helping. Quite the contrary. 1 Corinthians 12:11 emphatically states that all gifts "are inspired by one and the same Spirit, who apportions to each one individually as he wills." Although Ephesians 4:8 is sometimes cited to prove God intends only men to be apostles, prophets, evangelists, and pastors (v. 11), the word in Greek is *anthropos,* the generic term for all people, not just males. When a woman tried to get Jesus to affirm motherhood as "woman's role," he said, "Blessed rather are those who hear the word of God and keep it!" (Luke 11:28). Another time he commented, "Whoever does the will of God is my brother, and sister, and mother" (Mark 3:35). To do the will and work of God in the world is the task of all Christians.

"To each is given the manifestation of the Spirit for the common good" (1 Cor. 12:7). The decision to use or to squander our gift is not a purely personal one, but something that has ramifications for the entire Body. If anyone hides her talent or uses it for purely selfish ends, the Body is weakened, handicapped. But if each uses her gifts to build up the Body, then all benefit.

Shortly before his death, Jesus instructed his disciples with an interesting series of parables about servants, wise and foolish virgins, talents, and do-gooders (Matt. 24:45–25:46). He warned all his followers that they were expected to be faithful, diligent workers. Those who were not would be cast out of the kingdom. The parable of the talents is particularly applicable to our subject. Two servants, given gifts by their master, went out in his absence and doubled their worth. On his return they were praised and rewarded. The third had this to say:

> "Master, I knew you to be a hard man . . . so I was afraid, and I went and hid your gold in the ground. Here it is." "You lazy rascal!" said the master, ". . . you ought to have put my money on deposit, and on my return I should have got it back with interest. Take the bag of gold from him, and give it to the one with ten bags. . . . Fling the useless servant out into the dark, the place of wailing and grinding of teeth!" (Matt. 24:25–30, NEB).

How could God be so harsh on the poor timid soul, who did after all return the original gift in mint condition? Will he be as harsh on the woman who confesses:

I heard your call to preach your word, but when I sought advice from my pastor he ridiculed me.

I applied to a seminary, but they told me women were not permitted to enroll in the master of divinity program.

I requested ordination from our denomination, but they told me women were not called to the ministry.

I asked to candidate at a local church, but they said people in the congregation would not accept a woman pastor.

I applied to a mission board, but they turned me away when they learned my gift was evangelization, not nursing, secretarial work, or teaching children.

So I just gave up, got married, and had kids like everyone had been telling me to do all along.

We think rather that Christ's judgment will be turned on those who have denied women opportunities to develop and use their gifts —with words akin to those in Matthew 25:41!

The church does actively discourage women. If they report that the Holy Spirit has given them gifts for changing diapers, corralling seven-year-olds, baking cakes, or rolling bandages, the church has a place for them. But if their gifts are administration, accounting, theological investigation, or public speaking, forget it. A century ago a young woman of the Church of England wrote, "I would have given the church my head, my hand, my heart. She would not have them. She told me to go back and do crochet in my mother's drawing room." [19] Florence Nightingale had to go to another church in another country to find training to serve God.

In her teen years, Letha was invited into a wide variety of churches to play the trombone and give her testimony. Some Baptist elders took her aside and scolded her for her public speaking. Nancy as a teen-ager felt called to missionary service but visiting missionaries constantly discouraged her by saying, "Get married and we'll be happy to see you on the field." Clearly they did not want her, but her husband. Young women today still report similar experiences.

The church's pattern of discrimination leads to absurdities. Women are permitted to teach women and children. Yet if women are as weak-minded and prone to error as theologians say, does this mean we do not care if women and children are led astray? And at what age does a boy become a man? Why should it be all right for women to teach men in universities, even in Christian colleges, and yet not in church? Why do we hire women as directors of Christian education? (The observation that churches now tend to hire a man in the same capacity with the title "minister of education" and a higher salary is no sign of enlightenment!) One well-known woman missionary was permitted to speak only to the women of a certain church. But her speech was recorded and immediately played for the men assembled elsewhere in the building!

If women are supposed to keep silence in the church, why do we let them sing solos, play musical instruments, and even lead choirs? After all does not Colossians 3:16 link singing with teaching? If the church really took seriously the charge that women were unfit teachers, many fine hymns which teach doctrine and which were written by women would be ripped from our hymnals.

And why are women allowed to write Bible studies, Sunday school quarterlies, magazine articles, and books which instruct men as well as women?

Young women at an international youth organization's missionary convention responded to a call for volunteers to help distribute the elements at the climactic communion service. They were told that "biblically" only men could do so. Women can serve family suppers in the church, but not the Lord's Supper.

What are the results of these large and small discriminations? Many women take the easy, acceptable way out. After all, Christ's instructions not to hide one's light under a bushel must have been for men only too. The pious woman is supposed to be retiring, self-effacing, always ready to offer her husband's opinions rather than her own, to step aside from any position when a man becomes available for it, to make suggestions which male superiors can offer as their own. Women soon get the message and hide their gifts. Pride is often proclaimed as man's primary sin. For women it seems to be irresponsibility.

And manipulation. The church not only allows but encourages women to be devious, to exercise influence behind the scenes.

Women in the church are often pacified with the assertion that they wield immense power. But it is irresponsible power. We condemn such corruption in government and yet condone it in the church.

Many women cannot accept the circumscribed roles the church offers them. They become frustrated, depressed, and sometimes bitter. "The unfulfilled potential, the unlived experience, haunts consciousness, for deep down in every man lives the knowledge that the sin of unfulfillment is a sin against the Holy Ghost, the spirit of life whose breath is the Awakener." [20] Such women struggle to find avenues within the church through which they can serve God only to be met with suspicion and resistance. One seminary handbook warns the young minister that women in his congregation will want to work because they are neurotic, lonely, status-seeking, and guilt-ridden. They are usually unqualified for what they want to do, divisive, jealous, resentful, given to gossip, and their husbands may use their work as an excuse to stop giving. The young minister is cautioned to structure women's role in the church into a women's organization represented by one woman on the official board and responsible for domestic tasks.

Sometimes women simply conclude, as a college woman recently told us, "The church has no place for me." Another seminary wife commented, "I've been put down so many times in churches. For example, prayer is requested for someone and so someone comes up to three men around me and says, 'Let's pray.' They ignore me like I'm not there or like my prayers wouldn't do any good. I can't go into a local church and witness to a gospel that is not Good News for women as well as men." A woman seminarian with an established ministry expressed fears that those who have supported her in the past will discontinue their gifts when she marries. Despite the fact that her husband is a student, they will expect him to support her and her ministry, or for her to quit her ministry and devote her energies to supporting him.

Some of these women continue to attend church but invest their talents elsewhere.[21] Others, like the young convert at a major university who was excited about Christ until campus Christians began telling her that Christ opposed women's liberation, simply leave the church. Women who felt called into the ordained ministry have often had to leave the church of their birth and change to a more open denomination.

To deny one's own gifts or the gifts of others is to quench and grieve the Holy Spirit. Dietrich Bonhoeffer once warned, "A community which allows unemployed members to exist within it will perish because of them. It will be well, therefore, if every member receives a definite task to perform for the community, that he may know in hours of doubt that he, too, is not useless and unusable." [22] Feminine pronouns could easily be substituted here. Women are not asking to take over the church as many seem to fear. Instead their cry echoes the instruction of Paul (Rom. 12:6): "having gifts that differ according to the grace given to us, let us use them"!

14. The World Beyond the Home

> As they passed the rows of houses they saw through the open doors that men were sweeping and dusting and washing dishes, while the women sat around in groups, gossiping and laughing.
>
> "What has happened?" the Scarecrow asked a sad-looking man with a bushy beard, who wore an apron and was wheeling a baby-carriage along the sidewalk.
>
> "Why, we've had a revolution, your Majesty— as you ought to know very well," replied the man, "and since you went away the women have been running things to suit themselves. I'm glad you have decided to come back and restore order, for doing housework and minding children is wearing out the strength of every man in the Emerald City."
>
> "Hm!" said the Scarecrow, thoughtfully. "If it is such hard work as you say, how did the women manage it so easily?"
>
> "I really do not know," replied the man, with a deep sigh. "Perhaps the women are made of cast-iron."
>
> *The Marvelous Land of Oz* '

IN WHAT SEEMED a strange item of business at the 1970 American Political Science meetings, conferees were asked to try to solve the following riddle: A father and his teen-age son were involved in an auto crash that killed the father and critically injured the boy. At the hospital, the surgeon called to perform emergency surgery took one look and said, "I can't do it. That's my son!"

The riddle stumped most persons. Had its source not been so carefully concealed (a group of women concerned with equality in the professions), no doubt its answer would have been guessed more quickly. But as it was, the incident underscored how deeply ingrained are sex-role stereotypes in our thinking.

Because of cultural reinforcement, such attitudes form early— even in the most liberated families. Psychology professor Matina Horner tells of being startled when her small daughter expressed amazement upon learning that a female family friend happened to be a physician. The three-year-old's first question was, "Is she still a girl?" which was quickly followed by a second query, "Is she still Eric's mommy?" Then the child concluded, "She must be all mixed up." Dr. Horner was astonished, since the little girl not only had a mother actively engaged in a profession but had also known other

women physicians. Even so, society's expectations and sex-role
stereotyping had implanted the notion that doctors are men. And
women are mommies.[2]

The traditional view sees the matter simply. Woman's place is in
the home. It is *man* whose place is in the world. And if women venture into that world (except temporarily while waiting to get
married, or in cases of dire financial necessity), it is called "undesirable," "dangerous," "harmful to the family," "unfeminine," and
much more.[3]

Most people concede that there is a place in the world for certain
kinds of "women's jobs"—clerks, secretaries, domestics, waitresses,
schoolteachers, and nurses, for example; but the idea that women
should even *attempt* to equal men in a desire for leadership, involvement in the world's serious issues, and genuine commitment to
a career is considered a laughing matter. This in itself is a symptom
of how society feels about woman's place in the world. As one
sympathetic business executive put it: "When you talk about equal
employment of blacks, you no longer have Amos and Andy jokes.
But you still have jokes on the woman's issue. Society hasn't taken
the issue seriously." [4]

For many religious leaders, the matter of "working women" is
nothing to joke about. On practical grounds alone, women out earning a paycheck means having fewer women available to do volunteer
church work. Who will cook the church dinners, arrange flowers for
the sanctuary, conduct fund-raising projects, or even teach in the
Sunday school? Publishers of religious literature point out that one
reason traditional two-week vacation Bible school courses are now
offered in abbreviated, one-week editions is because so many
churches complained that the "working-mother problem" makes it
more difficult than ever to staff VBS. Shorter courses or evening
sessions seemed the only workable solution.

Most churches have trouble adjusting to working women,
whether single or married, because they simply cannot fit into the
traditional mold and schedule that is built around the housewife
ideal. Thus, all too often, the working woman is resented, if not
frankly criticized. Without realizing it, many Christians are very
close to Hitler's ideology which spelled out woman's "proper" and
limited sphere: *Kinder, Küche, Kirche.* The children, the kitchen,
and the church comprise her domain—and even there, she must be
careful not to step out of place.

SHOULD WOMEN BE INVOLVED IN THE WORLD?

Perhaps a better question than "Should women be involved in

the world?" would be this: Should human beings have a choice
about what they will do with their lives? Most people are quick to
say *yes* to that. After all, freedom is a highly esteemed value in our
society. Yet, they contradict themselves by encouraging one kind
of choice for males and another for females. Girls are expected
to choose marriage and motherhood. Yet if a little boy answered a
question about his future plans by saying, "I just want to be a
husband and father when I grow up," someone would quickly set him
straight. "Oh yes, but you'll also want to be something else. You'll
want to have a job like your daddy so that you can take care of
your wife and children. You'll want to do something important in
the world—like being a doctor or lawyer or astronaut. Or maybe a
great scientist." How many little girls would hear a response like
that? Few indeed. They would probably hear, "That's nice. You'll be
a good mommy someday. Now run along and play with your dollies
and toy dishes."

Yet this dichotomy of woman-in-the-home and man-in-the-world
was not always so rigid. In agricultural societies, women are involved
in economic production along with household duties. In our own
Western society, it was traditional (before mechanization) for
farm families to work together. Father alone wasn't considered the
breadwinner. Family businesses likewise utilized all family members, and often the home was located on the same premises as
the store or mill. Working with their husbands in various crafts
and trades, women played important roles in the bustling world outside the home. The notion of "full-time mothering" was unheard
of.

We have already seen that the Bible speaks of many women
who were active in the outside world—Deborah, the political leader;
religious leaders such as Phoebe, Priscilla, and Philip's daughters;
and Lydia, the businesswoman; to name only a few. If such examples explode the myth that women who love God shouldn't be
involved in the world, the ashes of that myth are driven under-
ground by Proverbs 31:10–31. Somehow, when the passage is used
for Mother's Day sermons, it comes through quite differently than it
does when we go directly to the Bible. The picture in Proverbs 31
is not that of a "clinging vine" or "helpless female," but rather portrays a mature woman of good business sense, capable of wise
thought and management, resourceful, responsible, and highly
esteemed by her husband who places his whole trust in her (see
v. 11).

Ministers often use this passage to describe an ideal wife and
mother. After all, the woman in Proverbs knows how to cook and
sew and dress tastefully (just like the ideal homemaker in the

women's magazines). And "like a ship laden with merchandise, she brings home food from far off" (v. 14, NEB). In other words, she does a good job with the weekly shopping and takes advantage of supermarket specials. She gets up early and goes to bed late (woman's work is never done!). Her children turn out well. Her husband thinks the world of her and is successful in his own career. And to top it all off, she's spiritually minded (v. 30). What more could anyone ask?

But many women *are* asking for more. So did the woman in Proverbs 31. She needed the sense of worth and achievement that comes from interests and activities outside the home. There are two main ways for women to become involved in the world: through voluntary, unpaid service (e.g., charitable, religious, or political work), or else through an actual occupation with monetary earnings. The woman in Proverbs chose both. "She opens her hand to the poor, and reaches out her hands to the needy" (v. 20). But she also has a wise head for financial management and investment. "After careful thought she buys a field and plants a vineyard out of her earnings" (v. 16, NEB). Furthermore, she set up her own weaving and garment business and supplied merchants with her goods (Prov. 31:17–18, 24, 31). The fact that she had servants indicates that she was not fearful that delegating certain household and childcare tasks to others would be detrimental to her family.

Yet, this dynamo of energy is not presented as an "unfeminine," "emasculating," scheming, aggressive female. She speaks kindly and wisely and seems to convey to her family a spirit of tranquillity, confidence, and happiness. Her husband isn't the least bit threatened by all her capabilities and activities. In fact, he's delighted. "He sings her praises: 'Many a woman shows how capable she is; but you excel them all.' " (vv. 28b–29, NEB). Her children likewise commend her.

This is not to say that all women must be involved in the world beyond home and family and that all women should be gainfully employed and career-oriented. We are only suggesting that women be given the *choice*—just as men are given choices. And we are pointing out that there is nothing "unchristian" or "unbiblical" in the decision of a woman who opts for an outside occupation instead of, or along with, family responsibilities. It is really the freedom to choose that the women's movement is all about.

Such freedom is not contrary to the Christian faith, which also lays much stress on the matter of choice. We are to *choose* to serve God, to *choose* to receive his offer of salvation, to *choose* to follow Christ. Individuals are encouraged to say, "*I* will follow God wherever he leads *me*." Yet at the same time, we contradict ourselves by implying that we know where he'll always lead women (into traditional domestic roles)—as well as *how* he leads women (by leading their husbands and asking that the women follow).

WHY WOMEN WANT INVOLVEMENT IN THE OUTSIDE WORLD

Many Christians, brought up to consider the traditional mold as the "normal" order of things, have difficulty understanding the discontent of so many modern women. What is it that women want?

Much of it has to do with the issue of freedom to choose one's destiny, as has already been mentioned. Increasingly, such freedom is thought to be a human right. A caste system is thoroughly out of keeping with the values we espouse today. It doesn't seem rational to assign whole groups of people to a certain place or sphere simply because of characteristics received by the accident of birth. Blacks and other groups have rebelled at the way society has blocked freedom of choice and opportunity for no other reason than a difference in pigmentation over which they had no control. And women too are awaking to the fact that they also have been forced into a particular mold, regardless of individual aptitudes and talents, simply because of having been born female rather than male. They too are asking for "freedom now."

The desire for self-fulfillment, for finding what one really wants to do with one's life—and then doing it, is not some phenomenon confined to women. Growing numbers of both men and women are returning to school, learning new skills, or changing careers in their middle years.[5] Sometimes the reasons are financial; but often they are attempts to find something meaningful—a way to use one's gifts and talents to make worthwhile contributions to the world. More and more individuals no longer are willing to accept passively "what fate has handed them." They see the possibility of rational control and manipulation of many of life's circumstances. They can envision second and third chances, rather than feeling they must continue in a dull rut or dead-end job. And they're willing to take risks and put forth great effort to make their dreams come true.

Behavioral scientists point out the linkage between occupational achievement and a sense of self-esteem. One of the first questions we ask about someone is, "What does he do?" And the answer to that question influences our opinion of him. With women, the question is usually, "What does her husband do?" Men are expected to define themselves in terms of their jobs, but women are expected to define themselves in terms of roles and relationships.

Yet, given society's value of occupational achievement and the rewards of money, prestige, and power, the items expected to comprise woman's self-image count for little. What kind of man has chosen her? How spotless does she keep her house? How attractive is she? How do her children behave? Women are sensitive to the low rating society places on their domestic endeavors; hence the apologetic statement, "Oh, I'm just a housewife." We may decry such self-denigration as wrong and unfortunate, but it is nevertheless a fact of life. As psychology professor Judith Bardwick expresses it: "In our masculine-oriented culture a person is worth the market value of his skills and personality. One's esteem depends not on the human qualities one possesses but on success in the competitive market place." [6] Therefore, many women feel that they should have the right to achieve (as do men) in the way that will allow maximum utilization of talents and bring the rewards that society gives for successful accomplishments, including the reward of enhanced self-esteem.

Some Christians may ask at this point, "Isn't that letting our-selves be squeezed into the world's mold? Isn't that what the Apostle Paul warned about in Romans 12:2? Why should we be in-fluenced by society's values? Why shouldn't we measure self-worth in terms of relationship to God rather than in relationship to the economic system?" There is much truth in this. To know that we "are of more value than many sparrows" and that the hairs of our head are numbered by the Father in heaven, to know that God created each of us as a unique person who is special in his sight, to know that Christ gave himself up in sacrifice for us—surely all of these assurances bolster one's self-image.

However, we must not lose sight of the fact that a Christian's sense of worthwhileness and self-esteem comes not only from aware-ness of the individual's importance to God but also from the knowledge that God created us in his own image. One aspect of that image, as we've already seen, is the capacity human beings have for relationship—both with God and with one another.

In addition to the "relation side" of God's image in male and fe-male, there is also a "creation side." God made human beings to be in a very real sense creators like him—to be like him in producing, achieving, subduing, controlling, and the like. In the Genesis account, there was the manual work of caring for the garden and the intellec-tual work of naming the animals. God has given us the ability to think, discover, create, explore, compose, make, cultivate, mold, and build. Such an ability is a reflection of what God is like and is thus an aspect of his image in mankind. Psalm 8:3–6 catches the wonder of this truth.

God intended that both men and women should reflect this aspect of his image by exercising dominion over the earth (Gen. 1:26–31). Yet, traditionally it has been considered a man's job to produce ideas and goods, while a woman's job is to produce babies. These verses from Genesis knock down that notion. God knew the woman couldn't be fruitful and multiply alone. Obviously, then, that statement wasn't intended for her only! Why should we think that God gave the commandment to subdue the earth to the man alone, as some Bible study guides suggest? It's foolish to say that half the human race, made in God's image and possessing talents he has bestowed, should have no part in the world he has placed in our hands.

This is the crux of the issue. All too many Christians label women "selfish" if they desire to work outside the home, or choose not to marry in favor of a career, or elect not to have children. It's assumed that working women are materialistic and intent only on making money for luxuries. Such critics have difficulty understanding that many women desire to work outside the home in order to use their talents and training creatively, in a way that brings meaning to their own lives and benefits society as well. Woman, made in God's image, should want to be a good steward and exercise the gifts God has given her—just as a man should. Perhaps both men and women together need to rethink the matter of "vocation" and formulate a "theology of work" that views all of us as being in charge of God's world and responsible to him for what we do with it.

It's wrong to criticize women for desiring to be a part of the world beyond home and family. Many women want to work not for what they can get but for what they can give. They want to serve—in politics, in medicine, in scientific research, in business, in education, and much more. And the world needs them. Why should it be denied their talents simply because God chose to place those talents in persons whose bodies are female?

Many Christians remain unconvinced, believing a woman's greatest contribution to the world is to be a good wife and mother. She is to be the family's haven from the cares and pressures of the outer world, the coordinator of family life to keep things running smoothly, the one who guides, trains, nurtures, and supports. Shouldn't this be enough for a woman? Isn't such a role sufficient to provide a woman with a sense of achievement and of having made a worthwhile contribution to the world? True, a homemaker doesn't get paid for what she does, but money isn't everything.

Those who reason this way like to point to examples of the past. Again, a favorite illustration is the life of Susannah Wesley. Sermons have been preached to show how this mother of nineteen children devoted her whole life to her family. "Think how tragic it would have been for the Christian church if Susannah Wesley had practiced birth control," announced a minister as he introduced a Charles Wesley hymn to his congregation, pointing out that Charles was the eighteenth child to whom she gave birth.

But another question arises. There is no denying that the world would have been poorer without Charles Wesley; but as matters now stand, might it not be true that in a sense the world is also poorer because Susannah Wesley was withheld from it? She was a very talented and brilliant woman, "indeed superior in mind and ability to her husband," writes Bishop Gerald Kennedy. "Born in a later time, she would have made a mark for herself. In the eighteenth century, she found fulfillment through her children and especially in the lives of her two famous sons, John and Charles." [7]

Mrs. Wesley poured her energies wholeheartedly into the task of rearing her children with strict but loving discipline, training them in both Christian doctrine and academic subjects (each child learned the alphabet on his or her fifth birthday and was expected to begin learning to read Genesis 1 the very next day). She wrote her own curriculum materials, including poems and books on theology to be used by her children, and she methodically sought to instill character-building habits in each son and daughter. Ten of her children died during infancy, but a strict regime was followed for the remaining nine so that all of them received individual instruction and time alone with their mother, talking things over with her, praying with her, and learning from her.

Susannah Wesley felt that this was the trust given her by God. She began her systematic plan of instruction out of a desire for something more to do for him, saying that since she was not a man nor a minister, perhaps this would provide a way of serving the Lord.[8]

But even this did not seem enough. Mrs. Wesley was disturbed that the assistant curate failed to hold evening services while her husband, the Reverend Samuel Wesley, was away. To correct this, she began inviting neighbors in on Sunday evenings for a time of Christian instruction. Soon more than two hundred began attending regularly and more were turned away due to lack of even standing room. Through this ministry of leadership and teaching, Susannah Wesley experienced a wonderful sense of achievement, fulfillment, and service to God. Yet, as has been the case with so many talented women, she felt a nagging guilt and uneasiness about what she was doing. Her husband disapproved for one thing, and there were the traditional interpretations of certain Scripture passages to contend with. Was she usurping the place of a man? Yet the people needed her ministry and she felt compelled to help them. Like so many of her modern sisters, she was pulled two ways.[9]

If even Susannah Wesley felt a need to utilize talents in ways other than child-care exclusively, how much more is this true of a woman today with only two or three children? She is likely to see her youngest go off to school while she is in her early or mid-thirties. Her husband is reaching the best years of his career. Her children grow increasingly independent and reach out to new worlds opening up through school, friends, and outside activities. Suddenly a woman feels alone and not so needed any longer. She begins to yearn for something more. Betty Friedan termed these feelings of emptiness and yearning so common among housewives, "the problem that has no name." [10]

An observation by psychologist Judith Bardwick is pertinent here. She points out that most attempts to define and measure achievement "derive from the academic-vocational-masculine model," but suggests that this should not be the *only* model used with regard to women. At certain times of their lives, according to Professor Bardwick, women desire achievement along other lines— particularly in matters relating to social success, internal development, and interpersonal relationships. If this is so, one kind of model (the internal-interpersonal achievement model) may be more salient for women at one stage of life, whereas the "masculine" model that emphasizes vocational achievement may be more applicable at another stage.

Dr. Bardwick says that this may explain a finding in certain psychological tests which have shown that, among women with some college training, there occurs after ten to fifteen years of marriage an increase in motives to achieve. At this stage, it isn't unusual for women to return to universities to complete degrees or to undertake graduate training. Or they may resume a career abandoned years before. Some may begin an altogether new type of occupation.

Behavioral scientists find it significant that this "motivation to achieve" appears at this particular point in life—especially in view of traditional achievement-motivation theories which have emphasized that the motive to achieve must develop during childhood or it will never develop. Bardwick suggests two possible explanations. Possibly an internalized motive to achieve develops later in women than in men and requires the security of having affiliative needs met first, thus reducing anxiety about achieving. "A stable marital relationship may permit the development of a secure and independent sense of self and the motive to achieve." Or, on the other hand, it may be that the women mentioned in the psychological testings above, *did* develop strong motives to achieve during childhood but did not act upon them behaviorally. Achievement motivation may have been suppressed because of anxieties about failing or because of fears of alienating other people (by not fulfilling traditional feminine roles, for example).[11]

Either possibility, of course, underscores the effects of how girls are socialized in our culture. But the point is that, even if the internal-interpersonal kind of achievement (success in social relationships) does seem to satisfy many women at one stage of life, there still appears to be a need—at least in the lives of women who have had some higher education—for achievement along the lines recognized and rewarded in our society, that is, academic and vocational achievement.

COMBINING A FAMILY AND CAREER— PROBLEMS AND REWARDS

Sidney Callahan points out that "developing a new theoretical approach to women is one thing, living it another." This is true for all women, but especially so in the case of a wife and mother. Mrs. Callahan (herself the mother of six children) writes that society supports a single woman in her career, expecting her to be seriously committed to her work and to be a responsible, active, and growing person. In contrast, society's expectations for a married woman often discourage rather than support her when she steps outside traditional feminine roles.[12]

In candidly describing her personal struggles and conflicts, Mrs. Callahan has shown herself to be a loving wife and mother who immensely enjoyed the rich family life she and her husband had worked together to build. Yet, she reached a point at which she began to experience a sense of boredom, frustration, and confusion about her role as a woman. "Ten years without formal intellectual work or study was all that I could bear," she writes. "During those years I had helped launch my husband and created a family and functioning household. Now I had to put myself first for awhile or sink."

But should a Christian woman ever "put herself first"? Doesn't the Bible say that the person who wants to be first should be the servant of all? It was precisely her commitment to such Christian ideals that intensified Sidney Callahan's conflict and forced her to do much soul-searching. She goes on:

My Christianity held up the ideal of self-sacrifice and service for the sake of love. Why could I no longer love enough to give up intellectual pursuits and intellectual work? The upheaval and inner questioning caused me suffering of a new kind. Out of that

agony I was finally able to come to some decisions. I decided there
was a fine line between sacrifice and suicide. I could not live without intellectual function and some systematic nondomestic work
in the adult world. To try to live the traditional feminine role
would be suicide and a betrayal as well of the ideals and equality
of our marriage.[13]

Mrs. Callahan's personal solution took the form of writing and
graduate school. Other women deal with the problem in other ways,
but it's important for them to know they are not alone in their
struggles. Nor do these struggles automatically disappear all at
once never to return again. "I still have many, many conflicts and
problems in combining work and family life," says Sidney Callahan,
"but they are better conflicts than my old self-destructive embittered
conflicts born of frustration and boredom. I chose them freely."

What many deeply dissatisfied and frustrated housewives consider to be self-sacrifice really *is* "suicide," as Mrs. Callahan pointed
out. They are destroying themselves. Witness the numbers of
married women, with husbands busy in their careers and no more
small children at home, who stream into physicians' offices with
varied complaints. They may hope the doctor will prescribe tran-
quilizers or antidepressant drugs, or that he'll suggest an operation
(a way of being the center of attention and something to talk about
afterwards). Some such women begin wondering if having another
baby might not bring new zest to life and make them feel useful
again.

Tired, bored, lonely, some women turn to alcohol or get involved in an extramarital affair. Some have "nervous breakdowns"
and require hospitalization. Others take out their frustrations on
their families; they nag, whine, complain, interfere, dominate, and
in general try to live through their husbands and children. As a
result, the whole family often feels sapped and trapped. It is not a
healthy situation.

Such women may think of themselves as martyrs, sacrificing
everything for their families. In actuality, they are committing
mental-emotional suicide, hurting both themselves and others.
Such mothers are not really giving themselves to their families.
They are denying their families the real personality, the richly fulfilled woman, the true self that could have been (and still could be)
if only they would be willing to face up to the problem. And then do
something about it.

A Woman's Options

Voluntary charitable, political, and church work provide avenues
that may meet the needs of some women. At the same time that

they are being "ministered unto," they are also "ministering" through performing helpful services. Other women find this solution insufficient—especially in cases where mere busywork crowds out opportunities to develop and use talents, training, and intellectual abilities.

A return to school is another possible solution. Interest in adult education is growing in today's world. No woman should feel it is ever too late to learn, to grow, to train or retrain for some career that interests her. A magazine survey once endeavored to discover the major regrets of adults in looking back over their lives. Heading the list was the statement, "I regret that I didn't get more education." But a missed opportunity at one stage of life needn't mean there can be no second chances. Sometimes opportunity *does* knock twice.

Yet often women are afraid to open the door. It takes courage and means hard work, sacrifices, and inconveniences for both the woman and for her family. But it's well worth it. Many women have found that a return to school brings a new zest to life, opens up a whole new world of ideas and interests, brings to light talents and abilities they never knew they had, and helps them better understand themselves, their families, and life in general. They find themselves better able to relate to their husbands and children and better able to converse with them. The whole family's life can be enriched by Mom's venture into the classroom. Her children may tease her about having to do homework right along with them in the evenings, and they'll be the first to ask what grade she received on a test. But they'll be proud of her and do all they can to help. Some women say their return to school helped bridge the "generation gap" with their teenagers. And a thirty-two-year-old Sunday school teacher says that since her return to college she has learned to understand her students as never before.

There are difficulties in resuming formal education—particularly if there are still young children in the home. Mothers who have returned to school warn that there is a real temptation to take a course load that is simply too heavy. They suggest that in most cases a woman who wants to combine student life with family responsibilities should seek wise counsel and only take a reasonable amount of course hours at a time. What is "reasonable" will vary with the individual, but realistic planning is in order in any case.

No woman interested in further education should be afraid to try. A dean at a major university says the fact that a woman has been out of the classroom for years needn't deter her. "Our experience shows us she can achieve. The good student remains a good student. The mediocre student often becomes a good student because of a different motivation." [14] Many universities have adjusted their programs to accommodate the mature student who can only attend part-time or who needs great flexibility in scheduling classes. Some universities offer evening courses and correspondence courses that may be applied toward university credit. Community colleges are springing up in many areas. All such programs are worth investigating.

In addition to becoming involved in the outside world through voluntary activities or further education, there is always the option of paid employment. Some women are interested in "just finding a job" so that they can get away from the house or earn some extra money—often to supplement family income for some specific purpose, such as travel, house payments, or the children's college education. For other women a mere "job" isn't challenging enough. They aren't interested in becoming secretaries or supermarket cashiers, but rather desire a professional career that can utilize their present training or the training they hope to get.

The problems of combining family and outside work are similar in both cases. But they seem to be intensified in the case of a woman who is totally immersed in a profession—something that cannot be conveniently laid aside after an eight-hour day. A woman scientist, for example, may feel a need to spend twelve or more hours at the laboratory as she works on an important experiment. Knowing there is a family at home—a husband and children who need her—can't help but produce conflict in her mind.

But the woman who works from nine to five in a clerical or sales job has her anxieties, too. She finds that in essence she has two jobs, because in most cases she continues to do all the cleaning, laundry, mending, and cooking, in addition to her outside occupation. Her husband comes home from work and grabs the evening paper. She comes home from work and grabs an apron and skillet. Even at that, her husband may complain that she is still doing housework long after he has gone to bed.

Some women have found that part-time work, where possible, is a workable solution. One variation on this theme is the arrangement one team of authors call "the tandem job." [15] Where cooperative employers can be found, two women take the same job, but divide the hours, responsibilities, and pay. The authors cite such examples as the two housewives who share a bank teller's job, with one working mornings and the other afternoons. Other women alternate days on their shared job. In some cities, special teaching partnership programs even permit tandem teaching arrangements. This would seem to work out quite well in nursery schools and kindergartens, for example.

Without ever hearing of such things as "tandem jobs," some husbands and wives have worked out similar systems out of sheer necessity. One registered nurse, with preschoolers still at home, accepted an offer to work afternoons in a physician's office. Her college professor husband arranged his class schedule so that he could arrive home shortly after lunch to take over the household when his wife left for work. He did his reading, writing, and lecture preparations while the children took their naps; and he even prepared the evening meal. Another couple split a forty-hour work week at a bookstore into two twenty-hour jobs, so that either the mother or the father was taking care of their children while the other worked.

In her book, *Academic Women,* Jessie Bernard predicts many more such arrangements in which husbands and wives will cooperate with regard to both outside occupations and home and child-care responsibilities. She cites examples of couples who feel that both their professional lives and their family life are benefited by their being husband-wife teams at work and at home.

Husbands and Working Wives

An understanding, considerate, cooperative, and supportive husband is essential if a married woman desires to become involved in the world outside the walls of home. Otherwise, there will be endless frustration and turmoil. Dr. Bernard tells of a college student who asked a married woman, just back from a trip to India, what advice she had for someone who wanted to specialize in Indian studies. The girl was outraged by the reply: "Think about the kind of man you might marry who would make a career in Indian studies possible." The advice seemed so irrelevant at the time. But later, married to a professor whose area of specialty complemented her own, which not only meant support and encouragement but also opportunities for collaboration, the young woman who had asked the question saw the wisdom in the advice she had been given.[16]

Ginzberg and Yohalem make the same point: "The fact that many men are willing to accept certain conditions at home—a less than spotless house, a limited amount of entertaining, the necessity to help with household chores and the care of children—frequently represents the margin of difference between whether women can or cannot work." [17] A husband who sees the importance of the wife's career and encourages her makes it possible for her to pursue her occupational endeavors without feeling guilty and overburdened.

How does one get such a husband? In a speech at Wellesley College, sociologist Alice Rossi said it is important for young women to be *looking* for such a man and not to marry anyone who isn't willing to stand with his wife and to encourage her in her career pursuits.[18] An unsupportive husband can be a millstone, dragging a woman down and holding her back from all she could otherwise be. A woman should determine *before marriage* what kind of husband can work together with her rather than against her. If such a man can't be found, a lifetime of singleness would seem preferable to a marriage in which a woman's gifts would be stifled and in which the husband and wife could not share fully their total selves.

Ginzberg and associates, after calling attention to the facts of high female employment in recent years and the various factors that encourage women to enter the labor force, list three counterforces pulling in the opposite direction. These are the rising standards and expectations for child-care and mother-child relationships, the problem of finding competent domestic help, and the difficulties posed by residency in suburban areas from which husbands commute to the cities but which leave wives cut off from work opportunities.[19] However, there are signs of change as many firms move out to the suburbs—a fact which aggravates inner city problems at the same time that it leaves the suburban wife a little less stranded.

For women with certain skills, working at home seems to offer an ideal solution. Free-lance writers, certain copy editors, and artists may find they can mesh their occupational and home responsibilities well. They are at home to greet the children after school (or keep an eye on preschoolers). They are able to put the laundry in the washer or the casserole in the oven during coffee breaks. And yet, they are "at work" all day as well. They are also available to care for a sick child who unexpectedly wakes up with a fever and can't go to school that day. They can also arrange their schedule to take a child to the dentist or arrange to attend an afternoon school program with a minimum of difficulty. Some women enjoy this work-at-home system. Others find it impractical and especially resent interruptions. One free-lance artist and mother of five has her studio in her home but nevertheless hires a babysitter several hours a day so that she can work undisturbed.

Music teachers provide another example of women who can earn money without leaving their homes. Imaginative women have found other ways as well. One mother who didn't want to leave her baby during the day came up with the idea that she could put her cooking skills to use. She makes hors d'oeuvres and pastries and provides a catering service for private parties. Her business is booming.

But for most women, working at home is not feasible. Their professions, like those of most men, require that they be present somewhere else—perhaps in a classroom or office or hospital. How then does a woman work out conflicts resulting from the demands of home and career? Ginzberg and Yohalem in their book, *Educated American Women: Self-Portraits,* described four basic categories of women with respect to the home career dilemma.[20]

There were first of all those whom the authors called "the planners"—women who have had clear goals from a young age and who directed their efforts toward their goals without allowing other things to interfere or deflect them. Second, there were the "recasters"—women who shift their interests, plans, and goals when something else is perceived as more desirable. Perhaps they had original dreams about what they wished to do with their lives, but obstacles and barriers have blocked them and they have settled for something else. Or maybe they simply changed their minds about what they once thought they wanted and purposely chose another way of life that seemed better.

The "adapters" are a third category described by Ginzberg and Yohalem. These women are highly flexible. Convinced that their adult lives will require many adjustments and changes, such women are prepared to adapt themselves—particularly to the different situations that arise at different stages of their marriages. They tend to resolve conflicts in the direction of the family and its needs, while at the same time using their resourcefulness to find fulfillment in their outside work.

Last of all, there is the category of women whose self-portraits show them to be among what Ginzberg and Yohalem call the "unsettled." These are women who may have been at one time in any of the other three categories but for whom plans have gone awry. They are now fumbling and searching, and often experiencing much discontent.

How a woman resolves the problem of home and career demands depends to a great extent on which of these four categories describes her. But even within the categories, the problem is handled in different ways. People and circumstances vary, and what works well for one family may be highly undesirable for another. In trying to develop a workable pattern, it helps to read about ways other women have met the challenges and coped with problems in relation to home and career. Books like that of Ginzberg and Yohalem just mentioned or Sidney Callahan's *The Working Mother* [21] permit women who are attempting to excel in both family and career to speak for themselves with candor and realism.

Once again, the husband's cooperation (or lack of it) cannot be overstressed. For example, would a husband be willing to pass up an opportunity for advancement if it required relocating in another city that would take his wife away from her law partnership or medical practice? Traditionally wives have followed husbands, but would a husband be willing to reverse this custom if his wife were offered greater opportunities in another location—even though his own career would be affected? These are the kinds of decisions increasing numbers of couples are being forced to face as more and more wives desire to utilize their talents and make contributions to the outside world.

Some couples make diligent efforts to find positions in the same area before *either* considers a job relocation. For example, a prominent theologian placed a classified ad in a national periodical in an effort to find a university where he could teach in his field and where his wife (also a Ph. D.) could teach literature. In still other cases, the husband and wife may choose to work in different locations and maintain apartments in two cities, commuting on weekends to be together. If there are no children, some couples report that this arrangement can be quite satisfactory. Their emphasis is on the quality rather than the quantity of their time together. (Christians who are critical of such couples are often the same ones who heap praise upon evangelists and missionaries who are away from their families for weeks at a time.)

Wives who are committed to achievement goals and who have career aspirations just as their husbands do never seem entirely to escape anxieties, doubts, occasional feelings of guilt and role conflict, and an ongoing questioning. "Am I doing what is right in regard to my family?" "Am I doing my best in my profession?" "Am I investing myself as I should in both areas of life?" Judith Bardwick points out that some women begin worrying about their own normality when freedom of choice replaces rigid definitions and cultural norms are no longer clear. Some women become uncertain about their femininity especially when they choose professions atypical for women.

According to Dr. Bardwick, women who have trained for a profession suffer various anxieties regardless of how they seek to resolve the family/career dilemma. Those who leave their professions while their children are small worry that they may become intellectually rusty and fail to develop their full potential or fail to keep abreast in their fields. Those who try, on the other hand, to combine the traditional mothering role with professional commitment often feel guilty because their working "evokes obvious, surface changes in the family." These changes, according to psychologist Bardwick, are occasioned by the mother's being too busy to take part in activities that her children and community consider to be normal responsibilities—leading a Scout troop, working with the PTA, and so on. Not being solely preoccupied with her children, she may begin wondering if she is harming them.[22]

Children and Working Mothers

The question of how a mother's working outside the home affects her children is a very salient one. This is particularly true in the case of Christians who have a strong commitment to family life and a conviction that God wants them to rear children "in the discipline and instruction of the Lord" (Eph. 6:4). Because of alarmist articles and sermons, the usual picture conjured up in the minds of many is one of crumbling homes, divorces, juvenile delinquency, emotional disturbances in youngsters, and visions of dirty-faced tots with runny noses and tattered clothing playing in the streets because their mothers are neglecting them in order to earn a paycheck.

There is no disputing the fact that such tragedies do occur; but as with most other social problems, the blame cannot be attributed to one cause alone. It is unfair to blame everything on "working mothers." Mothers who *don't* "work" but who rule their children's lives, nagging them and stifling their development with smother-love, also lie behind such problems. Likewise, fathers who show no interest in their children because they have shifted all responsibility onto their wives in order to devote all their energies to advancement in their careers must share the blame. Then there are the many cases where both parents are simply too wrapped up in other noncareer interests —church meetings, clubs, community activities, and organizational responsibilities. In the rush and busyness of everyday life, such parents have no time (or take no time) to share deeply with their children and to interact with them on a warm, personal, human level. They feed them, clothe them, scold them, tuck them into bed —but they never get to really know them.

Actually, studies are contradictory and uncertain with regard to the effects a mother's working has on her children. So much depends on such factors as social class, the reasons for her working, the financial situation of the home, where a family lives, the kind of work a woman does, the type of child-care arrangements available and what kind of mother-substitute is provided, and so on.

In general, it seems that mothers who feel intensely guilty about their working, or who dislike their jobs, will have somewhat negative effects upon their children. On the other hand, mothers who are committed to a profession and who thoroughly enjoy their work may find that their children are better off than if they weren't working. One teen-ager whose mother returned to college and became a schoolteacher says his life is better than ever. The mother is so happy and not bored and discontented as before, he points out. And besides, she has become a fascinating person and is able to share the interests of her husband and son as never before.

Much is being discussed today about child-care centers that would release mothers for working but at the same time would provide enrichment experiences for children. For many mothers, this may provide an excellent solution. Some churches see a real opportunity for ministry along these lines by putting Sunday school classrooms to use during the week as day-care centers, providing not only physical care for youngsters but also spiritual guidance under Christian teachers.

Even so, many mothers prefer to stay at home during their children's preschool years to be on call when their children need them. They want to be the ones to train their sons and daughters and to answer their questions about God or sex or death or any other deep issues for which children seek explanations—often unexpectedly during the course of a day. Such mothers just want to be there to take part in the once-in-a-lifetime experience of watching their children grow from babyhood to school-age.

Other mothers think differently. They feel they are better mothers if they have been away from their children part of the day and have been intellectually stimulated through working in their professional careers. To remain at home all day cut off from the adult world, they feel, would be stultifying and boring and they might end up "taking it out on the children," by acting annoyed and irritable. However, after a day on the job, they find they come home eager to be with the children and to relax with them and enjoy them. Such mothers feel that either a trustworthy babysitter (when one can be found) or good day-care arrangements can assure care for their youngsters that is just as good as what their own mothers could offer them.

Another solution is a commune set up. In this arrangement, several families live together sharing household tasks and child-care. Actually, it is just a new form of the old extended family idea in which various relatives lived together in a large home or on a farm or very nearby so that someone was always available to take care of the children. No one worried if a baby or small child wasn't with Mommy constantly; the youngster received plenty of love, attention, and care from aunts, uncles, grandparents, older siblings, and others. Some Christian couples are experimenting with such a system, which not only gives mothers freedom for outside interests, but also provides children with opportunities to know deeply and lovingly a variety of adults—each of whom can contribute much to their development.

All of this is a matter of individual choice. There is no one and only answer. Some women choose to marry and have children late after they have had several years in a career. Other couples choose not to have children at all so that a woman's commitment to her profession can continue without interruption. Some women manage career and pregnancies and small children concurrently without too much apparent difficulty. Others find it too physically exhausting and emotionally taxing; they prefer to take out a few years from their professions and return later. If such is the case, it's crucial that they keep learning, reading, and growing during that time-out period. Again, the choice must depend upon the individual couple involved.

There is no denying that women are concerned about being part of today's world with all its problems and challenges and opportunities. To judge them as straying from Christian principles because of this desire for involvement is unwarranted. There is the matter of stewardship of talents to consider—of using what God has given in order to benefit others and to serve the world in Christ's name. Related to this is the matter of the world's need; can we afford *not* to utilize the talents of women?

There is also, as we have seen, the fact that woman bears God's image; and like man, she too desires to create and build and discover. And lastly, there is the matter of self-fulfillment. A woman must love and respect herself and must experience the self-esteem that comes from successful achievement. This can, in turn, release her love and creative energies in a new way so that her family and society are benefited rather than hurt.

Jesus told us to love our neighbor as ourselves. The woman who is not being true to herself finds it extremely difficult to love herself. Until she learns to do this, she may never know what it really means to love others, even her own family, in spite of all her talk about sacrificing and living for them alone.

15. Where Do We Go from Here?

> Confusion has seized us, and all things go wrong,
>   The women have leaped from "their spheres."
> And, instead of fixed stars, shoot as comets along,
>   And are setting the world by the ears!
> In courses erratic they're wheeling through space,
> In brainless confusion and meaningless chase.
>
> Oh! shade of the prophet Mahomet arise!
>   Place woman again in "her sphere,"
> And teach that her soul was not born for the skies,
>   But to flutter a brief moment here.
> This doctrine of Jesus, as preached up by Paul
> If embraced in its spirit, will ruin us all.
>
> —MARIA W. CHAPMAN [1]
> *(Nineteenth-century feminist humorist)*

"CHRISTIANITY has done much to raise the status of women" is a persistent shibboleth. The infinite worth of all human beings and the possibility of their redemption *are* basic tenets of the faith.

But Christians must honestly face the historical fact that the church has erected many barriers—socially, legally, spiritually, psychologically—against women's advancement. By propagating the notion that God ordained women to be passive and dependent, lacking initiative and assertiveness, confined to kitchen and pew, the church has hampered growth and fostered low self-esteem in women. It has not challenged women to recognize their God-given gifts, encouraged them to fully use their talents, or helped them to gain a mature sense of personhood. In fact objective outside observers have concluded that "churches are one of the few important institutions that still elevate discrimination against women to the level of principle." [2]

Change is taking place rapidly and the church can't afford to lag any further behind the world in implementing the gospel we profess to believe. We should have learned from the history of slavery and racism. Those who assert an "order of creation" in which women are to be "functionally subordinate" to men, might study the precedents for their arguments in the sixteenth-century Spanish theologians who formulated a "natural law theology for inequality" in order to enslave Indians. They declared that each person has a most appropriate social function. Some individuals' function is to work rather than to think. These biologically distinct individuals are destined by nature to be slaves, a condition beneficial to them and to society. Southerners of the last century used similar arguments to keep blacks in slavery.

Those who declare that the gospel offers women spiritual equality in Christ but not in this world, find themselves arguing along with a theologian of the last century who wrote in defense of slavery: "Our design in giving them the Gospel is not to civilize them—not to change their social condition—not to exalt them into citizens or freemen—it is to save them. . . . Sweeten their toil—sanctify their lives—hallow their deaths." [3] How many women have been similarly treated to saccharine sermons on the blessedness of motherhood?

Some will argue that change is rebellious, that God has assigned women a subordinate role and made his will for them perfectly clear in Scripture. Women have been protesting such misinterpretations of the gospel since the first century. Their efforts came to a boil more than a hundred years ago when many women became active in antislavery efforts. They traveled about giving lectures in various public places, including churches. This brought stern disapproval from ministers who, even though possibly sympathetic to humanitarian causes and reform, felt women should keep silent. When Quaker Abby Kelly spoke out against slavery, one New England clergyman preached a sermon against her, using Revelation 2:20 (KJV) as his text: "I have a few things against thee, because thou sufferest that woman Jezebel, which calleth herself a prophetess, to teach and to seduce my servants to commit fornication."

When the Grimke sisters, Sarah and Angelina (also Quakers), tried to promote abolition, the General Association of Massachusetts Congregationalist Clergy (Orthodox) in 1837 issued a pastoral letter forbidding clergymen to allow them to speak. Woman's power lies in her dependence, the letter declared, and flows from "the consciousness of that weakness which God has given her for her protection." Women were commended for promoting piety in the home and Sabbath schools but rebuked for assuming "the place and tone of men as a public reformer." Because the Grimke sisters spoke of the sexual exploitation of their black sisters and the destruction of marriages under slavery, the divines deplored "the intimate acquaintance and promiscuous conversation of females with regard to things which ought not to be named." [4]

The Grimke sisters responded with a series of articles titled "Letters on the Condition of Women and the Equality of the Sexes," in which they answered the pastoral letter point by point and sought to show how Scripture, particularly the example and teachings of Jesus Christ, emancipates women as well as slaves. Actually the

feminist movement as such was born out of the persecution that
women abolitionists received because of their sex. Many of these
women campaigned against slavery because of their deep Christian
convictions, but they found themselves fighting allegedly "scriptural"
arguments for both slavery and antifeminism. In self-defense they
searched the Bible and discovered many of the same interpretations
which we have used in this book.[5]

Little by little their cause has prevailed. Some Christians, for
example, originally opposed education for women on the grounds
that 1 Corinthians 14:35 says that if a woman wants to know anything she can ask her husband at home. Education was considered
contrary to God's intention for the "weaker sex," whose minds had
not been created to withstand the rigors of learning. If women
studied mathematics, argued some clergymen, it might cause dis-
integration of family life. If women learned geography, they might
leave home (where God intended them to stay) and set off to explore
the world. Some said the only geography women needed to know
was how to get from one room to another in the house and the only
chemistry they needed was how to follow a recipe.

Christians similarly argued against the use of anesthesia in childbirth on the grounds that Genesis 3:16 taught that "God's will is
that women should suffer and die in childbirth." [6] In the same vein
Christians have opposed the whole idea of birth control because
"God's will for women is motherhood."

At the turn of the century when suffragists had pared down their
demands to merely the franchise, men declared that women should
not vote because they were to keep silent and not usurp male authority according to 1 Timothy 2:12.

As Martin Marty points out in *Righteous Empire,* "According to
all accounts evangelical clergymen were virtually unanimous in re-
jecting the feminist cause. . . . Feminists who were religious were
so repelled by conventional Protestantism's opposition that they
drifted off to Unitarianism or to some of the new free religious
groups to gain moral support." [7] Some have always wondered why
women seem more evident in the sects on the fringes of Christianity—perhaps they have been simply driven there by the main-
stream's rejection of their needs and gifts.

Will the church repeat its past errors or learn from them? Paul
laid the groundwork for social change in Galatians 3:28: "There is
neither Jew nor Greek, there is neither slave nor free, there is
neither male nor female; for you are all one in Christ Jesus." As
Krister Stendahl points out, "We would hardly expect to hear Paul
say, 'These statements apply to the question of individual salvation,
but in all other respects things are as they used to be.' " [8] Much of

Paul's energy was devoted to combating the Judaizers who declared that reconciliation of Jews and Gentiles was only a spiritual concept and that meanwhile on earth Gentiles would have to conform to Jewish customs. The first church council (Acts 15) was called to decide that issue. The principles of equality among all believers and freedom from specific cultural customs were affirmed—principles which would eventually extend to slaves and women. But implementation of these principles has been slow and painful.

Paul himself had difficulty with the issues, particularly when it came to women. And yet in the end he affirms, "Nevertheless, in the Lord woman is not independent of man nor man of woman; for as woman was made from man, so man is now born of woman. And all things are from God" (1 Cor. 11:11–12). Something happens in the new life in Christ that abolishes differences, that makes all persons one "in the Lord," mutually interdependent with one another and with him, mutually aware that "all things are from God." Assigning privileges, roles, and spheres of duty and ministry on the basis of sex would necessarily disappear if these teachings of Paul were carried to their logical end.

Today we stand at the crossroads. As Christians we can no longer dodge the "woman problem." To argue that women are equal in creation but subordinate in function is no more defensible than "separate but equal" schools for the races. The church must either be consistent with the theology it sometimes espouses and oppose all forms of women's emancipation—including education, political participation, and vocations outside the home—or it must face up to the concrete implications of a gospel which liberates women as well as men. To argue that women should have political and vocational freedom in the secular world while declaring that they should be subordinate in marriage and silent in church is to stand the gospel on its head.[9] The church must deal with its attitudes and practices in regard to women. To fail to come to grips with this issue is to fail both God and the world we profess to serve in his name.

It's time for Christian men and women to begin to take the women's movement seriously, rather than lightly or humorously, or contemptuously dismissing it. Every movement, Christianity included, has its lunatic fringes, but feminists today inside and outside the church are raising important issues with which we all must grapple. Some areas cry out for Christian theological and ethical insight: the nature of sexuality, the meaning of marriage, questions about vocation, ordination, friendship, homosexuality, abortion. Other issues need Christian involvement on the practical level: equal pay, employment discrimination, child care, educational opportunity, care for the aged, complete and creative use of all women's talents (including use in the church).

What are the basic issues of women's liberation? Do women want to become men? No, we simply want to be full human beings. In the minds of many, however, only men are human—women are their female relatives. Only men can participate in the full range of earth's activities—women have a "proper feminine sphere." Thus to ask for full humanity is, for many, to "want to be like men." Feminists, however, are not denying the basic biological differences between the sexes. We only ask that these differences no longer be used as the basis for judgments of superior/inferior, dominant/subordinate, wide-choices/rigid-roles, vast-opportunities/limited-spheres, and the like. Women are not asking to "become men." We only want to be persons, free to give the world all that our individual talents, minds, and personalities have to offer. Nor are we interested in taking over things or pushing men out of the way. We only ask to be recognized as equal partners, "joint heirs of the grace of life" (1 Pet. 3:7) and "fellow workers in Christ Jesus" (Rom. 16:3).

Nor is women's liberation simply a selfish drive to "do our own thing." We ask for the right to make our own choices, to define our own lives, not out of selfish motivations but because God calls us and commands us to develop the gifts he has given us. Too long we have let men define our lives. Now we must listen to the inner voice. Of course, women will sometimes make mistakes, will succumb to the lure of money, success, power. Men have also made these mistakes. But each of us is responsible for our lives, not to the wishes of others but to the voice of God.

Is it possible to be a feminist and a Christian? The early American abolitionists were. The English Quakers and such women as Catherine Booth, cofounder of the Salvation Army, definitely were. Many other women around the world have been. They have felt directly responsible to God for their gifts. And they have heard his command to use their gifts in service to the world. All Christians, men and women, must remain ever open to the reforming, renewing Word of God.

For men, it is true, women's liberation will mean a loss of power. The king has no place in a democracy. Christ always cautioned his followers about seeking power and authority. At creation God set an example for mankind by sharing with all of us his power and reponsibility for the earth. Men have usurped that power for themselves alone. Redeemed men must again learn to share responsibility with women, including their wives. While from one angle this represents a loss, from another it offers freedom and a lighter load.

We follow a man who once offered, "Take my yoke upon you, and learn from me . . . . my yoke is easy, and my burden is light" (Matt. 11:29–30). In turning over power to him we find the freedom to be our true selves. So men will find in helping to liberate women.

For Christian women, liberation may be a long and difficult process. Many women have not even begun to understand what the movement means to others or to themselves. As Mennonite author Lois Gunden Clemens notes, "Many of the older women in the church who have happily accepted the role assigned to them find it difficult to understand the attitude of the younger women. But these younger women regard this as a matter of Christian integrity. They are seriously concerned about the stewardship of their God-given powers, feeling that they should be using such abilities in the church as well as in the larger community." [10]

Liberation means an end to the self-hatred women have been taught, an end to the hatred we project on other women. Often women resist liberation because we have been taught that our bodies are weaker, our powers of reasoning defective, our intellects lighter, our skills inferior, our emotions frivolous. And we have believed our teachers. We suffer from low self-esteem and no self-confidence. Women's liberation has been termed an "identity crisis." Women are beginning to ask, "Who am I? What does it mean to say that *I* am created in the image of God?" Christ commanded us to love others as ourselves, but we women have been taught to despise ourselves.

And so we have mistrusted other women. We prefer a man to cut our hair, carve our meat, service our car, preach us a sermon. We say we wouldn't work for a woman executive or vote for a woman president. We really do believe that we and all other women are inferior to men. Men sometimes see other men as a part of the "team" but women usually view each other as the "competition." It's time we begin practicing sisterhood as well as brotherhood. Perhaps church circles, auxiliaries, or women's missionary societies could become "consciousness-raising groups" where we begin to share our experiences honestly and learn to appreciate each other as sisters in Christ. Those of us who have "made it" must stop pushing our sisters back with clichés like "Any woman who works hard enough can get to where I'm at—I've never felt discriminated against." We must begin to share our struggles and help each other, particularly those unable to help themselves.

The end of male chauvinism will also mean the end of chivalry in the traditional sense of men continually smoothing the way for the "weaker sex." Women can no longer expect doors to open, seats to become vacant, packages to be carried for them simply because they're women. Women can no longer rely on tears and manipulation rather than reason and hard work to achieve their ends. But hopefully courtesy and consideration will be extended to all persons on an equal basis. Each of us will learn to help the other, to reach out whenever aid is needed, to respond to all appeals for help.

No longer pampered and protected by men, we women must take responsibility for our own lives. We must shoulder our share of the cultural mandate God has given us for the development of our own talents and the preservation of the earth. The easy way out is closed. If we are to follow in Christ's footsteps, we must spend thirty years in the carpenter shop learning our trade; we must endure the wilderness testing; we must travel the land healing the sick, feeding the multitudes, teaching the disciples, preaching the gospel.

We cannot hide behind the skirts of our alleged inferiority or under our domestic bushels. We must speak out ourselves, not wait for men to do it for us. We must join with other women who are crusading for an end to discrimination and for freedom for all people. We must work side by side with men who are also seeking to see God's will done on earth.

Women today must begin to provide role models for younger women, rather than urging them to simply get a man, get married, and beget children. Women now must demonstrate for the next generation that we can be dedicated Christians as well as dedicated, competent achievers in the occupational realm. That Christian single women can be whole persons. That we can be supportive, loving wives without being subservient, self-denying and destructive. That we can successfully combine love of family, dedication to profession, and discipleship to Christ. We must offer both boys and girls a variety of choices, a full range of possibilities for serving God.

We must begin to implement Galatians 3:28, to transcend the limitations our culture has placed on us because of our sex. Jesus walked and taught in a temple which segregated Jew from Gentile, man from woman, priest from layman. But he came to change things. At his crucifixion, the veil of the temple was ripped from top to bottom. Through Christ we have direct access to God; he has abolished the distinction between priest and laity. In Ephesians 2:14 we are told that Christ is "our peace, who has made us both one, and has broken down the dividing wall of hostility," the "middle wall of partition," between Jew and Gentile. Only one barrier still remains—the "court of the women." It is time for the Christian church to tear it down once for all.

In Isaiah 43:4-7, God says to his people: "You are precious in my eyes, and honored, and I love you. . . . Bring my sons from afar and my daughters from the end of the earth, every one who is called by my name, whom I created for my glory, whom I formed and made." Jesus said, "Whoever does the will of God is my brother, and sister, and mother" (Mark 3:35). God does have daughters as well as sons; Christ does have sisters as well as brothers. Now is the time for the church to recognize this—and to act upon it. That's what the Christian woman's liberation is all about.

References

Chapter 1: Religion and the Male/Female Polarity

1. Karen Horney, *Feminine Psychology* (New York: W. W. Norton & Co., 1967), p. 116.
2. Mircea Eliade, *The Quest* (Chicago: University of Chicago Press, 1969), pp. 133–75.
3. William Theodore de Bary, Wing-Tsit Chan, and Burton Watson, eds., *Sources of Chinese Tradition* (New York: Columbia University Press, 1960), 1:59.
4. Eliade, *The Quest,* pp. 161, 175.
5. Ibid., pp. 169–70.
6. H. R. Hays, *The Dangerous Sex: The Myth of Feminine Evil* (New York: G. P. Putnam's Sons, 1964).

Chapter 2: Understanding the Bible

1. G. C. Berkouwer, "Understanding Scripture," *Christianity Today* 14 (22 May 1970): 40.
2. Ibid.
3. Julius Bodensieck, "Theological Principles Determining the Role of Christian Women in Church and Society," mimeographed for Lutheran Social Ethics Seminar, Valparaiso University, December 1955, p. 1. As quoted in Russell C. Prohl, *Woman in the Church* (Grand Rapids, Mich.: Wm. B. Eerdmans Publishing Co., 1957), pp. 18–19.
4. C. S. Lewis, "'Priestesses in the Church?'" in *God in the Dock,* ed. Walter Hooper (Grand Rapids, Mich.: Wm. B. Eerdmans Publishing Co., 1970), p. 237.
5. Eric Marshall and Stuart Hample, compilers, *Children's Letters to God* (New York: Pocket Books, 1966), as quoted in *Reader's Digest,* March 1967, p. 97.
6. John Chrysostom, *The Homilies of S. John Chrysostom on the First Epistle of St. Paul the Apostle to the Corinthians* (London: F. and J. Rivington, 1854), pp. 351–52.

Chapter 3: It All Started with Eve

1. Billy Graham, "Jesus and the Liberated Woman," *Ladies' Home Journal,* December 1970, p. 42.
2. Eva Figes, *Patriarchal Attitudes* (Greenwich, Conn.: Fawcett Publi-

cations, Fawcett Premier Book, 1970), pp. 40, 24, records the story of Lilith. According to seventeenth-century Jewish kabbalistic writings, "God then formed Lilith, the first woman, just as he had formed Adam, except that He used filth and sediment instead of pure dust. From Adam's union with this demoness, and with another like her named Naamah, Tubal Cain's sister, sprang Asmodeus and innumerable demons that still plague mankind." Actually this is surprising, for a twelfth-century midrash on Numbers declares: "Adam and Lilith never found peace together; for when he wished to lie with her, she took offence at the recumbent posture he demanded. 'Why must I lie beneath you?' she asked. 'I also was made from dust, and am therefore your equal.' Because Adam tried to compel her obedience by force, Lilith, in a rage, uttered the magic name of God, rose into the air and left him." The story of Lilith is also the subject of Lilly Rivlin, "Lilith: The First Woman," *Ms.*, December 1972, pp. 92–97; 114–15.

3. H. C. Leupold, *Exposition of Genesis* (Grand Rapids, Mich.: Baker Book House, 1950), 1:94. Plato declared that male and female were the halves of an original sphere. Jewish speculation along the same lines saw a double creature joined back to back which God sawed in half while Adam slept.

4. Emile Cardinal Leger, *Search* 2 (August 1963): 136. Sidney Cornelia Callahan, *The Illusion of Eve* (New York: Sheed and Ward, 1965), p. 60. Alfred Lapple, *Key Problems in Genesis* (Glen Rock, N.J.: Paulist Press, Deus Books, 1967), p. 60.

5. Prohl, *Woman in the Church,* p. 37. James Hastings, *A Dictionary of the Bible* (Edinburgh: T. & T. Clark, 1899), s.v. "Help."

6. Helmut Thielicke, *The Ethics of Sex,* trans. John W. Doberstein (New York: Harper & Row, Publishers, 1964), p. 4, quoting F. Delitzsch. Hastings, *A Dictionary of the Bible,* s.v. "Help."

7. Alexander Jones, gen. ed., *The Jerusalem Bible* (Garden City, N.Y.: Doubleday & Co., 1966). Leupold, *Exposition of Genesis,* 1:94, 137, suggests that "male" and "female" in Gen. 1:27 come from *zakhar,* which has no root meaning other than "male" and *neqebhaha* from *neqab,* meaning "to perforate." The words used in Gen. 2:23 are *ish* and *issha. Ish* is said to have a root meaning "to exercise power." *Issha* is not really grammatically related but is a Hebrew word play. Its roots are possibly Assyrian. *The Interpreter's Bible Dictionary,* s.v. "Sex," suggests *issanu,* as a root meaning "strong," but author O. J. Baab dismisses this immediately as "improbable" without explanation. A second possible root is *anasu,* which can mean either "to be weak or sick" or "to be inclined to, to be friendly, social." A word with the same Hebrew spelling *(anasu)* means "soft, delicate."

8. Paul King Jewett, "The Doctrine of Man: The Divine Ima⸗—Man as Male and Female," course outline for T21 Systematic Theol᾿ᴈy, Fuller Theological Seminary, Pasadena, Calif., 1973, p. 114.

9. Augustine, "The Good of Marriage," trans. Charles T. Wilcox, in *Treatises on Marriage and Other Subjects,* The Fathers of the Church, ed. Roy Joseph Deferrari (Washington, D.C.: Catholic University of America Press, 1955), 27:9.

10. J. B. Phillips, *The Ring of Truth* (New York: Macmillan Co., 1967), p. 28: "Sometimes you can see the conflict between the Pharisaic spirit of the former Saul (who could say such grudging things about marriage and insist upon the perennial submission of women) and the Spirit of God, who inspired Paul to write that in Christ there is neither 'Jew nor Greek . . . male nor female.'" Jewett, "The Doctrine of Man," p. 98: "Because these

two perspectives—the Jewish and the Christian—are incompatible, there is no satisfying way to harmonize the Pauline argument for female subordination with the larger Christian vision of which the great apostle to the Gentiles is the primary New Testament architect. Paul himself, judging from the evidence, was not wholly unaware of the tension in his thought." Richard N. Longenecker, "Can We Reproduce the Exegesis of the New Testament?" *Tyndale Bulletin* 21 (1970) :3–38.

11. Jewett, "The Doctrine of Man," p. 99.

12. Dick and Joyce Boldrey, "Women in Paul's Life," *Trinity Studies* 2 (1972) :13. Morna D. Hooker, "Authority on Her Head: An Examination of I Cor. XI.10," *New Testament Studies* 10(1963–64) :410–16.

13. Thielicke, *Ethics of Sex,* p. 10.

14. Augustine, *The Trinity,* trans. Stephen McKenna, The Fathers of the Church, 45:351–55 (bk. 12, chap. 7).

15. Marcus Dods, "The First Epistle to the Corinthians," *The Expositor's Bible* (Grand Rapids, Mich.: Wm. B. Eerdmans Publishing Co., 1940), 5: 681–2. Quoted by permission.

16. James Moffatt, *The First Epistle of Paul to the Corinthians* (New York: Harper and Bros., Publishers, n.d.), p. 151. Margaret E. Thrall, *The First and Second Letters of Paul to the Corinthians* (London: Cambridge University Press, 1965), pp. 79–80.

17. Peter Brunner, *The Ministry and the Ministry of Women* (St. Louis: Concordia Publishing House, 1971) has developed this argument most fully. John Reumann, "What in Scripture Speaks to the Ordination of Women?" *Concordia Theological Monthly* 44 (January 1973): 25–26 offers a reply.

18. For a biblical study of head vs. heart note such references as "Wisdom resteth in the heart of him that hath understanding" (Prov. 14:33, KJV); "The good man out of the good treasure of his heart produces good, and the evil man out of his evil treasure produces evil; for out of the abundance of the heart his mouth speaks" (Luke 6:45). See also Ps. 44:21; 1 Chron. 28:9; Rom. 10:9–10; Mark 2:6–8, etc.

19. Boldrey and Boldrey, "Women in Paul's Life," p. 11.

20. Martin Luther, *Luther's Commentary on Genesis,* trans. J. Theodore Mueller (Grand Rapids, Mich.: Zondervan Publishing House, 1958), p. 68.

21. E. A. Speiser, *Genesis* (Garden City, N.Y.: Doubleday & Co., 1964), p. 21.

22. Johanna Timmer, " 'Women's Lib'—A Misnomer?" *The Outlook* 23 (April 1973) :9–10: "The devil's first customer was Eve, who, horror of horrors! lent him a ready ear. . . . In a sense Eve may be said to have started the 'Women's Lib.' movement."

23. Aileen S. Kraditor, ed., *Up from the Pedestal* (Chicago: University of Chicago Press, Quadrangle Books, 1968), p. 38.

24. Dave Scaer, "What Did St. Paul Want?" *His,* May 1973, p. 13.

25. David Hubbard, "When Man Was Human," *His,* October 1971, p. 3.

26. John Peter Lange, *A Commentary on the Holy Scriptures,* trans. Philip Schaff (New York: Charles Scribner's Sons, 1905), 10:229. Augustine, *The City of God* (Garden City, N.Y.: Doubleday & Co., Image Books, 1958), p. 256 (bk. 19, chap. 2).

27. Leupold, *Exposition of Genesis,* p. 152.

28. Dietrich Bonhoeffer, *Creation and Fall; Temptation* (New York: Macmillan Co., 1959), p. 75.

29. E. J. Young, *Genesis 3* (London: The Banner of Truth Trust, 1966), pp. 70, 91.

30. Boldrey and Boldrey, "Women in Paul's Life," p. 33. The first reference to woman's "pain" in Gen. 3:16 is the Hebrew word *itstsabon*, which is used again in v. 17 of man's "toil" or "labor." Likewise, *etzev*, the second word of "pain" in 3:16 is translated "labor" in Gen. 5:29 (NEB) and Prov. 14:23 (KJV).

31. Young, *Genesis 3*, p. 124.

32. Leupold, *Exposition of Genesis*, p. 172.

33. Young, *Genesis 3*, p. 127. Cf. C. F. Keil and F. Delitzsch, *Biblical Commentary on the Old Testament* (Grand Rapids, Mich.: Wm. B. Eerdmans Publishing Co., n.d.), 1:103.

34. S. R. Driver, *The Book of Genesis* (London: Methuen & Co., 1911), p. 49.

35. Helen B. Andelin, *Fascinating Womanhood* (Santa Barbara, Calif.: Pacific Press, 1963), p. 89.

36. Prohl, *Woman in the Church*, p. 39.

37. Thielicke, *Ethics of Sex*, p. 8.

38. Luther, *Commentary on Genesis*, p. 82.

39. Andre Dumas, "Biblical Anthropology and the Participation of Women in the Ministry of the Church," in *Concerning the Ordination of Women* (Geneva: World Council of Churches, Department on Faith and Order, 1964), p. 32.

Chapter 4: Women in the Bible World

1. Richard Gilman, "Where Did It All Go Wrong?" *Life*, 13 August 1971, p. 48.

2. Simone de Beauvoir, *The Second Sex*, trans. and ed. H. M. Parshley (New York: Bantam Books, 1961), pp. 75–76.

3. See, for example, Phyllis M. Kaberry, *Women of the Grassfields* (London: Her Majesty's Stationery Office, 1952).

4. H. W. F. Saggs, *The Greatness That Was Babylon* (London: Sidgwick and Jackson, 1962), pp. 186–87.

5. Edward B. Pollard, *Woman in All Ages and in All Countries*, vol. 4, *Oriental Women* (Philadelphia: The Rittenhouse Press, 1907), pp. 104–5.

6. Saggs, *The Greatness That Was Babylon*, p. 214.

7. "Women's Rights Becoming Issue in Morocco," UPI report in *Bloomington* (Ind.) *Herald-Telephone*, 29 September 1971.

8. See Eva Matthews Sanford, *The Mediterranean World in Ancient Times* (New York: Ronald Press Co., 1938), pp. 45, 110; Pollard, *Oriental Women*, p. 106; Charles Seltman, *Women in Antiquity* (London: Thames and Hudson, 1956), pp. 30–32; "The Code of Hammurabi," in James B. Pritchard, ed., *The Ancient Near East* (Princeton: Princeton University Press, 1958), pp. 138–67.

9. de Beauvoir, *Second Sex*, pp. 78–79.

10. Seltman, *Women in Antiquity*, p. 42.

11. de Beauvoir, *Second Sex*, p. 79.

12. Seltman, *Women in Antiquity*, p. 43.

13. de Beauvoir, *Second Sex*, p. 80.

14. Roland de Vaux, *Ancient Israel*, trans. John McHugh (London: Darton, Longman & Todd, 1961), p. 20.

15. Ibid., p. 40.

16. Krister Stendahl, *The Bible and the Role of Women*, trans. Emilie T. Sander (Philadelphia: Fortress Press, 1966), p. 27.

17. Ze'ev W. Falk, *Hebrew Law in Biblical Times* (Jerusalem: Wahrmann Books, 1964), p. 111.

18. Ibid., p. 169.

19. de Vaux, *Ancient Israel,* pp. 54–55.

20. See David R. Mace, *Hebrew Marriage* (New York: Philosophical Library, 1953), pp. 230–31. Also William N. Stephens, *The Family in Cross-Cultural Perspective* (New York: Holt, Rinehart and Winston, 1963), pp. 225 ff.

21. Mary Douglas, *Purity and Danger* (Middlesex, England; Baltimore, Md.; Penguin, Pelican Books, 1970), p. 160.

22. de Vaux, *Ancient Israel,* p. 36.

23. Michael Grant, *The World of Rome* (New York: New American Library Mentor Book, 1960), p. 91.

24. de Beauvoir, *Second Sex,* p. 86.

25. E. M. Blaiklock, *From Prison in Rome—Letters to the Philippians and Philemon* (Grand Rapids, Mich.: Zondervan Publishing House, 1964), p. 47; and "Luke" in *Zondervan Pictorial Bible Dictionary* (Grand Rapids, Mich.: Zondervan Publishing House, 1963), p. 495.

26. Plato, *The Republic,* trans. Francis MacDonald Cornford (New York: Oxford University Press, paperback, 1945), pp. 149, 153.

27. Quoted in de Beauvoir, *Second Sex,* p. 81.

28. Seltman, *Women in Antiquity,* p. 115.

29. See for example Jerome Carcopino, *Daily Life in Ancient Rome* (New Haven: Yale University Press, 1940), pp. 92–93.

30. Suetonius, *The Twelve Caesars,* trans. Robert Graves (Middlesex, England; Baltimore, Md.: Penguin Books, 1957).

31. Grant, *World of Rome,* ch. 6.

32. Stendahl, *Bible and the Role of Women,* p. 25.

Chapter 5: Woman's Best Friend: Jesus

1. Seltman, *Women in Antiquity,* p. 184.

2. C. F. D. Moule, *The Phenomenon of the New Testament* (Naperville, Ill.: Alec R. Allenson, Inc., 1967), p. 65.

3. Dorothy Sayers, *Are Women Human?* (Grand Rapids, Mich.: Wm. B. Eerdmans Publishing Company, 1971), p. 46.

4. Charles Caldwell Ryrie, *The Place of Women in the Church* (Chicago: Moody Press, 1958), p. 23, quoting James Hastings.

5. Sacrifices under the levitical law were not all male, however. Note Lev. 3:1; 4:28, 32; 5:6.

6. Graham, "Jesus and the Liberated Woman," p. 46.

7. Sayers, *Are Women Human?,* pp. 46–47.

8. Interestingly Matthew, writing to the Jewish community, includes Joseph's genealogy and all that we know about him. Luke, on the other hand, a liberated physician writing to a Gentile, mentions many women, often placing them parallel with his mention of men:

	Luke	
Zechariah	1:5–22, 26–38	Mary
Simeon	2:25–38	Anna
Naaman	4:27, 25–26	widow of Zarephath
demoniac at Capernaum	4:31–39	Peter's mother-in-law
centurion's servant	7:1–17	widow of Nain's son

Simon the Pharisee	7:36–50	public sinner
Twelve	8:1–3	women followers
Garasene demoniac	8:26–56	woman with hemorrhage, Jairus' daughter
Good Samaritan	10:29–42	Mary and Martha
men of Nineveh	11:32, 31	queen of the South
man with dropsy	14:1–6; 13:10–17	crippled woman
man with mustard seed	13:18–21	woman with yeast
man with 100 sheep	15:4–10	woman with 10 coins
two men sleeping	17:34–35	two women grinding corn
Pharisee and publican	18:9–14, 1–8	importunate widow
scribes	20:45–47; 21:1–4	widow's mite
Joseph of Arimathea	23:50–56	women from Galilee
Emmaus disciples	24:13–35, 1–11	women at the tomb
Eleven, Jesus' brothers	Acts 1:13–14	women, Mary, Jesus' mother
sons, menservants	2:17–18	daughters, maidservants
Ananias	5:1–11	Sapphira
Aeneas	9:32–42	Tabitha (Dorcas)
Philippian jailer	16:25–34, 14–15	Lydia
Dionysius	17:34	Damaris
Apollos	18:24–28	Priscilla
Agabus	21:10, 9	Philip's four daughters

Other interesting parallels could be drawn between Nicodemus and the Samaritan woman (John 3:1–21; 4:1–42); the conscientious steward and the ten bridesmaids (Matt. 24:45–25:13); Judas who sold Christ for money and Mary who anointed him with the most costly thing she owned (Matt. 26:14–16; 6–13); the disciples in the upper room and Mary Magdalene at the tomb (John 20:19–29; 11–18). Such parallelism has been suggested by Helmut Flender, *St. Luke, Theologian of Redemption History* (Philadelphia: Fortress Press, 1967), pp. 9–10.

9. Paul ignores women in his summary of resurrection witnesses (1 Cor. 15:4–8). As Josephus records, "But let not a single witness be credited; but three or two at the least, and those such whose testimony is confirmed by their good lives. But let not the testimony of women be admitted, on account of the levity and boldness of their sex." *The Works of Flavius Josephus,* "The Antiquities," trans. William Whiston (London: William W. Nimmo, n.d.), p. 97 (bk. 6, chap. 8, v. 15). This anti-feminine tradition had grown up in Jewish law despite the fact that Deut. 17:6 and 19:15 say nothing about the inadmissibility of women's testimony.

10. This point was most movingly made in a devotional talk by Virginia Mollenkott at the Conference on Contemporary Issues, "Evangelical Perspectives on Woman's Role and Status," 30 May 1973, at Conservative Baptist Theological Seminary, Denver.

11. Noted by Paul King Jewett in a speech at the Conference on Contemporary Issues, 31 May 1973.

12. Is there any connection between the murderous rage displayed by the people of Nazareth in Luke 4:28 and the fact that "Joseph's son" had compared his mission to Elijah's being sent to a Sidonian widow or to Naaman's being healed on the suggestion of his Jewish maid? Note the reactions also in Matt. 26:8; Luke 7:39; 13:14; John 4:27; 8:9–10.

Chapter 6: Your Daughters Shall Prophesy

1. Lucy S. Dawidowicz, "On Being a Woman in Shul," *Commentary*, July 1968, p. 72.

2. In Romans 16 Paul mentions ten women: Phoebe (v. 1), Prisca (Priscilla, v. 3), Mary (v. 6), Junias (Junia, v. 7, see KJV), Tryphaena and Tryphosa (v. 12), Persis (v. 12), Rufus's mother (v. 13), Julia, Nereus's sister (v. 15). Junia(s) is sometimes considered a masculine name. However, Junia was a common woman's name and is more likely feminine rather than a shortened form of a very obscure man's name. The case ending on the name in the Greek could be either masculine or feminine.

3. Ruth Hoppin, *Priscilla: Author of the Epistle to the Hebrews* (New York: Exposition Press, 1969). Other scholars who share this opinion which was first proposed by Adolf Harnack are James Rendel Harris (*Sidelights on New Testament Research*), Arthur S. Peake (*A Critical Introduction to the New Testament*) and James Hope Moulton. Lee Anna Starr, *The Bible Status of Women* (Zarephath, N.J.: Pillar of Fire, 1926, 1955), pp. 392–415, reprints a translation of Harnack's essay.

4. Charles Caldwell Ryrie, *Place of Women*, pp. 87–88. Prohl, *Woman in the Church*, pp. 70–71. Boldrey and Boldrey, "Women in Paul's Life," p. 1. J. Massyngberde Ford, "Biblical Material Relevant to the Ordination of Women," *Journal of Ecumenical Studies* 10 (Fall 1973): 677, notes that the masculine form *prostates* (fem. *prostatis*) is used repeatedly in the LXX of stewards (1 Chron. 27:31), officers (1 Chron. 29:6; 2 Chron. 8:10), governors (1 Esdras 2:12; 2 Macc. 3:4).

5. Prohl, *Woman in the Church*, p. 70. Ryrie, *Place of Women*, pp. 85–86. Catherine Beaton, "Does the Church Discriminate Against Women on the Basis of Their Sex?", *Critic* 24 (June-July 1966): 25. Elsie Culver, *Women in the World of Religion* (Garden City, N.Y.: Doubleday & Co., 1967), p. 68. Apostolic Constitutions 2:57; 3:5; *Didascalia* 2:26, 3:12.

6. Ryrie, *Place of Women*, pp. 82, 84, 99–100, 128, 130.

7. Ibid., pp. 128, 131–32, 140.

8. Ford, "Biblical Material Relevant to the Ordination of Women," pp. 683, 685, 677–78. Though there is no biblical evidence that women also functioned as bishops, there are several inscription references to *presbutera* and *episcopa*, indicating women. See Joan Morris, *The Lady Was a Bishop* (New York: Macmillan Co., 1973), pp. 3–8.

9. Chrysostom, *The Homilies of St. John Chrysostom*, Nicene and Post Nicene Fathers, First Series (Grand Rapids, Mich.: Wm. B. Eerdmans Publishing Co., 1956), 11:555. Elsie Gibson, *When the Minister Is a Woman* (New York: Holt, Rinehart and Winston, 1970), pp. 9–10. Prohl, *Woman in the Church*, p. 72. Some suggest that Junia was not an apostle but simply one known by the apostles. This is not the best translation of the text.

10. Prohl, *Woman in the Church*, p. 55. Tertullian, *Ante-Nicene Fathers* (New York: Charles Scribner's Sons, 1885), 4:48.

11. Abel Isaksson, *Marriage and Ministry in the New Temple*, vol. 24 Acta Seminarii Neotestamentici Upsaliensis (Lund, Sweden: C. W: K. Gleerup, 1965), and James B. Hurley, "Did Paul Require Veils or the Silence of Women?" *Westminster Theological Journal* 35 (Winter 1973): 190–220, argue that the issue here is not veils but loose hair as opposed to hair braided in a manner indicative of marriage. The word for "veil" appears only in v. 15 where it says a woman's hair is given her instead of a veil. These authors note that the phrases used for head covered and uncovered

in 1 Cor. 11:4–5 are the same as those used by the LXX to translate "the hair of his head hang loose" in Lev. 13:45 and "unbind the hair of the woman's head" in Num. 5:18. They see a similar parallel in Ezek. 44:20 which explains why Paul prohibited long hair on men.

12. Johannes Weiss, *The History of Primitive Christianity,* trans. Frederick C. Grant (New York: Wilson-Erickson, 1937), p. 584. Clarence Tucker Craig, "The First Epistle to the Corinthians," in *The Interpreter's Bible* (New York: Abingdon Press, 1955), 10:126. Prohl, *Woman in the Church,* pp. 28, 51–52.

13. Eugenia Leonard, "St. Paul on the Status of Women," *The Catholic Biblical Quarterly* 12 (July 1950): 319. Moffatt, *First . . . Corinthians,* p. 149. Boldrey and Boldrey, "Women in Paul's Life," p. 28. Culver, *World of Religion,* p. 55.

14. Morna D. Hooker, "Authority on Her Head: An Examination of I Corinthians XI.10," *New Testament Studies* 10 (1963–64): 410–16. J. A. Fitzmyer, "A Feature of Qumran Angelology and the Angels of I Cor. XI.10," *New Testament Studies* 4 (1957–58): 48–58.

15. John Reumann, "What in Scripture Speaks to the Ordination of Women?", *Concordia Theological Monthly* 44 (January 1973): 16; Isaksson, *Marriage and Ministry,* pp. 179–80.

16. Joseph Yoder, *The Prayer Veil Analyzed* (Huntingdon, Pa.: Yoder Publishing Co., 1954).

17. See Hooker, "Authority on Her Head," and Fitzmyer, "A Feature of Qumran Angelology." H. A. Ironside, *Addresses on the First Epistle to the Corinthians* (New York: Loizeaux Brothers, Publishers, 1938), pp. 337–38. Thielicke, *Ethics of Sex,* p. 10.

18. Moffatt, *First . . . Corinthians,* p. 154. Chrysostom, *Homilies,* p. 349. Isaksson, *Marriage and Ministry,* suggests that Paul is thinking of Ezek. 44:20, where the priests serving God must not wear long, unkempt hair.

19. Scaer, "What Did St. Paul Want?" p. 12.

20. Moffat, *First . . . Corinthians,* pp. 231–32.

21. Dawidowicz, "On Being a Woman in Shul," pp. 73–74.

22. Boldrey and Boldrey, "Women in Paul's Life," p. 19.

23. Marga Buhrig, "The Question of the Ordination of Women in the Light of Some New Testament Texts," in *Concerning the Ordination of Women* (Geneva: World Council of Churches, Department on Faith and Order, 1964), pp. 51–53. Fred D. Gealy, "I Timothy," in *The Interpreter's Bible* (New York: Abingdon Press, 1955), 11:403–6.

24. Stendahl, *Bible and the Role of Women,* p. 32.

Chapter 7: He, She, or We?

1. Sigmund Freud, "Femininity," *New Introductory Lectures on Phychoanalysis* (New York: W. W. Norton, 1965), p. 113.

2. Christian Reformed Church, *Study Committee Reports,* "Report 39: Women in Ecclesiastical Office," 1973, pp. 388, 382, 383.

3. Betty Friedan, *The Feminine Mystique* (New York: Dell Books, 1964), pp. 37, 69.

4. Estelle Ramey, "Well, Fellows, What Did Happen at the Bay of Pigs? And Who Was in Control?", *McCall's,* January 1971, pp. 26, 81–83.

5. John Money, "Sexual Dimorphism and Homosexual Gender Identity," *National Institute of Mental Health Task Force on Homosexuality: Final Report and Background Papers* (Rockville, Md.: NIMH, 1972), pp. 45, 44.

See also Mary Jane Sherfey, *The Nature and Evolution of Female Sexuality* (New York: Random House, 1972), p. 46.

6. John Money, "Pubertal Hormones and Homosexuality, Bisexuality, and Heterosexuality," *NIMH Report*, p. 76. See also John Money, "Developmental Differentiation of Femininity and Masculinity Compared," in Seymour H. Farber and Roger H. L. Wilson, eds., *The Potential of Woman* (New York: McGraw-Hill, 1963), pp. 51–65.

7. E. Mansell Pattison in a speech at the Conference on Contemporary Issues, "Evangelical Perspectives on Woman's Role and Status," 30 May 1973, at Conservative Baptist Seminary, Denver, outlined eight variables which contribute to the formation of one's sexual identity. The first five are physiological: chromosomal sex pattern, gonads (the basic gender organs, ovaries or testes), hormonal balance, accessory internal organs (uterus or prostate), external genitals. As Money's research has indicated, a person's basic gender identity is not ultimately determined by these but rather by the final three variables: sex of assignment and rearing, core gender identity or self-image, and gender role identity (one's feeling of adequacy in the performance of social roles labeled "masculine" or "feminine").

8. Susan Fogg, "The Ups and Downs of Human Behavior Cycles," *Chicago Daily News*, 20 April 1973, p. 23 reporting on research by Michael Wallerstein, Jr., and Nancy Lee Roberts. Estelle Ramey, "Men's Cycles," *Ms.*, Spring 1972, pp. 8–15. David Reuben, *Everything You Always Wanted to Know about Sex* (New York: Bantam Books, 1969), pp. 360–85.

9. Dick and Joyce Boldrey in "Women in Paul's Life," p. 23, suggest that "weaker" does not mean physical or mental deficiency but one who is socially and politically *without honor*. Cf. 1 Cor. 1:27 where "weak" is equated with "base, despised, without boast," or 4:10 where it means "undistinguished, without honor." Compare Acts 20:35; 1 Cor. 2:3; 11:30; 15:43 (where weakness is paralleled with dishonor); 2 Cor. 11:21, 29, 30; 12:5, 9, 10; 13:3, 4, 9; 1 Thess. 5:14. Note that Peter in 1 Pet. 3:7 instructs husbands to "honor" wives. In traditional Jewish thinking honor went in only one direction: upward. But Christians were repeatedly instructed to honor those socially and politically beneath them as well.

10. Lionel Tiger, "The Possible Biological Origins of Sexual Discrimination," in Cynthia Fuchs Epstein and William J. Goode, eds., *The Other Half—Roads to Women's Equality* (Englewood Cliffs, N.J.: Prentice-Hall, 1971), p. 55, argues that animal studies show that males are the organizers of society. Naomi Weisstein, "Psychology Constructs the Female, or the Fantasy Life of the Male Psychologist," in Edith Hoshino Altbach, ed., *From Feminism to Liberation* (Cambridge, Mass.: Schenkman Publishing Co., 1971), pp. 153–54, notes that "humans are not non-humans" and secondly that researchers like Tiger ignore animal studies which show such things as competitive, aggressive females and nurturant males. The follies of animal studies and the whole biological question is dealt with in the first two chapters of Ruth Herschberger, *Adam's Rib* (New York: Harper & Row, Publishers, Har/Row Books, 1948), pp. 1–14.

11. Margaret Mead, *Sex and Temperament in Three Primitive Societies* (New York: William Morrow and Company, 1935, 1963), p. 280.

12. Michael Lewis, "There's No Unisex in the Nursery," *Psychology Today*, May 1972, pp. 54–57.

13. Dean Walley, *What Girls Can Be* and *What Boys Can Be* (New York: Hallmark Children's Editions, n.d.).

14. Sarah Bentley Doely, ed., *Women's Liberation and the Church* (New York: Association Press, 1970), pp. 119–24. Study by Miriam Crist and Tilda Norberg for the New York Conference Task Force on the Status of Women, United Methodist Church.

15. Patricia Cross, "The Undergraduate Woman," Research Report Number 5 from the American Association for Higher Education, 15 March 1971. Florence Howe, "Sexual Stereotypes Start Early," *Saturday Review,* 16 October 1971, pp. 76–82, 92–94.

16. William Law, *A Serious Call to a Devout and Holy Life* (London: Printed for the Proprietors and sold by all Booksellers, 1837), pp. 202–3.

17. Marlene Pringle, "Counseling Women," *Caps Capsule* 4 (Spring 1971): 11–15. Entire issue devoted to the subject. See also Eleanor E. Maccoby, "Woman's Intellect," in Farber and Wilson, *The Potential of Woman,* pp. 24–39. Also Alice S. Rossi, "Women in Science: Why So Few?" in Constantina Safilios-Rothschild, *Toward a Sociology of Women* (Lexington, Mass.: Xerox College Publishing, 1972), pp. 141–53.

18. Matina Horner, "Fail: Bright Women," *Psychology Today,* November 1969, pp. 36–38, 62. Judith M. Bardwick, *Psychology of Women* (New York: Harper & Row, Publishers, 1971), pp. 167–87.

19. Kate Millett, *Sexual Politics* (Garden City, N.Y.: Doubleday & Company, Inc., 1970), pp. 176–203.

20. Erik H. Erikson, "Inner and Outer Space: Reflections on Womanhood," in Robert Jay Lifton, ed., *The Woman in America* (Boston: Beacon Press, 1964), pp. 19, 5. For a criticism see Millett, *Sexual Politics,* pp. 214–15.

21. Donald and Inge Broverman, "Sex Role Stereotypes and Clinical Judgments of Mental Health," *Journal of Consulting and Clinical Psychology* 34 (1970): 1–7. Published in summary form by Jo-Ann Gardner, *The Face across the Breakfast Table* (Pittsburgh: Know, Inc., 1970). For similar studies concerning children see Eleanor Maccoby, "Is There Any Special Way of Thinking, Feeling, or Acting that Is Characteristically Female . . . ?" *Mademoiselle,* February 1970, pp. 180–81, 277–78.

22. Doely, *Women's Liberation,* p. 52.

23. Mead, *Sex and Temperament,* pp. 296, 292–93.

24. Alex Davidson, *The Returns of Love* (Downers Grove, Ill.: InterVarsity Press, 1970), p. 59.

25. Matthew Besdine, "Mrs. Oedipus," *Psychology Today,* February 1970, pp. 40–47, 67; "Mrs. Oedipus Has Daughters, Too," *Psychology Today,* March 1971, pp. 62–65, 99.

Chapter 8: Love, Honor, and _____?

1. William J. Lederer and Don D. Jackson, *The Mirages of Marriage* (New York: W. W. Norton & Co., 1968), p. 18.

2. John Stuart Mill, "The Subjection of Women," as reprinted in John Stuart Mill and Harriet Taylor Mill, *Essays on Sex Equality,* edited and with an introductory essay by Alice S. Rossi (Chicago: University of Chicago Press, 1970), pp. 235–36.

3. John Milton, *The Doctrine and Discipline of Divorce* (London: Sherwood, Neely, and Jones, 1820), p. 126.

4. "Women's Lib: Friend or Foe?" *The Alliance Witness* 28 October 1970, p. 23.

5. James Henley Thornwell, "The Rights and the Duties of Masters, A

Sermon Preached at the Dedication of A Church, erected in Charleston, S.C., for the Benefit and Instruction of the Coloured Population" (Charleston, S.C., 1850), as reprinted in Robert L. Ferm, ed., *Issues in American Protestantism* (Garden City, N.Y.: Doubleday & Co., Anchor Books, 1969), pp. 193, 191.

6. Sir William Blackstone's interpretation of English Common Law, as reflected in his *Commentaries* of the late eighteenth century, influenced the laws and customs of both Great Britain and America so that sex discrimination was legally sanctioned. Upon marriage, a woman lost her individual rights and became a nonperson in the eyes of the law. In his seventh edition (1775) Blackstone said, "By marriage, the husband and wife are one person in law; that is, the very being or legal existence of the woman is suspended during the marriage, or at least is incorporated and consolidated into that of the husband; under whose wing, protection, and *cover,* she performs every thing." Quoted in Mary T. Beard, *Woman as Force in History* (New York: Collier Books edition, 1962), p. 89.

7. Mill, "Subjection," pp. 168–69.

8. Johs. Pedersen, *Israel: Its Life and Culture, I–II* (London: Oxford University Press, Geoffrey Cumberlege, 1926), p. 343.

9. Falk, *Hebrew Law in Biblical Times,* p. 154. Also see Deuteronomy 24:1–4, which Jesus said was given because of the hardness of men's hearts (Matt. 19:7–8). The requirement of a *written* bill of divorce was perhaps a protection of sorts for women. At least she knew where she stood—as compared with an angry, spur of the moment demand by a husband that she get out. The requirement of signed papers probably made divorce a bit more difficult and forestalled capriciousness somewhat. But it was far from God's intended ideal (cf. Mal. 2:16).

10. de Vaux, *Ancient Israel,* p. 39.

11. Andre S. Bustanoby, "Love, Honor, and Obey," *Christianity Today* 13 (June 6, 1969): 4. Larry Christenson uses this same quotation to buttress his own similar arguments. See Christenson, *The Christian Family* (Minneapolis: Bethany Fellowship, 1970), p. 41.

12. Winnie Christensen, "What Is Woman's Role?" *Moody Monthly* 71 (June 1971): 83. Also see Bob Mumford, *Living Happily Ever After* (Old Tappan, N.J.: Fleming H. Revell Company, 1973), pp. 28–38.

13. Mumford makes the point that Sarah submitted to her husband even though she knew he was wrong. In obeying her husband she was obeying God, he writes. "Had she disobeyed, she would only have added her own disobedience to the disobedience of her husband." Elsewhere, Mumford uses the passage regarding vows (Numbers 30) to tell Christian husbands they may nullify a woman's promises to God. As an example, he speaks of a wife who announces to her husband she has promised the Lord to serve in some capacity in the local church (such as teaching Sunday school). The husband says she may not do it because the family needs her time and energies at home, assuring her that God will not hold her to her promise because the husband is her head and refuses to give her permission! See Mumford, *Living Happily Ever After,* pp. 29–30, 45.

14. John S. Newton, *Susannah Wesley and the Puritan Tradition in Methodism* (London: Epworth Press, 1968), pp. 84–93.

15. Expressing a similar point of view, Dick and Joyce Boldrey make the clever observation that the Ephesians 5 passage on marriage contains a built-in "self-destruct" with regard to authority. See Boldrey and Boldrey, "Women in Paul's Life," p. 22.

16. James Montgomery Boice, "Marriage by Christ's Standard," *Eternity* 21 (November, 1970) : 21.

17. Callahan, *Illusion of Eve,* p. 201.

18. Donald Grey Barnhouse, *This Man and This Woman* (Philadelphia: The Evangelical Foundation, Inc., 1958), p. 10.

19. Donald Grey Barnhouse, "The Wife with Two Heads," *Eternity* 14 (July, 1963) : 3. (Reprinted from the December, 1958 issue.)

20. Kathryn Kuhlman, "Healing in the Spirit" (an interview with Miss Kuhlman), *Christianity Today* 17 (20 July 1973) : 7.

Chapter 9: Living in Partnership

1. Jessie Bernard, *Women and the Public Interest* (Chicago: Aldine-Atherton, 1971), pp. 88 ff. Psychotherapists of the transactional analysis school also emphasize the need for stroking in human relationships. It is a need for recognition and approval which Harris calls "the psychological version of the early physical stroking" so crucial to infants. See Thomas A. Harris, M.D., *I'm OK—You're OK* (New York: Harper & Row Publishers, 1967), Chapter 3. Also see Eric Berne, M.D., *Games People Play* (New York: Grove Press, 1964), "Introduction."

2. "Talk of the Town," a morning call-in program on an Indianapolis radio station. This interview was heard March 15, 1967.

3. Paul H. Landis, *Making the Most of Marriage* (New York: Appleton-Century-Crofts, 1965), p. 476.

4. The Masters and Johnson research shows that there is only one kind of orgasm, which we may simply call a sexual orgasm (rather than trying to make a distinction between a "clitoral" orgasm and a "vaginal" orgasm, as was the custom in the past—particularly among those of Freudian persuasion). The most sensitive organ of erotic arousal is the clitoris, with the surrounding labia and mons area also being quite sensitive. The vagina itself is supplied with very few nerve endings in contrast to the richly supplied vulva (external female genitalia). During orgasm, the reaction involves and is generalized throughout all the pelvic sex organs regardless of the mode of stimulation, with the clitoris having the role "as the center of female sensual focus." In other words, all orgasm involves clitoral-body stimulation—whether it is direct manual or mechanical stimulation applied to the clitoral shaft or glans, or indirect stimulation through mons area manipulation, breast stimulation, or actual intercourse. See William H. Masters, M.D. and Virginia E. Johnson, *Human Sexual Response* (Boston: Little, Brown, 1966).

5. For a detailed discussion of what the Song of Solomon has to say to married couples today, see Letha Scanzoni, *Sex Is a Parent Affair* (Glendale, California: Regal Books, 1973), pp. 22–33.

6. See A. H. Maslow, "Dominance, Personality and Social Behavior in Women," *Journal of Social Psychology* 10 (1939) : 3–39; and "Self-Esteem (Dominance Feeling) and Sexuality in Women," *Journal of Social Psychology* 16 (1942) : 259–94. Betty Friedan summarizes Maslow's findings in her book, *The Feminine Mystique,* pp. 306–14.

Chapter 10: Womb-Man

1. Augustine, *De Genesi ad Litteram*, VII, 3; and IX, 5, as quoted in Daniel Sullivan, "A History of Catholic Thinking on Contraception," in William Birmingham, ed., *What Modern Catholics Think About Birth Control* (New York: Signet Books, 1964), pp. 32–33.

2. Sigmund Freud, "Femininity," in his *New Introductory Lectures on Psychoanalysis*, trans. and ed. James Strachey (New York: W. W. Norton & Co., College paperback edition, 1965), p. 128.

3. Gerhard Lenski, *Human Societies* (New York: McGraw-Hill Book Co., 1970), p. 156.

4. John Langdon-Davies, *A Short History of Women* (New York: Viking Press, 1927), pp. 149–51.

5. Mircea Eliade, *The Sacred and the Profane* (New York: Harcourt, Brace & World, Harvest Books, 1959), p. 145. Also see Lenski, *Human Societies*, pp. 219–21.

6. See the section entitled, "The Birth of Reason," in Langdon-Davies, *Short History of Women*, pp. 162–65.

7. Horney, *Feminine Psychology*, pp. 114–15.

8. Ashley Montagu, *The Natural Superiority of Women* (New York: Macmillan Co., 1952), p. 33.

9. Hays, *Dangerous Sex*, p. 23.

10. Margaret Mead, *Male and Female* (New York: Dell Publishing Co., Laurel ed. 1968), pp. 119–20.

11. Max Weber, *Ancient Judaism*, trans. and ed. Hans H. Gerth and Don Martindale (New York: The Free Press, 1952), p. 190.

12. *Artharva Veda*, XIV, 2, 14, as quoted in Eliade, p. 166.

13. *Koran*, II, 225, as quoted in Eliade, p. 166.

14. Sophocles, *Oedipus the King*, in David Grene and Richmond Lattimore, eds., *Greek Tragedies*, vol. 1 (Chicago: University of Chicago Press, 1942), p. 166, lines 1256–58.

15. Aeschylus, *The Eumenides*, in David Grene and Richmond Lattimore, eds., *Greek Tragedies*, vol. 3 (Chicago: University of Chicago Press, 1953), p. 28.

16. Paul Isaac Hershon, *A Rabbinical Commentary on Genesis* (London: Hodder and Stoughton, 1885), p. 33.

17. de Vaux, *Ancient Israel*, p. 271.

18. Ibid., p. 460.

19. William Graham Cole, *Sex and Love in the Bible* (New York: Association Press, 1959), pp. 281–83.

20. See Fred E. D'Amour, *Basic Physiology* (Chicago: University of Chicago Press, 1961), pp. 477–78.

21. *The Babylonian Talmud*, 'Erubin, translated under the editorship of Rabbi Dr. I. Epstein (London: The Soncino Press, 1936), pp. 697–98.

22. P. Thomas, *Indian Women Through the Ages* (Bombay: Asia Publishing House, 1964), p. 163.

23. See the chapter entitled, "The Abominations of Leviticus," in Douglas, *Purity and Danger*, pp. 54–72.

24. Ibid., p. 179.

25. *The Babylonian Talmud*, 'Erubin, pp. 697–98.

26. *The Babylonian Talmud*, Niddah, pp. 218–19. Also see *Midrash*, "Genesis," translated under the editorship of Rabbi Dr. H. Freedman and Maurice Simon (London: Soncino Press, 1939), 1:166.

27. S. H. Kellogg, "The Book of Leviticus," *The Expositor's Bible,* 1:316.

28. Ibid., p. 318.

29. Cole, *Sex and Love in the Bible,* p. 283.

30. Hays, *Dangerous Sex,* p. 44.

31. de Vaux, *Ancient Israel,* p. 41.

32. *The Babylonian Talmud,* Niddah, section 31a, pp. 218–19.

33. Ibid., pp. 208 ff.

34. Ibid., p. 213.

35. Panos D. Bardis, "Family Forms and Variations Historically Considered," in Harold T. Christensen, ed., *Handbook of Marriage and the Family* (Chicago: Rand McNally & Co., 1964), p. 417.

36. *Midrash,* Thazria, "Leviticus," 4:187.

37. Troeltsch makes the point that Christian teachings on virginity and the institutionalization of it in the convents gave value and position to the unmarried woman, providing a sphere of great influence that had a part in raising the position of women generally. See Ernst Troeltsch, *The Social Teaching of the Christian Churches,* vol. I, trans. Olive Wyon (London: George Allen and Unwin, 1931), p. 131.

Chapter 11: Reproduction and the Modern Woman

1. U.S. Department of Health, Education, and Welfare, *Monthly Vital Statistics Report: Annual Summary for the United States, 1972—Births, Deaths, Marriages, and Divorces* 21 (27 June 1973):1.

2. Arthur A. Campbell, "Three Generations of Parents," *Family Planning Perspectives* 5, no. 2 (Spring 1973): 110.

3. Letty Cottin Pogrebin, "Motherhood!" *Ms.* 1, no. 11 (May 1973):97.

4. David M. Kennedy, *Birth Control in America* (New Haven: Yale University Press, 1970), p. 42.

5. Ibid., p. 183.

6. Up until 1969, the official manual of the American College of Obstetricians and Gynecologists recommended a number of restrictions with regard to the sterilization of women for contraceptive purposes. Most hospitals followed these guidelines or even stricter regulations, although many have eased them since 1969 when the official manual removed references to such requirements for sterilization. These requirements had related permission to perform contraceptive sterilization with a woman's age and number of children. Women of 25 years of age must have five living children, women 30 years old must have four living children, and women of 35 could not be sterilized unless they had three living children. See Harriet B. Presser and Larry L. Bumpass, "The Acceptability of Contraceptive Sterilization among U.S. Couples: 1970," *Family Planning Perspectives* 4, no. 4 (October 1972):20.

7. Charles F. Westoff, "The Modernization of U.S. Contraceptive Practice," *Family Planning Perspectives* 4, no. 3 (July 1972):10.

8. Richard Bube, "Frozen for the Future," *Eternity* 18, no. 6 (June 1967): 36.

9. R. F. R. Gardner, *Abortion: The Personal Dilemma* (Grand Rapids: William B. Eerdman's Publishing Co., 1972), p. 126.

10. Walter O. Spitzer and Carlyle L. Saylor, eds., *Birth Control and the Christian* (Wheaton, Ill.: Tyndale House Publishers, 1969).

11. One scientist, pointing out that fertility depends on the proportion

of women to men, suggests that the quickest way to curb population growth would be to cut down on the number of women in the world! Thus, he has proposed a "boy birth pill" which would bring about selective fertilization, assuring that 90 percent of babies born would be male. Associated Press report on British scientist John Postgate of Sussex University, "Scientist Proposes 'Boy' Pill," *Bloomington* (Ind.) *Herald-Telephone,* 12 July 1973.

Chapter 12: The Single Woman

1. Evelyn Goldfield, Sue Munaker, and Naomi Weisstein, "A Woman Is a Sometime *Thing,*" in *The New Left,* ed. Priscilla Long (Boston: Porter Sargent Publisher, 1969), p. 256.

2. Herbert J. Miles, *Sexual Understanding Before Marriage* (Grand Rapids, Mich.: Zondervan Publishing House, 1971), p. 177.

3. Goldfield, "A Woman Is a Sometime *Thing,*" p. 255.

4. Jessie Bernard, *The Future of Marriage* (New York: World Publishing Company, 1972), pp. 29–30, 34, 296–97. Hugh Carter and Paul C. Glick, *Marriage and Divorce: A Social and Economic Study* (Cambridge, Mass.: Harvard University Press, 1970), p. 347.

5. Bernard, *Future of Marriage,* pp. 32–36.

6. Germaine Greer, *The Female Eunuch* (New York: McGraw-Hill Book Co., 1970), p. 316.

7. *Family Weekly,* 29 August 1971, p. 2.

8. Dorothy Payne, *Women Without Men* (Philadelphia: Pilgrim Press, 1969), p. 72.

9. Laura Hutton, *The Single Woman* (London: Barrie & Rockliff, 1960), pp. 46–51.

10. Studies have shown that masturbation is not harmful to women and may even be beneficial. See Hutton, *Single Woman,* p. 58. Paul Gebhard, et al., *The Sexuality of Women* (London: Andre Deutsch, 1970), p. 18. Sex Information and Education Council in the U.S., *Sexuality and Man* (New York: Charles Scribner's Sons, 1970), p. 67.

11. Phil Landrum, "But What About Right Now?" an interview on masturbation with Letha Scanzoni, Charlie Shedd, Jim Hefley, M. O. Vincent, Herbert J. Miles, *Campus Life,* March 1972, pp. 38–42. See also Letha Scanzoni, *Sex Is a Parent Affair* (Glendale, Calif.: Regal Books, 1973), pp. 180–93.

12. Charlie Shedd, *The Stork Is Dead* (Waco, Texas: Word Books, Publisher, 1968), p. 73. Miles in *Sexual Understanding,* chaps. 9–10, takes this view of men but denies masturbation as a proper outlet for women.

13. Paul H. Gebhard, "Incidence of Overt Homosexuality in the United States and Western Europe," *National Institute of Mental Health Task Force on Homosexuality: Final Report and Background Papers* (Rockville, Md.: NIMH, 1972), p. 26.

14. Marc H. Hollender, "The Need or Wish to Be Held," *Archives of General Psychiatry* 22 (May 1970):447–48.

15. Payne, *Women Without Men,* pp. 33, 35.

16. John and Mary Ryan, *Love and Sexuality: A Christian Approach* (New York: Holt, Rinehart and Winston, 1967), pp. 137–38.

17. Erich Fromm, *The Art of Loving* (New York: Harper & Row, Publishers, Colophon Books, 1956), p. 9.

18. Ibid., p. 22.

19. Erich Fromm, *Psychoanalysis and Religion* (New Haven, Conn.: Yale University Press, 1950), p. 86.

20. Fromm, *Art of Loving,* p. 46.

21. Frances M. Bontrager, *The Church and the Single Person* (Scottdale, Pa.: Herald Press, 1969), p. 28.

22. Mary Bosanquet, *The Life and Death of Dietrich Bonhoeffer* (New York: Harper & Row, Publishers, 1968), p. 64.

23. O. Hobart Mowrer, *The New Group Therapy* (New York: Van Nostrand Reinhold Company, Insight Book, 1964), p. 31.

24. Among those suggesting communal living for single women are Margaret E. Kuhn, "Female and Single—What Then?" *Church and Society,* March-April 1970, p. 27, and Dorothy Payne, Sister Mary Hilary and others in *The Church Woman,* February 1967.

Chapter 13: Wasting the Church's Gifts

1. "Point of View," afternoon call-in program on WBRI, Indianapolis, March 21, 1967.

2. In the United States, the Congregational Church and Disciples of Christ have the most consistent record for ordaining women. The United Methodist Church granted local preachers' licenses to women in 1919, ordained them in 1924, and finally granted them equality with men as members of annual conferences in 1956. The United Church of Canada (Methodist, Presbyterian, and Congregational) ordained its first woman in 1936. In 1956 the United Presbyterian Church U.S.A. began ordaining women and in 1964 the Southern Presbyterian Church (U.S.) followed suit. In 1970 both the Lutheran Church in America and the American Lutheran Church ordained women. The Baptist Church of Great Britain and the American Baptist Convention ordain women. According to *Christianity Today,* 10 November 1972, p. 62, the Southern Baptist Convention acquired a black woman pastor previously ordained by another Baptist association. The Episcopal Church at the 1970 Houston Convention recognized women as deacons on a par with men, but in 1973 they refused to take the next step and admit women to full orders of priest and bishop. Conservative groups which ordain women include the Assemblies of God, Church of God, Church of the Nazarene, Churches of Christ in Christian Union, International Church of the Foursquare Gospel, United Missionary Church, and the Salvation Army. *Christianity Today,* 21 February 1973, p. 43, reports that a woman has also been licensed by the North American Mennonites.

3. Basic sources on the question of the ordination of women are: Peter Brunner, *The Ministry and the Ministry of Women* (St. Louis: Concordia Publishing House, 1971), Lutheran, negative. *Concerning the Ordination of Women* (Geneva: World Council of Churches, Department of Faith and Order, 1964), ecumenical. Margaret Sittler Ermarth, *Adam's Fractured Rib* (Philadelphia: Fortress Press, 1970), Lutheran Church in America, positive. Emily C. Hewitt and Suzanne R. Hiatt, *Women Priests: Yes or No?* (New York: Seabury Press, 1973), Episcopal, positive. John Reumann, "What in Scripture Speaks to the Ordination of Women?" *Concordia Theological Monthly* 44 (January 1973): 1–30, Lutheran, scholarly, positive. Stendahl, *The Bible and the Role of Women,* Swedish, hermeneutical, positive. Few of the arguments in these books are really new. Many of them were outlined in the last century in such books as Phoebe Palmer's *Prom-*

ise of the Father (1859), Catherine Booth's *Female Ministry* (1859), B. T. Roberts's *Ordaining Women* (1891) and Frances Willard's *Woman in the Pulpit* (1888). They founded, respectively, the "Holiness Movement," the Salvation Army, the Free Methodist Church and the Women's Christian Temperance Union.

4. "The practice of excluding women from ecclesiastical office cannot conclusively be defended on biblical grounds"—Christian Reformed Church, *Study Committee Reports,* "Report 39: Women in Ecclesiastical Office," 1973, p. 453. "Although the ordination of women raises new and difficult questions, there is no decisive theological argument against the ordination of women"—American Lutheran Church seminary position paper, in Ermarth, *Adam's Fractured Rib,* p. 113. ". . . the objections rest on a rather literal approach to the Bible and fail to take into account the degree to which the Bible is conditioned by the circumstances of its time"—The Episcopal Church, progress report to the House of Bishops, October 1966, in Hewitt and Hiatt, *Women Priests?* p. 114. See also N. J. Hommes, "Let Women Be Silent in Church," *Calvin Theological Journal* 4 (April 1969): 6.

5. Catherine Beaton, "Does the Church Discriminate Against Women on the Basis of Their Sex?" *Critic* 24 (June–July 1966): 22.

6. Mary Daly, *The Church and the Second Sex* (New York: Harper & Row, Publishers, 1968), p. 121. Mossie Allman Wyker, *Church Women in the Scheme of Things* (St. Louis: Bethany Press, 1953), pp. 50–52.

7. Leonard Hodgson, "Theological Objections to the Ordination of Women," *The Expository Times* 77 (April 1966): 212–13. Hewitt and Hiatt, *Women Priests?* pp. 75–76. Gertrud Heinzelmann, "The Priesthood and Women," *Commonweal,* 15 January 1965, p. 507.

8. From a statement to the press dated 25–8 April 1967 by the Orthodox Presbyterian Church. H. Goedhard, "Women in the Pulpit?" *Journal of Ecumenical Studies* (Fall 1968): 826. From a report concerning the Lutheran Church—Missouri Synod, *Chicago Daily News,* 25 November 1970, p. 12.

9. Nicolae Chitescu, "The Ordination of Women," in *Concerning the Ordination of Women,* p. 58. He cites the second canon of Denis of Alexandria (Synt. At., 4:7) and the sixth and seventh canons of Timothy of Alexandria (Synt. At., 4:333–36).

10. See chapter 2. This position is blatantly argued by C. S. Lewis, "Priestesses in the Church?", pp. 234–39. And by C. Kilmer Myers, Episcopal Bishop of California, "Should Women Be Ordained? No," *The Episcopalian,* February 1972, pp. 8–9. See also James L. Steele, "Caligula's Horse," *Advance,* January 1973, pp. 6–7.

11. Andre Dumas, "Biblical Anthropology and the Participation of Women in the Ministry of the Church," in *Concerning the Ordination of Women,* pp. 14–15.

12. Hodgson, "Theological Objections," p. 211.

13. Hewitt and Hiatt, *Women Priests?,* p. 121, footnote 9. Doely, ed., *Women's Liberation and the Church,* p. 41.

14. Stendahl, *Bible and the Role of Women,* pp. 19–20.

15. Heinzelmann, "The Priesthood and Women," p. 507. Eugenia Leonard, "St. Paul on the Status of Women," *The Catholic Biblical Quarterly* 12 (July 1950): 313–14.

16. Culver, *Women in the World of Religion,* p. 71. See also Morris, *The Bishop Was a Lady.*

17. See Culver, *Women in the World of Religion;* Edith Deen, *Great Women of the Christian Faith* (New York: Harper & Bros. Publishers, 1959); Roland Bainton, *Women of the Reformation in Germany and Italy* (Minneapolis: Augsburg Publishing House, 1971); Roland Bainton, *Women of the Reformation in France and England* (Minneapolis: Augsburg Publishing House, 1973).

18. Elsie Gibson, *When the Minister Is a Woman* (New York: Holt, Rinehart and Winston, 1970), cites many examples, as does Hewitt and Hiatt, *Women Priests?* Many women ministers are members of The International Association of Women Ministers, which publishes *The Woman's Pulpit.*

19. Prohl, *Woman in the Church,* p. 77.

20. Elizabeth O'Connor, *Eighth Day of Creation: Gifts and Creativity* (Waco, Texas: Word Books, Publisher, 1971), p. 57, quoting Frances G. Wickes, *The Inner World of Choice* (New York: Harper & Row, 1963), p. 53.

21. Christensen, "What Is a Woman's Role?" p. 82.

22. Dietrich Bonhoeffer, *Life Together* (New York: Harper & Row, Publishers, 1954), p. 94.

Chapter 14: The World Beyond the Home

1. L. Frank Baum, *The Marvelous Land of Oz* (New York: Dover Publications, Inc., 1969 edition), pp. 170–71.

2. Matina Horner, "Fail: Bright Women," *Psychology Today,* Reprint series No. P–42 (from the November, 1969 issue), as told in the author's biographical information.

3. Larry Christenson, for example, claims that a woman is not equipped by nature to sustain the psychological and emotional pressure of career commitment and leadership in the world "and still fulfill her God-appointed role as wife and mother." Christenson, *The Christian Family,* p. 45.

4. Dr. Henry Morgan, manager of the human relations division of the Polaroid Corporation, as quoted in the *Chicago Tribune,* 28 June 1971.

5. See for example Dale L. Hiestand, *Changing Careers after 35* (New York: Columbia University Press, 1971).

6. Bardwick, *Psychology of Women,* p. 166.

7. Gerald Kennedy, "John Wesley's Life and Times," introduction to *The Journal of John Wesley,* as abridged by Nehemiah Curnock (New York: Capricorn Books edition, 1963), p. viii.

8. *Journal of John Wesley,* p. 132.

9. Ibid., p. 133.

10. Friedan, *The Feminine Mystique,* chapter one.

11. Bardwick, *Psychology of Women,* p. 171.

12. Callahan, *Illusion of Eve,* p. 91.

13. Sidney Cornelia Callahan, "A Christian Perspective on Feminism," in Doely, *Women's Liberation and the Church,* p. 40.

14. Dean Eunice Roberts, Indiana University, quoted in the *Bloomington* (Ind.) *Herald-Telephone,* 9 November 1969.

15. Joan Scobey and Lee Parr McGrath, "The Tandem Job," *Family Circle* (October, 1969), pp. 8 ff.

16. Jessie Bernard, *Academic Women* (University Park, Pa.: Pennsylvania State University Press, 1964), p. 237.

17. Eli Ginzberg and Alice M. Yohalem, *Educated American Women: Self-Portraits* (New York: Columbia University Press, 1966), p. 135.

18. Alice S. Rossi, "Deviance and Conformity in the Life Goals of Women," lecture delivered at Wellesley College, 12 March 1970.

19. Eli Ginzberg et al., *Life Styles of Educated Women* (New York: Columbia University Press, 1966), p. 13.

20. Ginzberg and Yohalem, *Self-Portraits.* The entire book is planned around these four categories. Other insightful books on combining careers and family life are Lynda Lyttle Holmstrom, *The Two-Career Family* (Cambridge, Mass.: Schenkman Pub. Co., 1972) and Michael P. Fogarty, Rhona Rapoport, and Robert N. Rapoport, *Sex, Careers and Family* (London: George Allen and Unwin Ltd., 1971).

21. In addition to introductory chapters on problems, challenges, and responsibilities involved in combining motherhood and an outside occupation, Mrs. Callahan's book contains the detailed stories of sixteen contemporary women who tell how they successfully combine careers and/or further education with child rearing. See Sidney Cornelia Callahan, *The Working Mother* (New York: Macmillan Co., 1971).

22. Bardwick, *Psychology of Women,* p. 213.

Chapter 15: Where Do We Go from Here?

1. From "The Times that Try Men's Souls," a tongue-in-cheek poem written by Maria Weston Chapman in answer to the pastoral letter directed against the Grimke sisters, as quoted in Alice Felt Tyler, *Freedom's Ferment* (New York: Harper & Row Publishers, Torchbook, 1962), p. 445. The poem is quoted in full in E. C. Stanton, S. B. Anthony, and M. J. Gage, *The History of Woman Suffrage,* 6 vols. (n.p., 1881–1922), 1:82–86.

2. *The New York Times,* 17 May 1970.

3. Thornwell, "The Rights and Duties of Masters," p. 197. An interesting parallel is to be found in Luther's response to the German peasants who thought that the priesthood of all believers made them equal to their landlords. In a savage tract *Against the Thievish and Murderous Hordes of Peasants,* Luther encouraged the princes to use brutal force to put down the peasant rebellion, citing New Testament passages on spiritual warfare and texts from Romans 13 on civil order and police power. But to the peasants his appeal was to the Sermon on the Mount. They were to turn the other cheek, not resist evil, endure hardship without complaint. He even went so far as to say that the peasants' claim that Genesis 1 and 2 taught that God had made men equal and created the world equally for all were not texts to be taken seriously in the New Testament age when "Moses counts for nothing." See H. Richard Niebuhr, *The Social Sources of Denominationalism* (Cleveland: The World Publishing Co., Meridian Books, 1957), pp. 34–37. See also V. H. H. Green, *Luther and the Reformation* (New York: Capricorn Books, 1964), pp. 137–39.

4. Gage, *History of Woman Suffrage,* 1:81, as quoted in Tyler, *Freedom's Ferment,* pp. 444–45.

5. Letha Scanzoni, "The Feminists and the Bible," *Christianity Today,* 2 February 1973, pp. 10–15.

6. See A. D. White, *The History of the Warfare of Science with Theology in Christendom* (New York: Appleton-Century-Crofts, 1955), 2:63.

7. Martin E. Marty, *Righteous Empire* (New York: Dial Press, 1970), p. 98.

8. Stendahl, *Bible and the Role of Women,* p. 33.

9. Ibid., p. 39.

10. Lois Gunden Clemens, *Woman Liberated* (Scottdale, Pa.: Herald Press, 1971), p. 141.

Index

Study Guide

Many Christians today are asking: What does it mean to be a woman, to be a man? What does it mean for women to participate fully and equally in home, church and world? What does it mean to be *All We're Meant to Be?* Since we wrote this book, we have talked with many sisters and brothers around the country. Many others have written to us to rejoice in their own thoughts which they found articulated in this book, to share their own struggles, and to ask deeper and more personal questions. We have tried to give honest answers based on our study of the Bible, church history, psychology and sociology. Sometimes we have simply shared the questions we still have, the struggles which continue.

The purpose of this study guide is to help you as an individual or a group of readers to understand, evaluate, and struggle with the concepts presented in our book, to share your own experiences, to learn from the experiences of others, and to apply the insights gained to your own life or lives. This book might well be studied by an existing group interested in the women's issue, a group gathered just to study this book, or a group resulting from interest aroused among people who have already read the book. Women of all ages and life styles will find the study challenging and helpful. Men will also find discussion of the issues profitable and liberating.

All We're Meant to Be contains both scholarly discussion of the Bible and practical applications of biblical principles to daily life. The first six chapters are primarily concerned with exploring what Scripture has to say; the remainder tries to apply it to women's lives today. Although this study guide supplies questions for each chapter in order, readers and group leaders may prefer to approach the book in a variety of other ways. One could begin with Chapter 6 "He, She, or We?" and work forward, backtracking to the more exegetical chapters as the group feels the need. One could combine various chapters which deal with similar issues. For example:

- *What is feminism?* Introduction and Chapter 15 "Where Do We Go from Here?"
- *How can we approach the issues?* Chapter 1 "Religion and the

Male/Female Polarity" and Chapter 2 "Understanding the Bible"

- *Finding basic principles.* Chapter 3 "It All Started with Eve" and Chapter 5 "Woman's Best Friend: Jesus"
- *Old Testament teaching.* Chapter 3 "It all started with Eve," Chapter 4 "Women in the Bible World," Chapter 8 "Love, Honor, and _____?" pp. 92–96, Chapter 10 "Womb-Man" pp. 119–33, Chapter 14 "The World Beyond the Home" pp. 184–85
- *New Testament teaching.* Chapter 5 "Woman's Best Friend: Jesus," Chapter 6 "Your Daughters Shall Prophesy," Chapter 3 "It All Started with Eve" pp. 27–31, 36–37, Chapter 7 "He, She, or We?" pp. 85–87, Chapter 8 "Love, Honor, and _____?" pp. 101–5, Chapter 9 "Living in Partnership" pp. 106–11, Chapter 10 "Womb-Man" pp. 133–36, Chapter 13 "Wasting the Church's Gifts" pp. 170–73, 177–81
- *Made in God's image.* Chapter 3 "It All Started with Eve," Chapter 7 "He, She, or We?" and Chapter 14 "The World Beyond the Home" pp. 187–88
- *Singleness.* Chapter 12 "The Single Woman"
- *Marriage.* Chapter 8 "Love, Honor, and _____?" and Chapter 9 "Living in Partnership"
- *Motherhood.* Chapter 10 "Womb-Man," Chapter 11 "Reproduction and the Modern Woman," Chapter 14 "The World Beyond the Home"
- *Career.* Chapter 12 "The Single Woman" pp. 159–63, Chapter 13 "Wasting the Church's Gifts," Chapter 14 "The World Beyond the Home"
- *The church.* Chapter 6 "Your Daughters Shall Prophesy" and Chapter 13 "Wasting the Church's Gifts"

Regardless of the size, composition or goals of the group, it will need someone to act as discussion leader and guide on a permanent, shared or rotating basis. The person who leads the first session should have read the entire book and perhaps some reviews of it in order to introduce the study in an enthusiastic way which will stimulate interest and curiosity. Questions have been included for the first session (Introduction and chapter 1) which will help members of the group introduce themselves to each other. This is particularly important if the members of the group do not know each other previously, but it is also helpful even if they are friends in other contexts. The questions will help them share their views on the women's movement and their own stance in regard to it.

The group should covenant together to read the assigned chapters so that discussions will not simply center around unsupported opinions. The leader may wish to assign certain key Scripture passages the week before they are to be discussed so that group members may be studying them beforehand. Members should be encouraged to bring a Bible to each session. Paper and pencils should also be available when the questions necessitate their use.

The leader at each meeting should have read the chapter or chapters under consideration as well as the major Scripture passages alluded to by the authors. She should also consider the various members of the group—their life styles, needs, gifts, bruises—in order to gear the study in a way that will be most helpful to everyone present. The leader's aim should be to listen to the group's reactions and interpretations of the authors' thoughts, to clarify and/or summarize the authors' viewpoint when appropriate (be prepared to read key sections if it appears a majority of the group have not done their homework), to make sure the group takes seriously the book's contributions as well as encouraging all members of the group to share their own opinions, reactions, experiences. It is good to have in mind specific goals for what the group should accomplish in each session: knowledge that they should gain from the book, feelings which they should explore and action which might appropriately result.

The leader should open each session with a succinct statement of the topic to be discussed. She should then throw out as an opening question the one which she thinks will most stimulate her group. She should not hesitate to pick and choose among the questions or make up her own in order to draw out or speak to the needs of her group. The goal of each session should not be to get through a given chapter or so many questions but to explore the issues which interest the group. A good leader will be able to formulate additional questions to follow up on an issue raised in the discussion, to uncover assumptions or prejudices, to help clarify generalizations.

All We're Meant to Be will at times arouse heated discussion in any group. Don't be afraid to let everyone express their views, and don't be hasty in trying to patch up disagreements or harmonize opposing ideas. The leader, however, should try to maintain a certain objective perspective on the discussion, to affirm each member of the group, to help each one clarify their own views and listen sympathetically to the views of others. No one person (leader included) should dominate the group. Nor should one faction (singles, marrieds, men, educated people) be allowed to monopolize the discussion. Another pitfall is getting hung up on one or two biblical texts to the exclusion of all others. If this happens, the group's leader should exercise her right to table the issue until more homework can be done, expert advice sought, or the group reassembles in Heaven (some issues just have two sides that are irreconcilable).

A group of evangelical Christian women in Chicago who became
interested in the issues discussed in this book are continuing the
discussion in a bi-monthly newsletter *Daughters of Sarah*. For a
sample copy write 5104 North Christiana, Chicago, IL 60625.

INTRODUCTION and Chapter 1:
RELIGION AND THE MALE/FEMALE POLARITY

1. Finish the statement "I am . . ." in ten different words or
phrases. Share your answers with the group.

2. Of the ten answers you gave to question 1, which do you consider the most significant? Discuss why.

3. What does the phrase *women's liberation* mean to you? Do you
think that the term *feminism* means the same things or something
different? Would you identify yourself as a "women's libber," an
"advocate of women's rights," a "feminist"? The authors sometimes
speak of themselves as "Christian feminists" or "biblical feminists."
What do you think that means?

4. Do you agree or disagree with the authors' statement on p. 11
that "Jesus' attitude toward women gave promise of liberation from
the chains of custom"? Why?

5. Reading this book and studying these issues will make changes
in your life. List the ways you hope to change. Make another list of
changes you fear. Share your lists with the group.

6. The authors on p. 15 claim that the four approaches to male-
female interaction described in Chapter 1 are all intermingled in the
Judeo-Christian tradition. (The leader should be prepared to define
and illustrate with appropriate Scriptures the four approaches.)
Which of the four do you think predominates?

Chapter 2: UNDERSTANDING THE BIBLE

1. What is "hermeneutics"? (See pp. 17–20). Why is hermeneutics
so crucial to arriving at a Christian perspective on the women's
movement?

2. On p. 18 the authors note that "Christians who claim to follow
'exactly what the Bible says' are nevertheless *interpreting* its meaning." Tell why you agree or disagree. Can you give examples other
than those cited?

3. Compare the statements of G. C. Berkouwer on pp. 17 and 19.
How do you think they relate to taking a new look at the Bible's
teaching concerning women?

4. Jot down five major principles which you think the Bible *as a
whole* is trying to teach. Compare and discuss answers. Which of

these principles should guide us in understanding the women's issue?

5. Scripture uses many images for God—for example, Father, Rock, Lamb. List as many such symbols as you can think of. Which picture of God means the most to you? Why?

6. What does it mean to say that all language about God is metaphorical?

_____ We can think about God only by picturing God in human terms.

_____ All language about God is inadequate.

_____ We should not take any of the language we use for God literally.

7. Does the Trinity reflect a "chain of command" or are all of the persons of the Godhead equal? (See p. 22.)

8. In the past it was common practice to use masculine words with the intention of referring to both women and men. We sometimes unconsciously fell into that habit ourselves in this book. But increasingly women are becoming offended by such usages. Do you as a woman feel excluded by such hymns as "In Christ There Is No East or West" when the third verse reads:

> Join hands, then, brothers of the faith,
> Whate'er your race may be!
> Who serves my Father as a son
> Is surely kin to me.

Can you think of other such examples of "noninclusive" language in hymns, popular gospel songs, or other worship material? Can you think of ways to change such songs? How about following the verse above with something like this?

> And you, dear daughters of our God,
> Join hands and hearts with me;
> Who serves in love our Lord above
> My sister, too, will be.

For further suggestions concerning worship, see Thomas and Sharon Neufer Emswiler's *Women and Worship: A Guide To Non-Sexist Hymns, Prayers and Liturgies* (New York: Harper & Row, 1974), and Arlene Swidler's *Sistercelebrations: Nine Worship Experiences* (Philadelphia: Fortress Press, 1974). McGraw-Hill Book Company has put out "Guidelines for Equal Treatment of the Sexes" for their writers and others who request it. These guidelines give helpful hints on how to make language more inclusive. The American Bible Society is even trying to use inclusive language in the translation of the Good News Bible. (Compare translations of such

passages as 1 John 3:1, 2 Cor. 5:17, and Rom. 16:1–2 to see some
of the issues involved.)

Chapter 3: IT ALL STARTED WITH EVE

1. To say that male and female were both created in the image
and likeness of God means
—— Women and men are basically alike.
—— All human beings are children of God.
—— Men and women resemble God in the abilities to communi-
cate intelligently and to love other persons.
—— That _____.
2. What part, if any, do sexual differences play in the image of
God?
—— Men are in the image of God; women derive their image from
men.
—— God contains all the qualities our culture has labeled "masculine" and "feminine."
—— None at all because God is not a sexual being.
—— They make possible human reproduction which reflects God's
ability to create life in the beginning.
3. Does the fact that Eve was created as a "help meet" for Adam
mean that they were assigned "different functions" or "separate
spheres"? (See pp. 24 and 26.)
4. How did Jesus harmonize the two accounts of creation found
in Genesis 1 and Genesis 2?
5. Is there any significance to the fact that in Genesis 2 woman is
described as being created after the man? Does Genesis 5:1–2 shed
any light on this?
6. Many Christians equate the word "head" in the New Testament
with the concept of ruling. However, the authors on pp. 30–31 cite
various Scriptures to suggest that "head" "points overwhelmingly,
not to a corporate organizational chart, but to a dynamic, organic,
living unity." All of the Scriptures cited are talking about Christ's
relationship with Christian believers and emphasize Christ's self-
sacrificing role as Savior rather than his role as Lord. What new
perspectives on your relationship to Christ and to other believers
do you gain from a study of Colossians 1:15–18, 2:19 and Ephesians
4:15–16. (Note: Another perspective on the concept of "headship"
in regard to marriage is found on pp. 98–101, but we would suggest
that you reserve discussions of marriage and Ephesians 5:21 ff.
until the group reaches those chapters.)
7. Theologians through the centuries have blamed Eve for the
Fall. Do you think this blame is warranted by the account found in

Genesis 3? How is the Fall interpreted in Romans 5:12–19 and 1 Corinthians 15:22, 45–49?

8. I always thought that original sin was

—— the first time Adam and Eve had sexual relations.

—— Eve's decision to listen to the serpent without consulting her husband.

—— Adam's loving Eve more than he loved God's word.

—— Eve's seduction by the serpent.

—— Adam and Eve's act of disobeying God's specific command not to eat the fruit from a certain tree.

—— Adam and Eve's assertion of their independence from God.

9. What were the consequences of Adam and Eve's sin? Were the results the same or different for all human beings? How are these consequences still manifest today?

10. Does Genesis 3:16 say that male domination was God's intention from the beginning of creation? (See p. 35.) For further discussion of the Genesis accounts see the work of Phyllis Trible: "Biblical Theology as Women's Work" in *Religion in Life* (Spring 1975), "Depatriarchalizing in Biblical Interpretation," *Journal of the American Academy of Religion* (1973), "Eve and Adam: Genesis 2–3 Reread," *Andover Newton Quarterly* (March 1973).

Chapter 4: WOMEN IN THE BIBLE WORLD

1. In what respects was the position of women in ancient Israel higher or lower than their position in surrounding cultures?

2. How was a woman in ancient Israel expected to find her identity? (See p. 42.) Discuss modern parallels.

3. What are some laws which seem to have discriminated against women in ancient Israel?

4. Exodus, Leviticus, Numbers and Deuteronomy are just as much a part of the Bible as the Gospels or Paul's epistles. Do we apply to our lives today the commands given in the Old Testament in the same way we accept those in the New Testament? Should we? Why or why not?

5. In what ways were boys and girls educated differently during Old Testament times?

6. What Old Testament evidence do we have for women's participation outside the home?

7. Compare and contrast Greek, Roman and Jewish cultural attitudes toward women during New Testament times.

8. Does this material concerning various cultures simply help us to understand the Bible better, or are we expected to re-create today any of these cultural patterns?

Chapter 5: WOMAN'S BEST FRIEND: JESUS

1. Why do you think Charles Seltman called Jesus a "feminist"? (For additional material the group may wish to read Leonard Swidler's article "Jesus Was a Feminist," *The Catholic World,* January 1971, pp. 177–83.)

2. What image of Mary the mother of Jesus is presented in the Gospel accounts? How do you think she can be a model for women today?

3. Why do you think the Messiah was a male? Do the New Testament writers stress Christ's maleness in any way? Why was the Greek word *anthropos* used to describe the Incarnation? (See p. 56.)

4. Cite examples showing how Jesus' attitudes and behavior toward women contrasted with those of his male contemporaries. What do you think Jesus thinks of you as a woman? What word best describes how you think of Jesus?

—— Brother   —— Stranger   —— Friend
—— Lover   —— Acquaintance   —— Merciful Judge
—— Lord   —— Teacher   —— Other _____

5. Why does Dorothy Sayers claim that the church has preferred Martha to Mary? (See p. 56.) Do you agree? Do you think of yourself as a Mary or a Martha?

6. What significance do you think there is to the fact that Jesus chose to reveal himself first to women after his resurrection and commanded them to tell this vital good news to the other disciples? (For a beautiful account of this event you might want to read together Virginia Mollenkott's article "Jesus, Women and the Resurrection" in *Eternity,* March 1975, pp. 16–19.)

7. If you could have been one of the women described in the Gospels, who would you like to have been? Why? Pretend that you are that woman and write a letter to Jesus describing your feelings.

Chapter 6: YOUR DAUGHTERS SHALL PROPHESY

(Note: Your group may prefer to study this chapter in conjunction with chapter 13.)

1. Compare and contrast the ministries and responsibilities in your church with those of women in the early church.

2. Compare the translations of Romans 16:1–2 in all the versions of the Bible available to you. Does the expression "Phoebe, a servant" convey the same meaning to you as "Paul, a servant [of the church]"? The feminine form, "deaconess," did not come into usage until centuries later. Until then, both women and men were simply called deacons.

3. What were some of the Jewish and Greek customs concerning head coverings and hairstyles? (See pp. 64–65.)

4. In first-century Greek, there were no quotation or question marks, nor were questions necessarily identified by a typical word order. Such punctuation marks have been supplied by scholars over the years, not all of whom have agreed. Joseph Yoder (cited on p. 66) suggests that in 1 Corinthians 11, Paul is simply restating traditional Jewish teachings in order to begin modifying them at verse 11. Other scholars suggest that from verses 2b through 10 we have a question from the Corinthian church which Paul quotes in order to answer, with the answer beginning at verse 11. (Note: Paul does the same thing in 1 Cor. 6, 7, and 8.) 1 Corinthians 11:13–14 may be read as either statements or questions. Does this help solve the apparent contradiction between verses 8–9 and 11–12? Does this also shed light on why modest hairstyles rather than head coverings become the focus of attention in 1 Peter 3:3 and 1 Timothy 2:9?

5. 1 Corinthians 14:34–35 has likewise been seen as a quotation from Paul's questioners rather than a statement of Paul's beliefs. His answer then may be seen in verses 36–40. Contrast and compare this possibility with other interpretations such as those given on pp. 67–69. Which of these interpretations do you favor?

6. How does 1 Timothy 2:8–15 differ from 1 Corinthians 14:34–40? If the Timothy passage was meant to forbid the improper usurping of authority by a false teacher, is it reasonable to use it to forbid the ordination of a woman who has been called by God and duly educated, examined, and certified by a church?

7. The authors on p. 72 declare that "social distinctions are meant to be transcended—not perpetuated—within the body of Christ." Can you think of examples in the history of the church where such distinctions have been transcended? Where they have been perpetuated?

8. Do the verses referred to at the bottom of p. 71 have only "spiritual" meaning, or do they have practical significance for the everyday lives of Christians?

For additional study in this whole area see Mary L. McKenna's *Women of the Church: Role and Renewal* (New York: Kenedy, 1967), George Tavard's *Women in Christian Tradition* (Notre Dame: University Press, 1973), or Jessie Penn-Lewis, *The Magna Charta of Woman* (Minneapolis: Bethany Fellowship, 1975). The latter is a welcome and significant reprint which contains excerpts from a work by Katherine Bushnell, first published about 1919.

Chapter 7: HE, SHE, OR WE?

1. List the first ten words or phrases that pop into your mind when you hear the word *man*. When you hear the word *woman*.

2. Define the following: (a) female, (b) male, (c) feminine, (d) masculine. How do your definitions of *female* and *feminine* differ? How do your definitions of *male* and *masculine* differ? How do your definitions of *masculine* and *feminine* differ?

3. To what degree are these distinctions biologically innate? To what degree are they learned?

4. Why have parents in our culture tended to train their sons to be aggressive and their daughters to be gentle? Do parents in all cultures train their children similarly? (See pp. 76–77.)

5. Share examples of sex-role stereotyping from your personal experiences with Sunday school curricula, children's books, advertisements, etc.

6. Look up Galatians 5:22–23; Romans 12:9–21; Ephesians 6:10–18; and 1 Corinthians 9:24–27. Would you describe these lists of characteristics as "masculine" or "feminine"? Are these qualities limited to one sex or the other, or are they expected of all Christians?

7. Professors John Money and Anke Ehrhardt, authorities on psychohormonal research, offer reassuring words to persons who worry that children will be confused about their gender identity if sex roles are not rigidly segregated. They do not deny that growing children need to realize that there are two distinguishable sexes but, they point out, "nature herself supplies the basic irreducible elements of sex difference which no culture can eradicate, at least not on a large scale." They refer to primary sexual characteristics (associated with reproduction) and secondary sexual characteristics (such as beards on males, voice pitch differences between the sexes, etc.). In the words of these scientists:

> Provided that a child grows up to know that sex differences are primarily defined by the reproductive capacity of the sex organs, and to have a positive feeling of pride in his or her own genitalia and their ultimate reproductive use, then it does not much matter whether various child-care, domestic, and vocational activities are or are not interchangeable between mother and father. It does not even matter if mother is a bus driver and daddy a cook. (John Money and Anke Ehrhardt, *Man and Woman, Boy and Girl*, Baltimore: Johns Hopkins University Press, 1972, Mentor Books paperback edition, p. 14.)

How does this statement show that emphasizing male-female differences beyond the physical is not important or even necessary? Do you find this viewpoint reassuring or disturbing? Why?

8. In what ways do rigid sex-role stereotypes foster homosexuality? (See pp. 83–84.)

Note: When the authors speak in chapter 7 of Christlikeness rather than culturally stereotyped sex roles as the Christian's model for personality, they are speaking on the universal level. As human beings we are all alike. But as individual persons we are each unique. We are all made in God's image and we are each given a unique configuration of traits and talents. We love and admire certain persons for the qualities that are uniquely theirs—gender is only one of those qualities.

Chapter 8: LOVE, HONOR, AND ———?

(Note: Your group may wish to study chapters 8 and 9 as a unit.)

1. Why do so many Christians believe that an egalitarian marriage is contrary to the will of God?

2. Discuss the two main reasons that so many Christians fear equal husband-wife authority. (See p. 90.) How were similar arguments once used to support such ideas as the divine right of kings or the institution of slavery?

3. Contrast the Old and New Testament views of a spouse's willingness to sacrifice for the other. (See bottom of p. 92 and Ephesians 5:25.)

4. 1 Peter 3:6 has been used to imply that Sarah gave unquestioned obedience to her husband. Did she? (See Genesis 12:10–20; 20:1–18; 16:1–6; 21:9–13.)

5. What does the example of Sapphira in Acts 5 teach us about a wife's obedience? (See p. 96.)

6. In what sense is 1 Peter 3:1–6 simply presenting a strategy for evangelism rather than offering a patriarchal model for Christian marriage?

7. In what sense does Ephesians 5:21–33 present a unique picture of marriage? (Consult pp. 98–99.)

8. How does Ephesians 5:21–33 establish a new pattern encouraging the development of "marriage as God intends it" (p. 99), with each spouse affirming and building up the other? Many Christians have assumed that this passage teaches that husbands are to rule over their wives and that the statement "the husband is the head of the wife" was simply intended to reinforce the prevailing cultural pattern of male dominance. However, the authors suggest that the

apostle was simply starting where the people were and proceeding from there to show *how* the husband is to be "head," with the result that "the headship-subjection pattern was transformed" (p. 100). What do they mean? According to this interpretation, what cycle is set in motion? (See pp. 100–101.)

9. In what ways has Ephesians 5:21–23 been misused?

Chapter 9: LIVING IN PARTNERSHIP

1. Does viewing marriage as a partnership of equals destroy or enrich your understanding of the relationship between Christ and the church? (See p. 106.)

2. Why didn't the New Testament writers call for immediate social change? Give examples.

3. In a cartoon, the minister asked the couple: "Do you promise to love, honor, and negotiate?" Discuss whether this idea is contrary to Christian principles.

4. It is sometimes said that a marriage must have one person in final authority in the event that the husband and wife cannot agree in some matter. How do the authors answer this argument through the use of John Stuart Mill's business illustration and through the example of two-person rulership during the Roman Republic? (See pp. 91–92, and 108.)

5. What does the Bible say about a division of labor according to sex? Consult such passages as Genesis 1:27–28; 3:16–19; and Titus 2:5, and discuss in connection with pages 108–11.

6. How can a wife's sexual assertiveness enhance marital relations? Look up the Scripture reference mentioned in the section from pp. 113–18. (For a more detailed discussion of a biblical perspective on marital sex, you might want to consult Letha Scanzoni's sex education book, *Sex Is a Parent Affair,* Glendale, California: Regal Books, 1973, especially chapter 2.)

Chapter 10: WOMB-MAN

1. Why do you think the authors chose this chapter title? Do you think it describes the way people have traditionally thought of women? Tell why or why not.

2. How did the ancient cultures view woman's reproductive capacities? (See pp. 119–22.)

3. What are some possible explanations for the taboos surrounding menstruation in the Old Testament? (See pp. 125–29.) Contrast these ideas about ritual uncleanness with Jesus' attitude toward the woman with the issue of blood. (See p. 135.) What attitudes might

the Christian woman today have toward menstruation? Is the view of the human body presented in Psalm 139:13–18 helpful in this regard?

4. Why was the period of purification twice as long after the birth of a daughter? (Or if we assume, as some Bible scholars do, that the longer period of purification was originally required for both sexes, the question may be restated: Why was the period of purification cut in half if the infant was of the male sex?)

5. Is there a difference in the way motherhood was viewed in the Old and New Testaments? (Note: In addition to the section which begins on p. 133, see also p. 139 in the next chapter.)

Chapter 11: REPRODUCTION AND THE MODERN WOMAN

1. Have someone in your group read aloud the opening quotation from Letty Cottin Pogrebin. Discuss together any times when you have had similar mixed feelings about children.

2. On page 138, the authors raise the question: "Does the de-emphasis on her childbearing role bring woman new freedom? Or does it threaten to take away her whole purpose for living?" How would you reply? Why?

3. In the section entitled, "A Woman's Choice" (pp. 140–41), a number of questions are raised with regard to decisions about marriage and children—including whether and when to have children and how many. How would you reply to someone who says that asking such questions indicates selfishness? Can you give personal examples of wrestling with these issues?

4. In recent years, articles have been written by both Protestants and Catholics suggesting that voluntary childlessness could serve a function in a life of Christian ministry comparable to the choice of celibacy. Just as the purpose of the committed celibate life has been to free the *individual* to serve God with greater flexibility in time, energy distribution, and geographical mobility, and to devote oneself to God's service with an intensity of concentration that would be difficult in the midst of family demands, so it is proposed that intentional childlessness would free a *couple* to pursue special areas of service to God and humanity. (See section 11 of "Singleness in Ethical and Pastoral Perspective," mimeographed paper by John Howard Yoder, Associated Mennonite Biblical Seminaries, 3003 Benham Avenue, Elkhart, Indiana 46514; also "Childless Marriages: A New Vocation?" by William and Julie Everett, *U.S. Catholic,* May, 1975, pp. 38–39.) What is your opinion of this viewpoint? How would you counsel a young couple who say they have decided never to have children?

5. How does the statement by Dr. Richard Bube (p. 142) have relevance for a Christian in thinking through decisions about contraception, sterilization, and abortion?

6. The authors close this chapter by asserting that "motherhood freely chosen and creatively implemented can be one of the most exciting and joyous experiences a woman can know." Tell why you agree or disagree. If possible, illustrate your answer with anecdotes about childbirth, breast-feeding, adoption, child-training, and so on from your own experience or from that of others known to you.

Chapter 12: THE SINGLE WOMAN

1. List the first ten descriptive words or phrases you think of when someone says "a single man." When they say "a single woman."

2. Were you reared with the expectation that you would certainly get married? How do you think the expectations of your family, relatives, teachers, friends, ministers, etc., affected your life in this regard?

3. Theologian John Howard Yoder has said, "It needs to be taught as normative Christian truth that singleness is the first normal state for every Christian. Marriage is not wrong, and existing marriages are to be nurtured. Yet there exists no Christian imperative to become married as soon as one can, or to prefer marriage over singleness as a more whole or wholesome situation. . . . Marriage is fine . . . singleness is better." Discuss this statement, consulting such Scriptures as Matthew 19:10–12 and 1 Corinthians 7:7–9, 17, 25–35.

4. If you are single, which of the attitudes outlined on pp. 147–50, best expresses your feelings?
—— I freely chose this life and I enjoy it thoroughly.
—— I suppose I'd rather be married, but I accept my singleness at the moment.
—— I will never stop hoping—and working—to get married.
—— I think my singleness is a punishment for being outside the will of God.
—— I'm single because I'm not pretty, I have a bad figure, I didn't have the opportunity to get a good education, I'm too intelligent and have more education than most of the men I meet, or _____.
—— I just live each day as it comes.

5. Although over 90 percent of all women eventually marry, the majority of them will also become single again through separation, divorce or widowhood. If you are currently married, what preparations are you making for the likely possibility of future singleness?

List those assets you already have for living the single life. Make another list of those you would like to work on.

6. I think masturbation is

—— an immature sexual expression which may establish patterns which are harmful to good marital relations.

—— wrong for the Christian because it is self-centered, self-indulgent.

—— morally neutral, a matter which each Christian has the liberty to decide for themselves with the guidance of the Holy Spirit.

—— a very helpful source of release for the single adult, potentially a source of joyful celebration of one's sexuality.

7. Do you think that the sexual guidelines for mature single adults should be the same as or different from those suitable for teenagers? Why? Do you agree or disagree with the authors' comments on sexuality on pp. 152–57? Why?

8. I feel comfortable about touching, hugging

—— a special person of the opposite sex.

—— children.

—— a special person of the same sex.

—— any friendly person who touches or hugs me in a loving manner.

—— none of the above.

9. I get a feeling of self-worth, of pride in myself, from

—— the love and support of the man in my life.

—— the love and support of my friends of either sex.

—— competence in my career.

—— my children.

—— the fact that God loves me.

—— other _____.

10. Psalm 68:6 says that "God setteth the solitary in families." List the people that you consider your "family." Are your "legal" kin or your "chosen" kin more important to you? Why?

11. In what ways can a single person achieve loving intimacy? In what ways did Jesus experience intimacy?

12. In what ways do you think your church could become more of a community in which people without spouses or those whose spouses are uninterested in the Christian faith could be made to feel more welcome?

For further reading and study in the area of singleness, see Margaret Evening, *Who Walk Alone* (Downers Grove, Ill.: InterVarsity Press, 1975).

Chapter 13: WASTING THE CHURCH'S GIFTS

1. What roles are open to women in your church? Are there other roles which you think women should be filling?

2. If women are not ordained by your denomination, what do you think are the reasons for this?

—— The majority of members feel that Scripture prohibits women's ordination.

—— Our ministers represent God, and women are inappropriate for this.

—— The Twelve and the leaders of the early church as described in the New Testament were all men.

—— We have just never done it before. (To make sure read "Women as Preachers: Evangelical Precedents" by Donald and Lucille Sider Dayton, *Christianity Today,* May 23, 1975.)

—— The ministry is too difficult for women; their talents are not suited for it.

—— Other _____.

3. List the qualities that you think are most essential in an ideal minister for your church. Are there any qualities that a woman could not possibly have? If so, which ones?

4. Read the parable of the talents aloud from Matthew 25:14–30. List the talents you think God has given you which could be useful to the building up of the body of Christ. Share your list with the group. Let others add gifts which they think you have.

5. Consider the little story about Florence Nightingale on p. 178. (Nancy Hardesty has written about the experiences of other women in the history of the church in a series entitled "Great Women of Faith." These articles appeared in *Eternity* magazine from September 1974 through June 1975.) Can you think of any similar experiences women have today? How can we encourage and support women who want to serve the church full time?

6. What action could this group take to give women a more active part in the worship of your church, a more decisive voice in its decision-making processes?

Chapter 14: THE WORLD BEYOND THE HOME

1. On page 183, the authors say that "most churches have trouble adjusting to working women." Do you agree? Can you give examples?

2. Has the description of the "ideal woman" in Proverbs 31:10–31 (as presented on pages 184–85) provided any new insights in your thinking about outside careers for married women? Why do you

think this passage of Scripture has been used in sermons to reinforce the traditional dependent housewife role for women, when in actuality a much broader role is depicted?

3. What is meant by what the authors call the "relation side" and the "creation side" of the image of God in which both females and males were created? How does this speak to the issue of a woman's involvement in the world beyond the home?

4. Discuss Susannah Wesley's life. (In addition to pp. 189–90, review the section beginning on p. 96.) How do you react to the minister's statement at the bottom of page 188 about how tragic it would have been for the Christian church if Susannah Wesley had practiced birth control? Do you think Mrs. Wesley should have been satisfied with her wife-mother role rather than experiencing a restless yearning to do something more? Why do you think she felt guilty about using her talents to serve God? Can you provide other examples of women who have experienced doubt and misgivings while attempting to do what they believe God wants them to do? How would you counsel such women?

5. Do you agree with the suggestion made by psychologist Judith Bardwick that women may need to achieve first in the area of interpersonal relationships and then, building on the foundation of a stable marital relationship, they can go on to educational and occupational achievement at a later point in life (p. 190)? Where do single women fit into this view? Discuss the statement on page 190: "Possibly an internalized motive to achieve develops later in women than in men and requires the security of having affiliative needs met first, thus reducing anxiety about achieving." Do you agree? What alternative explanation does Dr. Bardwick suggest? Some psychologists say that the development of achievement motivation appears to be more of a problem in females than males. What are some reasons for this? Do you think the situation may be changing? (Helpful resource materials for this question are these: Matina Horner, "Fail: Bright Women," *Psychology Today,* November, 1969; Lois Wladis Hoffman, "Early Childhood Experiences and Women's Achievement Motives," *Journal of Social Issues* 28, No. 2 [1972]: 129–55.)

6. Express your opinion of Sidney Callahan's statement about the fine line between self-sacrifice and suicide. Can you give examples illustrating the kinds of frustration and dissatisfaction described on page 192?

7. In thinking of a woman's involvement in the world beyond the home, three categories of options are suggested: voluntary work, enrolling for more education, or taking paid employment (pp. 192–95). Make a list of advantages and disadvantages of each category.

Is any particular option attractive to *you* at the moment? Are there any fears or hesitancies about taking this step—feelings you might wish to share with the group and gain support? (In addition to this section, review also the section beginning with the bottom two paragraphs on page 160.)

8. Sociologists Eli Ginzberg and Alice Yohalem have described four basic categories of women with respect to the home/career dilemma (p. 197). Discuss these categories and tell which, if any, comes closest to describing you.

9. Describe the misgivings many Christians have about employment for mothers. What are some ways a mother's employment might be beneficial to her and her family? What are some ways a mother's employment might not be beneficial? What are some ways a father's employment might be beneficial to him and his family? What are some ways a father's employment might not be beneficial?

10. Dr. Carl Henry has written that, while some women have a calling to serve God through full-time devotion to motherhood, other Christian women may find that motherhood diverts them "from their fullest creative possibilities" at a time in history when their talents are needed in a wide range of professions. He goes on to ask: "Can it be that Christian women who delight in homemaking as a divine calling can fill a role also as godparents to the children of others who are divinely gifted and burdened to pursue a career alongside motherhood?" (Carl Henry, "Reflections on Women's Lib," *Christianity Today* 19 [Jan. 3, 1975]: 345–46.) What do you think of Dr. Henry's suggestions?

11. What responsibility does the church have for providing child-care centers in view of the fact that government figures show that 50 percent of married women with children between the ages of six and seventeen and 30 percent of those with children under six years are already in the labor force?

Chapter 15: WHERE DO WE GO FROM HERE?

1. What is your reaction to the statement: "Christianity has done much to raise the status of women"?

2. In what ways were arguments in favor of slavery similar to arguments used to keep women in a subordinate position?

3. What are some ways Christians in the past have used Scripture to limit the potential of women? (See p. 204.) How have new interpretations brought about a change of thought in these areas? Do you believe a similar change is taking place today with regard to other areas concerning women? Give specific examples.

4. Does the women's movement mean that women want to become men? (See p. 206.)

5. At the bottom of page 206, the authors write: "For men, it is true, women's liberation will mean a loss of power" because power and rights will come to be distributed more equitably. However, many men are pointing out that men stand to *gain* more benefits than they lose through what they say is not only "women's liberation" but "human liberation." Whereas women have been hampered with regard to freedom to be committed to careers, men have not been free to choose *not* to work as women have been able to do by becoming housewives and having husbands to support them. Males have been reared traditionally to be tough, strong, protectors of women so that feelings of tenderness, fear, sadness, self-doubt, and so on have been locked inside. Men often find it difficult to display emotions (except so-called "masculine" ones like anger). Moving away from gender-role stereotypes could be freeing to men. List as many different ways as you can think of that the aims of the feminist movement will be to the advantage of males. (Helpful resource materials are these: Marc Feigen Fasteau, *The Male Machine,* New York: McGraw-Hill Book Co., 1974; Joseph Pleck and Jack Sawyer, eds., *Men and Masculinity,* Englewood Cliffs, N.J.: Prentice-Hall, Spectrum paperback, 1974; Warren Farrell, *The Liberated Man,* New York: Random House, 1974.)

6. Do you agree or disagree with Lois Gunden Clemens's statement on p. 207 in which she claims that many older women find it difficult to understand the dissatisfaction younger women feel about women's traditional roles in the church? Give reasons for your answer.

7. Discuss the symbolism of the Jerusalem temple described at the bottom of page 208, noticing especially the barriers it set up between certain groups. List the categories that were separated. In what sense did Christ come to tear down these barriers? (See Matt. 27:51; Heb. 10:19–20; Heb. 4:14–16; 1 Pet. 2:9; Rev. 1:6; Eph. 2:11–22; and Gal. 3:28.) Also discuss Galatians 3:28 in connection with the categories mentioned in the old Jewish prayer that is described on page 72.

8. What does it mean to you personally to know that God has daughters as well as sons, and Christ has sisters as well as brothers?

9. Look back over your answers to question 5 in the first lesson of this study guide. Have your goals in studying this book been achieved? What are some specific ways in which your life has been changed with regard to your self-concept, your relationships with others, your present life style, your future plans, and other areas of concern to you personally?

FOR ADDITIONAL READING

Many of you may wish to explore further the various issues raised by this book or by the discussions of your group. We suggest the following:

On Christianity and the women's movement in general. The July-August, 1973, issue of *The Other Side* was devoted entirely to the "woman question." The August-Sept., 1974, issue of the *Post American* was built around the theme of "evangelical feminism" and contains a detailed annotated bibliography prepared by Nancy Hardesty which lists a wide range of books and articles relating to feminism. If you like lively dialogue and enjoy reading debates and different points of view, try these: "A Dialogue on Women, Hierarchy and Equality" by Thomas Howard (traditionalist view) and Donald Dayton (egalitarian view), *Post American,* May 1975; "Why I Favor the Ordination of Women" by Paul King Jewett, and "Why I Oppose the Ordination of Women" by Elisabeth Elliot, *Christianity Today* 19 (June 6, 1975); "Women: Second Class Citizens?" by Nancy Hardesty, with responses from eleven Christian leaders, *Eternity* 22 (January 1971); and "The Women's Movement Challenges the Church" by Virginia Ramey Mollenkott, with reactions by three respondents and Dr. Mollenkott's comments on these critiques, *Journal of Psychology and Theology* 2 and 3 (Fall 1974 and Winter 1975), published by the Rosemead Graduate School of Psychology, 1409 N. Walnut Grove Ave., Rosemead, CA 91770.

On marriage. See John Scanzoni's arguments for egalitarian marriage in "Authority in Christian Marriage," *Reformed Journal* 24 (November 1974), published by Wm. B. Eerdmans Publishing Co., 255 Jefferson S.E., Grand Rapids, Mich. 49502. Also see the June 1975 issue of *McCall's* for an analysis and critique of "The Books that Teach Wives to be Sexy and Submissive" by Barbara Grizzuti Harrison.

On male-female roles and relationships. See *Sexual Bargaining: Power Politics in the American Marriage* by John Scanzoni (Englewood Cliffs, N.J.: Prentice-Hall Spectrum Books, 1972) and *Men, Women, and Change—A Sociology of Marriage and Family* by Letha and John Scanzoni (scheduled for January 1976 publication, New York: McGraw-Hill Book Company).

On friendship. A subject that has concerned both women's and men's liberation groups is the fear of homosexuality as persons learn to relate deeply to one another. (See the men's liberation books listed earlier in this study guide; also see the chapters on sisterhood and brotherhood in Nona Glazer-Malbin, ed., *Old Family/ New Family,* New York: D. Van Nostrand Co., 1975.) One way of

approaching this subject from a Christian perspective is presented
in Letha Scanzoni's "On Friendship and Homosexuality," *Christianity Today* 18 (September 27, 1974). Another is Paul Hinne-
busch's *Friendship in the Lord* (Notre Dame, Ind.: Ave Maria Press,
1974).